MW01240505

Ten years after 9/11, most Americans remain as baffled, unsure, and even hostile to Islam as they were at the start of the decade. Yet, as Dr. Manzoor Hussain has illustrated, the relationship between Islam and America can be a positive and beneficial one to both. More than ever, the Muslim intellectual has to play the role of an Ambassador and I am delighted that Dr. Hussain by offering us this illuminating and timely book is doing so.

Ambassador Akbar Ahmed
Ibn Khaldun Chair of Islamic Studies
American University
Author of *Journey in to America: The Challenge of Islam*

Come, Reader, as this well organized author takes you byw the hand. Open his book and let him walk you right past the usual mountains of misinformation about Islam, onto the wide, straight path of what the world's second largest faith is really all about. It's a painless and fulfilling journey. Experience the enjoyment of replacing blank stereotypes with functional understanding. This is the kind of book mainstream American readers have been waiting for. Reading it will make your life easier. I promise.

Michael Wolfe
Co-Founder & Co-Executive Producer
Unity Production Foundation
Author of *Taking Back Islam: American Muslims reclaim their Faith*

ISLAM

An Essential Understanding
for Fellow Americans

ISLAM

An Essential Understanding
for Fellow Americans

MANZOOR HUSSAIN PHD

*I dedicate this book to my parents
who taught me to love and obey God,
be truthful and honest, and
love, respect and help people*

CONTENTS

ACKNOWLEDGMENTS

I GRATEFULLY ACKNOWLEDGE the moral support of my wife Jana, without whose encouragement and valuable suggestions I might not have been able to write this book.

I wish to express my most sincere appreciation to Mr. Saffet Abid Catovic, a contributing scholar to a project of the Center for Muslim-Christian Understanding at Edmund A. Walsh School of Foreign Service at Georgetown University, for his critical review of a major part of my book and his valuable suggestions.

Appreciation is extended to Dr. Iqbal Unus, Director of The Fairfax Institute, Washington, D.C. for his review of the manuscript and helpful comments, and for his help in the selection of the title of the book. I am also grateful to Ms. Safia Hussain for reviewing portions of this book in its early stages and for her helpful comments.

I am greatly indebted to Professor Akbar Ahmed, Ibn Khaldun Chair of Islamic. Studies and Professor of International Relations, American University, Washington, D.C. and author of *"Journey in to America: The Challenge of Islam"* for his kind words about the book.

My sincere thanks also go to Mr. Michael Wolfe, Co-Founder, Unity Production Foundation and Author of *"Taking Back Islam: American Muslims reclaim their Faith"* for writing words of praise for my book.

I am grateful to Sayyida Seema Ahmad (http://seemasart. blogspot.com) who has granted me permission to reproduce her illustration in arabesque design on the cover page of this book.

INTRODUCTION

ISLAM IS THE second largest religion of the world, very close behind Christianity. With a global population of 1.5 billion, Muslims are living in almost every country. They speak many languages and come from a variety of cultural and ethnic backgrounds. Therefore, it would be naïve to believe that they all think alike. Like any other people of the world, Muslims range between fundamentalist and ultraconservative to progressive and reformist in their religious and socio-cultural outlook.

People in the West are surprised to learn that, like Jews and Christians, Muslims are monotheists and trace their lineage to Abraham through his son Ishmael. They believe in the same One God that Christians and Jews believe in. They also believe in all of the Biblical prophets and scriptures, albeit, in their original forms and languages.

Islam is fundamentally a religion of peace and loving submission to the Will of God Almighty, teaching Muslims to live with their fellow humans in peace and tranquility. However, there is a great deal of diversity within Islam. Not all Muslims think and act alike, and approaches to Islam among Muslims vary quite a bit.

There is also a range of opinions with respect to the question of how Muslims should relate to non-Muslims, especially the Western world; it is similar to the range of attitudes people in the West have towards Muslims. There are people in the Western world who are very friendly towards Muslims, but there is still hostility towards Muslims, even from people who have never known any.

The fundamental teaching in Islam is that God has created diverse peoples and cultures for a purpose, which indicates that He intended the world to remain pluralistic in religion as well. It is incorrect to believe that all Muslims hate Western people for their beliefs and who they are.

Muslims are not anti-West. Many of the teachings of Islam are compatible with modern concepts and ideas that are commonly identified with the Western culture. For example: love of God and the neighbor, respect for life and liberty, human rights, freedom of expression, freedom of religion, democracy, social justice, and environmental stewardship are all found in teachings of Islam.

Islam teaches tolerance and understanding towards people of other religions, especially towards Jews and Christians, the fellow "people of the Book." A study of history shows that Muslims, Jews, and Christians have lived and worked together, and Muslims have saved the lives of many Christians and Jews.

In the 15th century Spain, Reconquesta forces told Jews that they had to convert to Christianity and undergo baptism, or be forcibly expelled from the country. Thousands of Jews refused to convert, and were expelled. Many were tortured and killed by execution or were publicly burned at the stake. Muslims, on the other hand, came to rescue many Jews. When the Muslim ruler of the Ottoman Empire, Sultan Bayazed II, heard about the plight of the Jews, he dispatched his navy to evacuate the Jews of Spain and settle them in Turkish towns, where they were allowed to practice their religion and their occupations in peace and safety.

Similarly, thousands of Maronite Christians were saved in Damascus, Syria by the forces of Sufi Sheikh Amir Abdel Kader (for whom the town of Elkader, Iowa was later named). Muslims also saved many Jews in North Africa during World War II. Also, Muslims saved Jews and allied soldiers from the Nazi forces in Europe, in many cases, at the risk of their own lives.

Islam encourages its followers to ponder over the wonders of God's creation and explore the universe for the benefit of mankind by using principles of science and technology, and the Qur'an admonishes man to advance his knowledge. Muslims have contributed very significantly to the advancement of human civilization; many modern day scientific and technological inventions are based on the ideas of the Muslim science and technology of the Middle Ages.

Many of these achievements were realized from the 8th to 13th centuries when Muslims, Jews, and Christians lived and worked together, especially in Abbasid Caliphate in Baghdad and in Spain under Muslim rule. Muslims of that period contributed to knowledge in science, mathematics, medicine, philosophy, astronomy, and many other areas of human development.

There are between 6 and 8 million Muslims in America, and they are productive and loyal American citizens. Many are contributing to the American dream as doctors, engineers, lawyers, legislators, business people, social scientists, teachers, athletes, and in other professions. Many serve in the Armed Forces of the United States.

However, the American public has remained largely uneducated about the faith of Islam and its followers. Many people who wish to learn about Islam rely on stereotypes projected by the media, which focus on dramatic events such as terrorism, oppression, and extremism. The terrorist attack of September 11, 2001 served to further deteriorate the image of Islam and Muslims in America, and all Muslims seem to have become targets of suspicion and scrutiny.

Religious identification rarely occurs when non-Muslims commit acts of terror. For example, when Timothy McVeigh and his collaborators bombed the Murrah Federal Building in Oklahoma City in 1995, or when the Norwegian terrorist Anders Behring Breivik slaughtered 77 innocent people in Oslo and on the Island of Utoya on July 22, 2011, they were not referred to

as "Christian terrorists." In fact, in both cases until their identity was known, it was assumed that Middle Eastern terrorists
had carried out these attacks. The Oklahoma attack whipped up
anti-Muslim hysteria.

Negative, misleading stereotypes of Islam have created a
deep misunderstanding of this religion in people's minds in the
Western world. Particularly in America, Muslims are characterized as extremists, terrorists, and outsiders who disrupt the
American way of life. This misrepresentation causes confusion
and hostility in the minds of the American public, depriving
them of a fair assessment of one of the greatest religions of the
world. At the same time, incidents of backlash against innocent
Muslim Americans and their institutions are increasing at an
alarming rate.

Misunderstanding of Islam and the Muslims in the West has
given rise to a wave of Islamophobia spreading throughout
America. It manifests as Qur'an burning, anti-Shariah movements, hostility towards building mosques and Islamic Centers,
direct assaults on American Muslims, and expression of hate for
Islam and the Muslims in a variety of forms. The main reason for
Islamophobia is a Western lack of knowledge about Islam and
the Muslims—particularly in the USA.

However, it is reassuring for American Muslims to see that
despite the spread of Islamophobia, many people and groups,
especially Christian and Jewish organizations, have stepped
forward in the true spirit of America to defend Muslims as fellow Americans and followers of their common Judeo-Christian-
Islamic heritage.

This book is a humble attempt to educate the American public about Islam and its 1.5 billion followers, to strengthen the
connection between the three Abrahamic faiths—the other two
being Judaism and Christianity. An attempt has also been made
to answer some of the most frequently asked questions, with

the hope of dispelling ignorance and cultivating a better understanding of Islam and of Muslims in the West.

It is hoped that this effort will help to decrease Islamophobia
and hatred of Muslims. It is expected that once the American
people realize that Islam is a religion of peace and not a threat to
any civilization, perceptions will change.

ISLAM

An Essential Understanding
for Fellow Americans

1

ISLAM—THE MOST MISUNDERSTOOD RELIGION IN THE WEST

IN THE WESTERN world, especially in America and Europe, few non-Muslims are familiar with Islam; fewer still have a sophisticated understanding of the religion. Many rely on media stereotypes, seeing Islam through distorted lenses that focus on terrorists, oppression, religious extremists, and so forth. Some conservative politicians and media outlets associate Islam with violence, extremism, and militancy.

As a result, the average citizen in the Western world is deprived of the right to learn the facts about Islam, which teaches compassion, justice, and peace. It is an Abrahamic faith that teaches belief in One God. It is sad to note that most non-Muslims in the West are unfamiliar with the basic teachings of Islam, and very few are even interested in learning about the religion.

MISCONCEPTIONS ABOUT ISLAM AND MUSLIMS

Very few non-Muslims understand that Muslims worship the One and Only God, and that Islam is the second largest religion in the world, close behind Christianity. Islam is not a cult or a new religion, but a religion with deep historic roots that has followers numbering over 1.5 billion people worldwide, from different nationalities and cultural backgrounds. They are spread over almost every part of the world, and include an estimated 7 - 8 million American Muslims.

Some non-Muslim writers have used the term Mohammadanism for Islam. It is an incorrect term because it implies that Muslims worship the Prophet Muhammad, which is not correct. Prophet Muhammad was a human, not divine. Muslims only worship One God.

Westerners continue to be astonished to learn of Islam's similarities to Judaism and Christianity. For example, people often do not know that Islam is an Abrahamic faith. Like Jews and Christians, early Muslims were descendents of Abraham, but while Jews and Christians are the prophet's descendents through his son Isaac, Muslims trace their lineage to Abraham through his son Ishmael.

In addition, Western people are often surprised to learn that Muslims revere and honor prophets of Judaism and Christianity, including: Abraham, Isaac, Ishmael, Jacob, Joseph, Jonah, Job, Moses, David, Solomon, John the Baptist, and Jesus (may peace and blessings of God be upon them), as well as God's revealed books in their original forms. However, while it is common to hear about the Judeo-Christian tradition, it is rare to hear about the Judeo-Christian-Islamic tradition.

Westerners have many misconceptions about Islam. According to a survey conducted by Genesis Research in August 2004, about 25% Americans believe in several anti-Muslim falsehoods. For example: that Islam teaches violence, that Muslims value life less than others, they teach their children to hate, and that they want to change the American way of life. A large number of Americans support restrictions on the civil rights of Muslims.

There seems to be a general misunderstanding of Arabs, Muslims, Islam, and the Qur'an.

Some Western people believe that in the history of Christianity and Judaism, progress has been made in sociopolitical areas such as human rights, the status of women, and democracy, but it has been assumed that such developments are not possible with Islam.[1]

Many scholars of world religions agree that Islam is a misunderstood religion. Huston Smith, an internationally known scholar of world religions sums it up by quoting a reporter of Newsweek magazine who wrote: "no part of the world is more hopelessly, systematically and stubbornly misunderstood by us than that complex of religion, culture and geography known as Islam."[1]

Similarly, John Kaltner, Professor of Religion at Rhodes College in Memphis, Tennessee correctly pointed out that no religion in recent times has suffered more stereotypes than Islam.[2] Finally, as John Esposito, Professor of Religion and International Affairs at Georgetown University has observed in his book on Islam, many people who wish to know about Islam learn about it from media stereotypes, which often associate Islam with terrorism, religious extremism, and oppression.[3]

The aftermath of the events of September 11, 2001 has demonstrated the lack of awareness of Islam in the West and has further deteriorated the neutral or negative impression people already had of Islam and the Muslims. Since the individuals implicated in these attacks had Muslim names, all Muslims have become targets of suspicion and scrutiny.

Religious identification rarely occurs when non-Muslims commit terrible deeds. For example, Christians bombing abortion clinics, such as Eric Rudolph, or committing other violent acts, such as Timothy McVeigh, are not seen as discrediting Christianity. However, in many cases if a Muslim commits a wrongful act, the incident is promptly reported as a threat to America by followers of a particular religion.

When Timothy McVeigh and his collaborating terrorists bombed the Murrah Federal Building in Oklahoma City on April 19, 1995, it was immediately assumed by many that "Middle Eastern terrorists" had carried out the attack. Within hours of the bombing, former Congressman Dave McCurdy was on CBS talking about "very clear evidence of fundamentalist Islamic terrorist groups." The media, including CNN joined the fray.

The Federal law enforcement authorities were more careful. They were reported on the front page of New York Times of April 20, 1995 to have stated that they "had no suspect," and that the investigators "did not know whether the bombers were domestic or international terrorists."

The initial faulty assumption sparked a wave of anti-Muslim hysteria that resulted in almost 250 incidents of harassment, discrimination, and actual violence against American Muslims or those perceived to be Middle Eastern.[4]

There were two types of victims of the Oklahoma City bombing: The innocent dead and the falsely accused. When an alleged Oklahoma City bomber was captured a few days later, and he was not a Muslim, a story titled *"Muslims' Burden of Blame Lifts"* was carried by Laurie Goodstein and Marylou Tousignant in the April 22, 1995 issue of the Washington Post. This gave rise to a question: If the burden was lifted from the Muslims, on whom did it fall? The religion of the alleged bomber was not mentioned.

When it became clear that the attack was carried out by terrorists from the Midwest, not the Mideast, the opportunity arose for America to redefine terrorism and terrorist to include people who look like "regular" Americans, yet that opportunity was not seized and Muslims continue to be vilified as terrorists.

THE ROLE OF WESTERN MEDIA

Elements of Western media have played a leading role in spreading misinformation and stereotyping Muslims. As a result, there is a limited amount of unbiased information on Islam available in the West. The media seems to lack the will to obtain accurate information about Islam, and so spread misinformation about the religion and its followers. To illustrate, Islam is routinely linked with violence in news reports and articles.

People who demonize Islam and Muslims know the power of bad press. As a result of bad press, a majority of the people in the West have a negative perception of Arabs and Muslims.[5] Objective reporting about Islam often falls victim to political and personal agendas that distort the facts and obscure the truth.[3]

Stereotyping and dehumanizing Arabs and Muslims in television shows and Hollywood movies seem to have become a permanent feature. Only Native Americans seem to outdistance Arabs and Muslims in being denigrated and vilified in Hollywood movies. Arabs and Muslims are either portrayed as terrorists ("Black Sunday," "The Siege") or bumbling comics (Ishtar, Protocol, Jewel of the Nile). Scenes from these movies leave an impact on viewers' minds, creating negative thoughts and feelings about Arabs, Muslims, and Islam.

Some media sources have even gone to extremes and published derogatory and insulting caricatures of Prophet Muhammad, generating global outrage. Islam teaches respect and reverence for Abraham, Moses, Jesus, Muhammad and all other prophets and messengers of God. As a result, an attack on the character of any of them is offensive to Muslims. For the same reason, some movies depicting Jesus were not shown in some Muslim countries because they were considered to be insulting Jesus.

Any media outlets that report hostile and biased material against Islam and Muslims are not *following* the basic ethics of factual reporting. The Western public needs to know the truth and facts. For example, the media do not make an effort to hear thoughtful voices opposed to U.S. imperial policies vis-à-vis the Muslim countries. One seldom sees on any major TV news or talk shows the likes of former U.S. Attorney General Ramsey Clark, Professor Naom Chomsky, historian Howard Zinn, or journalist Robert Fisk.

THE ROLE OF WESTERN LEADERSHIP

It is disturbing to see some prominent American political, military and religious leaders attacking Islam, calling it a "fraudulent religion," "monumental scam," "religion of violence," "religion of idol worshipping" and so forth.[4] There is a relentless attack on the character of Prophet Muhammad, calling him a "wild-eyed fanatic," a "robber," a "brigand," and a "killer."

The culmination of the aforementioned forces gives the impression of a systematic effort to create hateful images of Islam and Prophet Muhammad. These misunderstandings, as well as anti-Islamic and anti-Muslim inflammatory statements are not harmless. They create a high incident of crime, and can affect the lives of innocent Muslim Americans in a profound way.[6]

The number of hate-crimes against Arabs and Muslims in America skyrocketed soon after 9/11. A report from the FBI indicated an increase in these incidents by 1,600 percent. Aggravated assault shot up dramatically and the growing tensions are not showing signs of stopping. Similarly, in a study called "Unequal Protection," the Council on American-Muslim Relations (CAIR) reported an increase in anti-Muslim incidents in the United States of more than 50% during 2004. These included 1522 cases involving anti-Muslim violence, discrimination, and harassment.[7]

In recent years, there has been increase in Islamophobia, defined as "an irrational fear and hostility towards Islam and Muslims." Islamophobia is fueled by anti-Islamic evangelists and preachers, right wing politicians, online bloggers, and the like. Consequently, American Muslims have suffered, and continue to suffer, from discrimination, profiling, hate crimes, violent offences, violation of their constitutional rights, and anti-Muslim rhetoric.

The image of American Muslims is further tarnished, and their safety and freedom put at risk when political leaders make baseless claims that a majority of the American Muslim community is radicalized, and insinuating that 'they are an enemy living among us.' A Congressman from Georgia said his state should 'arrest every Muslim that comes across the state line.' He later apologized for his remark. A former Speaker of the House equated Islam with Nazism. Such troubling rhetoric cannot be harmless; it puts the safety of American Muslims at risk. Anti-Muslim rhetoric has the potential for serious international repercussions—the United States has deep relations with several Muslim countries, and is heavily dependent on the oil that is imported from some of them.

In view of the anti-Muslim climate in the USA, there is a greater need for Americans to understand Islam and the Muslims than ever before. The events of 9/11 have also led to an increased interest in Islam by average Americans. It is reassuring to know that hatred and religious intolerance are not shared by everyone in the West, and many non-Muslim writers are trying to present a more factual image of Islam and the Muslims in their writings.[1, 2, 3, 8]

It is reassuring for American Muslims to see increasing numbers of leaders, especially religious leaders, deploring anti-Muslim sentiments and supporting Muslim causes in this country (see chapter 28 on Islamophobia). Those who want to learn about Islam need to take special care to approach the subject objectively and with an open mind. Once Islam is studied with neutrality, it becomes easy to relate to its followers with under-standing and fellowship.

2

WHAT ISLAM IS ALL ABOUT?

ISLAM IS A universal religion and a way of life. It is practiced by followers from all races, nationalities, and ethnicities in virtually all countries of the world. It is, however, important to recognize that all Muslims are not alike. Just as in Christianity there is great diversity of belief and practices, resulting in so many Christian churches or sects that exist in different cultures (Anglican, Baptist, Coptic, Eastern Orthodox, Greek Orthodox, Lutheran, Methodist, Protestant, Roman Catholic church, and others), so is there also some diversity in Muslims. It results from different interpretations of the teachings of Islam. However, all Muslims believe in the same One God, the same Qur'an, and Prophet Muhammad. They all pray five times a day, fast during Ramadan, pay mandatory charity (Zakat), and perform pilgrimage to Mecca once in lifetime.

There is only one divinely revealed Islam, but there are several interpretations. All Muslim sects and schools of theology express the same religion of Islam in different ways, within a variety of cultures that extend from North Africa to Southeast Asia, as well as across Europe and North America. Arabs constitute only 20% of the Muslim population worldwide. With a population of 220 million, Indonesia is the largest Muslim country of the world. Other Muslim countries include: Afghanistan, Algeria, Bangladesh, Egypt, Iraq, Iran, Jordan, Kuwait, Libya, Malaysia, Morocco, Nigeria, Pakistan, Qatar, Saudi Arabia, Senegal, Sudan, Syria, Tunisia, Turkey, United Arab Emirates, Yemen, and many other countries.

There are two major sects, Sunni (85 percent of the world's Muslims) and Shia (15 percent). Within these are diverse schools of theology and interpretations of the Islamic law or Sharia. Islam also has a rich mystical tradition that includes many Sufi Orders or Tariqas.

There is much to learn about Islam, but one of the most important points is the diversity of the religion's followers. It is often difficult to recognize this fact because of the lack of sophisticated media coverage about the religion. It would be wrong to believe that all 1.5 billion Muslims think and behave exactly alike.

WHAT DOES ISLAM MEAN AND WHAT DOES IT TEACH?

Religion is a way of worship to God or gods. Islam is not limited to just a particular method of worship; it is a harmonious way of life. In this way, it is more than just a religion in the traditional understanding of the word, although religious obligations are a part of Islam. Indeed, Islam is a complete way of life or deen, as it is called in Arabic, which governs not only religious practice, but also all other facets of life: ethical, moral, social, political, economical, spiritual, intellectual, and so forth.

The Arabic word "Islam" itself derives from the Arabic word 'silm', which means peace and submission. Thus, "Islam" means to achieve peace—peace with God, with His creation, and within oneself—through existential submission to the Will of God and to willingly accept His Guidance.

Most major world religions derive their names from their founders. For example, Judaism takes its name from the tribe of Judah, Christianity from Jesus Christ, and Buddhism from Gautam Buddha. However, Islam is unique because it derives its name from the moral attitude it represents, i.e., achievement of peace through submission to the Will of God.

The obvious question arises as to how Islam's position as a religion of peace can be reconciled with acts of terrorism carried out in its name. The answer to this would be that it would be as unfair to associate with Islam acts of violence committed by a tiny minority of extremist Muslims as associating with Christianity acts of terrorism and violence committed by extremist Christians.

Just as the Jewish terrorist groups such as Kach and Kahane Chai do not represent Judaism and Christian terrorist groups in the USA, Burma, India, Lebanon, Ireland, Serbia, Uganda and other countries do not represent Christianity, Muslim terrorists do not represent mainstream Islam. Terrorists, whether they are Muslims, Christian, Jewish or of any other religion, always represent an extremist group at the fringes of a population. Islam should not be judged by its small number of extremist followers, but by what the religion teaches and by the majority of its peaceful followers.

Islam teaches us about the nature of God and His creatures, and about the physical laws that God has made to sustain and govern the universe and everything in it. Islam addresses the biological and spiritual aspects of human life, including moral and ethical codes that apply to human conduct about family life; matters of marriage, divorce, inheritance, and the rights of man, woman, parents, children, relatives and neighbors. In addition, it gives guidance on some of the mundane aspects of human life. Islam addresses matters related to the individual, the family, the community, the government, and international relations, and teaches how we are supposed to do everything in life. It also teaches about the life after death.

ISLAM IS AN ABRAHAMIC FAITH

People in the West are astonished to discover that Islam is another Abrahamic faith besides Judaism and Christianity. The three belong to the same Abrahamic family of faith traditions.[1,3] Islam is a return to the pure monotheistic faith of Abraham; and early Muslims, like Jews and early Christians, were the children of Abraham. While Jews and Christians trace their roots to Abraham and his wife Sarah through their son Isaac, Muslims are descendents of Abraham through Ishmael (in Arabic Ismail), his first-born son by his wife Hagar.

According to both the Bible and the Qur'an, when Sarah could not conceive a child she urged Abraham to have a child by Hagar, who was her bondswoman. So Abraham took Hagar as his wife, and Ismail was born as a result of that union.[1] Sometime after Ismail's birth, Sarah also became pregnant and gave birth to Isaac. God commanded Abraham to take Hagar and Ismail to the Valley of Becca (modern day Mecca) in Arabia, and Abraham obeyed God's command. While it was a desolate place with no food and water, Abraham took comfort in God's promise that He would make Ismail the father of a great nation. He saved them by causing a spring to miraculously gush forth in the middle of the desert.

Abraham used to visit Hagar and Ismail now and then. During one such visit, Abraham and Ismail built the Ka'ba (located in the present day city of Mecca), as a house of worship of One True God. Today, the Ka'ba is considered the most sacred place in the Muslim world. Muslims around the world face in the direction of the Ka'ba when they pray as a unifying act of worship of the One True God. Additionally, Muslims are required to perform pilgrimage to Mecca and the surrounding areas at least once in their lifetime, if they can afford it.

WHEN AND HOW DID ISLAM ORIGINATE?

Islam is the original pure form of the same monotheistic faith system that was practiced by Jews and Christians. Although it is identified as the youngest of the three monotheistic faiths, Islam represents the same original truth that God revealed through all of His Prophets and Messengers.

Muslims believe that all Prophets and Messengers of God were sent to people of their respective ages to preach that there is no one worthy of worship except God Almighty, so mankind should submit to His Will, worship Him alone, obey His commands, do good deeds, abstain from committing sins, and practice social justice.

In the history of humanity, whoever surrendered to God's Will entered Islam and became a Muslim. For this reason, many Prophets and those who followed them, until the arrival of a new Prophet, are identified in the Qur'an as Muslims.

The reason for new Prophets was that as time passed, people corrupted the teachings of their Prophet. New Prophets were sent as reformers. All Prophets of God (including Abraham, Moses, Jesus, and Muhammad) taught the same message, namely to worship God Almighty alone, without any partners or associates, to do good deeds, to abstain from evil, and to practice social justice.

Prophet Muhammad was born in the year 570 in Mecca, Arabia among people who had drifted from God's way. The true religion had been forgotten or distorted all over the world. At the time of his birth, people of Arabia had become polytheists, and worshipped idols. They practiced vice and superstition of every kind. There was a growing division between the rich and the poor and injustice was prevalent in the society. People considered it dishonorable to have daughters, and so many baby girls were simply buried alive.

The polytheists of Mecca also lived in ignorance of the reality of One True God and His Will. Over time, even Jews and Christians had distorted God's original message to Moses and later to Jesus. The scriptures were altered and adulterated by mixing original revelation with human additions, such as elevation of Jesus from a Prophet to the son of God. Prophet Muhammad grew up among these people as a man of God and, according to the Qur'an, God sent him as His last Messenger to preach to mankind about One God and His Will (Qur'an 33:40, 46).

WHO ARE MUSLIMS?

The followers of Islam are called Muslims. Muslim literally means anyone who submits to the Will of God (and thereby accepts Islam as a way of life). By definition, all people, regardless of the period in history in which they lived, who surrendered to the Will of God, were Muslims. Like Jews and Christians, Muslims are monotheists. They believe in One God, the Creator and Sustainer of all creation, and Ruler of the Day of Judgment.

Usually Muslims are identified by their Arabic sounding names, and Islam is often judged from the actions of a few Muslims. The extent to whether someone can be Muslim depends upon the degree to which the person is following the true teachings of Islam and submitting to the will of God Almighty. A Muslim should not be judged by his name, but by his beliefs and actions.

It can be summarized that Islam a divinely revealed religion and a way of life. It is the second largest religion, right behind Christianity, with 1.5 billion followers called Muslims. Islam is universal in scope and Muslims are found in almost every country of the world. It is one of three Abrahamic faiths: the other two being Judaism and Christianity. Like Jews and early Christians, early Muslims traced their roots to Abraham. Muslims believe that Prophet Muhammad was the last messenger and Prophet of God Almighty, and there will be no more prophets after him. Muslims do not worship Muhammad, who was a human.

THE CONCEPT
OF GOD IN ISLAM

MUSLIMS BELIEVE IN One God: the Creator, Sustainer, and Ruler of the universe, and Master of the Day of Judgment. Like Jews and Christians, Muslims are monotheists who believe in and worship the same One God that Abraham, Moses, Jesus and Muhammad believed in and worshiped. Although people refer to God using different terms, it does not mean that they are referring to different gods. For example, some people call Him Jehovah (Yahweh) and others call Him Our Father in Heaven. Muslims call Him Allah, which is the personal name of Almighty God in the Arabic language. Allah is the Arabic term that translates literally as "the God." Arab Jews and twenty million Arab Christians refer to God as Allah, and it is the word Allah in Arabic that appears on the walls of churches in Arab countries.

In Aramaic, a language closely related to Arabic and Hebrew, and the language that Jesus spoke, God is referred to as Alaha.[9] It is interesting to note that in all three languages combination of the three letters, equivalent of English letters A, L, and H (ALH), gives the name of God. In Arabic it is Allah, in Aramaic Alaha, and in Hebrew it is Eloah.

The Arabic word Allah is formed by joining the definite article al (meaning "the") with Ilah (God). So, Allah (Al-Ilah) simply means "the God,"[10]not a god. Since Allah is the Arabic name that refers to the same monotheistic God in Whom Jews and Christians also believe, they should have no problem calling God Allah.[11] This is particularly true since Muslims do not believe that Allah is the God of Muslims alone, but the God of all people and all creation. Non-Muslims scholars have recognized this fact as well.

Professor John Kaltner has cautioned non-Muslims that they should be aware that when Muslims talk about Allah, they are talking about the same God as the God of the Bible.[2] Dr. Charles Kimball, a Religion Professor at Wake Forest University in Winston-Salem, N.C., has said that teaching about Allah involves "the same God that Jews and Christians are talking about." He added: "When you're talking about God of Abraham, Moses, Jesus and Mohammad, you're talking about the same God."[12]

Islam is a strictly monotheistic faith that teaches the existence of only One God Who has no son or partner, and that every other deity is false. The centrality of monotheism in Islam is best described in the following verses of the Qur'an:

"Say, He is God, the One and Only.
God, the Eternal, Absolute.
He begetteth not, nor is He begotten.
And there is none like unto Him."
(Qur'an 112:1-4)

"And your God is One God;
there is no God except Him, the Beneficent, the Merciful."
(Qur'an 2:163)

Muslims believe that no one shares God's divinity or His attributes and so no one has the right to be invoked, supplicated, prayed to, or shown any act of worship in any form, but God alone. To associate partners with God or to take others as gods besides Him contradicts the Islamic principle of the Oneness of God, and is considered a grave sin in Islam.

Additionally, no words, in any language, can accurately describe God. His essence or nature is so sublime, so transcendent, that the most intelligent human mind is incapable of totally grasping it. The Qur'an says:

"There is nothing whatsoever like unto Him,
and He is the One Who Hears and Sees all things."
(Qur'an: 42:11).

"No vision can grasp Him, and His grasp is over all visions;
and He is the Subtle, the Aware."
(Qur'an: 6:103).

From Islam's point of view, God is not limited and so has no finite form. In fact, God does not have any image because He is not physical. There is nothing that we could think of that is comparable to God, because He is infinitely different from the creation. He is transcendent, yet at the same time imminent and personal. He states in the Qur'an that there is nothing whatsoever that can be used as an example to describe Him. Human mind cannot even comprehend Him because He is beyond the human comprehension, which is limited.

God's divine attributes, however, could be within reasonable reach of human comprehension. In fact, our ability to know about Him is through His Attributes. Some of His ninety-nine Attributes are described in the following verses:

"He is God, the One that there is no deity but He,
the Knower of the unseen and the Apparent;
He is the Most Beneficent, Most Merciful.

He is God, the One that there is no deity but He,
the Sovereign, the Holy, the Source of All Peace,
the Guardian of Faith,
the Preserver, the Mighty, the Compeller, the Majestic;
Glory to God, Who is beyond their associations
(of partners with Him).
He is God, the Creator, the Maker, the Fashioner;
to Him belong the most beautiful names.
All that is in the heavens and the earth glorifies Him.
And He is the Mighty, the Wise."
(Qur'an 59:22–24)

Islam teaches that God is the Almighty, the Creator, the Sovereign, and the Sustainer of the entire universe. He manages all affairs, and stands in need of none of His creatures, and all His creatures depend on Him for all that they need. God did not just create the universe and then leave it. Creation is a continuous and on-going process. God existed before everything and He will remain existent after the end of time. He is Eternal, lives forever, and will not die. If He is subject to death, even on a temporary basis, who would run the universe in His absence, and who would bring Him back to life?

There is no parallel in Islam to the idea that 'on the seventh day God ended his work which he had made, and he rested on the seventh day from all his work which he had made.' From Islamic view, God does not have the need to rest. He is not subject to human weaknesses such as fatigue and sleepiness. Islam does not endow anthropomorphic qualities on God. It also rejects the idea that God is incarnate in any human being.

From Islam's perspective, God is Omniscient and All-Knowing. He knows not only what is manifest and tangible, but also the slightest thoughts that pass through our minds. In this respect the Qur'an states:

"And whether you hide your words or proclaim them,
He certainly has knowledge of the secrets of all hearts.
Should He not know? He is the One Who has created.
And He is the One Who understands the finest mysteries
and is well-acquainted with them."
(Qur'an 67:13,14)

Islam teaches that God is just and swift in retribution. Yet, the Islamic concept of God is also that He is loving, merciful, and compassionate. The result is that Islam teaches a balance between the fear of God's punishment and hope for His Mercy and Love. According to a saying of Prophet Muhammad: "God's mercy prevails over His wrath." This teaching protects one from complacency and despair.

Despite God's infinite qualities, humans can relate to Him. He is not remote or impersonal, but is very close to us and so we can call upon Him whenever we wish to do so. A Muslim (or any human being, for that matter) has a relationship of voluntary loving and conscious submission to God. If someone wants something from God, he or she can ask God directly without asking anyone else to intercede with God for him or her.

It can be summarized that Muslims believe in the same One True God that Jews and Christians believe in. Jews call Him Yahweh, Christians call Him Our Father in Heaven, and

Muslims call Him Allah. Allah is an Arabic word for God, and Jews and Christians in the Arab world also call Him Allah.

4

ISLAMIC BELIEFS

LIKE OTHER MAJOR religions, Islam entails both holding certain beliefs and putting them into practice. For Muslims, it is very important to have not only proper beliefs, but also proper actions. Without proper belief, actions may be inconsequential. Actions, on the other hand, express and articulate faith. The Qur'an teaches that a believer's fate after death will be determined on the basis of how he/she puts faith into action in this life.

The foundation of the Islamic faith is based on six articles. These are the basic beliefs that one must have in order to be considered a true Muslim. They are belief in: (1) One God, (2) all of the Messengers (Prophets) of God, (3) all of the original scriptures revealed to Prophets including Abraham, Moses, David, Jesus, and Muhammad, (4) the angels, (5) resurrection after death and the Day of Judgment, and (6) the divine decree (or destiny). Islam is unique among world religions in requiring Muslims to believe in the articles listed above.

In addition to the Oneness of God, as discussed above, Muslims believe in Prophets and Messengers of God. They do not just believe in the Prophet Muhammad but also other Prophets, starting with Adam, and including Noah, Abraham, Ishmael, Isaac, Jacob, Joseph, Job, Jonas, Moses, Aaron, David, Solomon, John the

Baptist, Jesus and others. Islam's understanding of God's Prophets is that they were human beings who reflected divine qualities i.e. Mercy, but were not divine. Also, they were the best among men.

It is noteworthy that Islam makes belief in the Books of other faiths a necessary condition for its own faith. Other books revered by Muslims include revelations, in their original forms, to Abraham, Moses, and David, as well as the original Gospel of Jesus. However, Muslims believe that God's final message to man, a reconfirmation of the eternal message, was revealed to the Prophet Muhammad in the form of the Qur'an.

Like most Jews and Christians, Muslims believe in the existence of angels and that they are honored creatures, created from Noor, the special light of God. According to Islam, angels worship God alone, obey Him, and act only by His command. Unlike humans, who have free will, angels have no free will. They are assigned a variety of functions and they perform their duties diligently. For example, Angel Gabriel (in Arabic Jibraeel) brought divine revelation to Prophet Muhammad, Angel Michael (in Arabic Mikaeel) makes available sustenance for humans, Angel Azraeel is responsible for taking life at death, and Angel Israfeel will blow the trumpet at the final hour. In addition to these famous angels, Muslims also believe that each human is assigned two guardian angels that remain with him and record everything he says or does. These recordings in his book of deeds will be presented for his accountability on the Day of Judgment.

The Day of Judgment (the Day of Resurrection) in Islam is when all people will be resurrected for God's judgment according to their beliefs and deeds. Based on the result of God's judgment, people will be sent to their final destination of either Heaven or Hell. Some will go to Hell for a period and after paying for their bad deeds and purification, will go to Heaven.

Muslims belief in Al-Qadr is based on the concept of Divine predestination. Islam teaches that human beings are free to do right or wrong, and will be held responsible for their choices accordingly. The belief in divine predestination also encompasses the belief that God knows and has a record of everything that has happened or will happen. Whatever He wills to happen, happens, and whatever He wills not to happen, does not and will never happen.

Humanity is free in this life to believe or not to believe in the One God, and has the choice to do good or evil. Everyone will be judged on the Day of Judgment for his or her faith and deeds. Muslims are not fatalists. The fact that God sent revelations to humanity through His Prophets and Messengers indicates that humans are expected to listen, make choices, and adjust their lives accordingly. Free will is the most fundamental ingredient of human activity. It empowers humans to demonstrate their morality. Without it there would be no such thing as good or evil conduct.

The actions that people will be will be judged by include not only their deeds, but also those we taught to others. For example, if I teach someone to do a beneficial deed, and he does it, I'll receive a part of the credit for that at the time of my accountability.

As for the final article of faith, Muslims believe that after their earthly life, human beings enter into a new state of existence, known as Akhirah or afterlife. Belief in the afterlife provides a very real motivation for us for our conduct in this life. It is the most serious deterrent to those who may contemplate doing something wrong. The true Muslim motivation is not the fear of God but His love. We do not want to do something God forbids because God loves us and we are afraid to displease Him by committing a forbidden act.

ISLAM'S VIEW ON THE DAY OF JUDGMENT, HEAVEN AND HELL

Like most Christians, Muslims believe that the present life is temporary and is just a preparation for the permanent life that will come after death. Life on earth is a test for each of us for the life in the hereafter.

With death, the body returns to the earth, but spiritual life does not cease to be. Indeed, the soul enters another stage of human life cycle or Barzakh, which is a state between the time of death and the Day of Resurrection. The length of time in the state of Barzakh may be centuries in earth time, but for the "dead," this period passes without a sense of time.

On the Last Day, everything and everyone who is alive will die, everything will come to an end, and nothing will remain, except for God Himself. No one knows when that day will be, but there will be signs to indicate its approach. According to Muslim belief, one of the major signs will be the second coming of Jesus.

On the Day of Resurrection, or the Day of Judgment as it is also sometimes known, all bodies will be resurrected. On that day, mankind will be brought before God for accountability of their faith and deeds in their earthly life. Souls will be reunited with their bodies. God says in the Qur'an (75:4) that He will restore us to our fingertips. In the life to come, we will be resurrected in forms unknown to us and our mode of living will be beyond our present comprehension. The Qur'an also teaches that we shall be in the company of those we loved and continue to love.

God will Judge people according to their future state of existence, and will sorted them to either Heaven or Hell. People's deeds will be judged by intentions and motives. The Qur'an (49:13) states: "the best among you in the sight of God are the ones who are the most righteous." Those who believed in One God and followed the message brought by His Prophets and Messengers, will be rewarded and admitted to Paradise. The Qur'an (2:82) states: "And those who believe and do good deeds, they will be dwellers of Paradise, they will dwell therein for ever."

Those who rejected One God and His message, and died in a state of disbelief, will have a painful punishment. With respect to such individuals the Qur'an (3:91) states: "Those who disbelieved and died in a state of disbelief, the earth full of gold would not be accepted from any of them if it were offered as ransom. They will have no helpers."

The Muslim's understanding of Paradise is that it is a heavenly place of peace and bliss, with beautiful gardens with rivers flowing underneath. Inhabitants of Paradise will recline on couches and will be served refreshing drinks that will not intoxicate them. They will enjoy the company of beautiful companions, and abide therein forever.

Hell is understood as a place of endless pain, suffering, torment, and agony, with roaring flames and scorching winds. The dwellers of Hell will be given boiling water to drink and awful tasting thorny bushes to eat. It will be the eternal destination for those who refused to accept God's Grace and His offer of forgiveness. They will be damned to eternal punishment, a result of their own choices made in life on earth.

Many sinners will not go to Hell because they repented for their sins, were genuinely sorry, and cried out to God for forgiveness. For this reason, Muslims are encouraged to continuously seek forgiveness for sins they committed knowingly or unknowingly.

Islam places great emphasis on the importance of moral responsibility in this life and its connection with accountability and eternal reward in the hereafter. Every soul will be held accountable for its actions on earth; each action we take in this life has the potential for eternal consequences. The best action is to choose to submit to God's Will, observe His Commands, and perform deeds that please Him, regardless of the difficult circumstances we may encounter.

Islam classifies actions on a sliding scale into those that are obligatory (in Arabic fard), actions that are recommended or praiseworthy (mustahab), actions that are inconsequential but permitted (mubah), actions that are frowned upon (makrooh), and actions that are forbidden (haram). Most Muslims know where they stand with respect to their actions.

Importantly, Muslims do not believe that anyone is predestined to end up in the Paradise because God has destined them for that, and that others are born for Hell. Our eternal fate is not sealed at the time of our physical birth, but only at the time of our physical death.

So long as we are alive and have not hardened our hearts to the point where we can no longer acknowledge the compassionate love of God, we are capable of receiving His gift of eternal success and well being (falah), repenting our sins and leading a new life. The road to heaven is not easy, and finding it often involves struggle and hardship.

5

THE FIVE PILLARS—FORMAL ACTS OF WORSHIP IN ISLAM

THERE ARE FIVE formal acts of worship in Islam. Sometimes these are called religious duties or five pillars of Islam, from which the house of Islam is constructed. These are compulsory religious duties, prescribed in the Qur'an, and must be undertaken with the best of effort in order to be considered a true Muslim. They are the most visible ways of expression of a Muslim's devotion to Islam and distinguish Islam from other religions. These include:

1. Shahadah—the testimony of belief and declaration: "I testify that there is no god but Allah and I testify that Muhammad is His servant and His (final) Messenger.
2. Salat—performance of the obligatory prayer five times each day.
3. Zakat—sharing of wealth with the needy by paying a fixed amount (2.5%) of one's wealth to them each year.
4. Sawm—fasting daily during daylight hours during the month of Ramadan.
5. Hajj—performance of pilgrimage to Mecca at least once in the lifetime, provided one is physically and financially able to do so.

THE FIRST PILLAR OF ISLAM: THE SHAHADAH

Islam's creed, the Shahadah, articulates Islam's essence and belief system. The declaration "there is no god but Allah and Muhammad is His servant and Messenger" has two parts: the first part negates the existence of all deities except the Only, One, True God. It is an expression of pure monotheism, which is the hallmark of Islam. Anything that violates the belief in divine unity is idolatry and an unpardonable sin, called 'shirk.' For example, it would be shirk to associate with God, the Creator, in worship anything or anyone from His creation.

Shirk is a very serious sin in Islam, and it is only up to God to decide the punishment for it. However, the following verse of the Qur'an says something about its gravity:

> *"God does not forgive anyone for associating anyone*
> *(or anything in worship) with Him; whereas,*
> *He may forgive whomever He wants to for any other sin.*
> *And whoever associates anything with God,*
> *he/she commits an enormous sin."*
> (Qur'an 4:48)

Shirk has been categorized as greater shirk or lesser shirk. Associating anything or anyone with God in worship is the greater shirk. The lesser shirk can be described as the preoccupation with material things, such as one's job, business, entertainment, family and friends to the extent that one forgets about God, who is the real Bestower of all blessings. Prophet Muhammad once said that he was very concerned about his followers committing the lesser shirk because one can be committing the lesser shirk and not realize it.

The second part of the creed is the belief and declaration that Muhammad is the (final) Messenger of God (to mankind).

Among the Messengers of God mentioned in the Qur'an are Abraham, Moses, David, Jesus, and Muhammad. Only some of the Prophets were Messengers of God. Allah has sent Prophets or Messengers to all people in the history of humanity, to teach them about God and His Will.

Muslims recite the declaration of faith on specific occasions. For example, a new convert to Islam recites the Shahadah as an expression of his faith and his membership in the Muslim community (Umma). Muslims recite the Shahadah in the ear of a newborn baby. It is also recited when one hears the call to prayer, during each Salat (prayer), and during a funeral procession to the cemetery. Finally, it is the hope and desire of every Muslim to recite the Shahadah with his/her last breath before dying.

THE SECOND PILLAR OF ISLAM: THE MUSLIM PRAYER

Five times each day, hundreds of millions of Muslims all over the world face towards the Ka'ba in Mecca, Saudi Arabia to perform the mandatory act of prayer called Salat. The Qur'an repeatedly mentions the injunction for the Muslims to pray. Each Salat can be performed only at a prescribed time period of day. The first prayer is performed before sunrise, the second at just past mid-day, the third in the afternoon, the fourth at sunset, and the fifth at night. The performance of the Salat five times every day keeps the Muslim conscious of God in the midst of all the activities and distractions of the material life on earth. It reminds man that the main purpose of his creation is to worship his Creator and that he is totally dependent on God.

At the start of each prayer time a caller, the Muazzen, chants out Islam's call to prayer (Azaan) from the minaret of the mosque or in a prayer hall. The call for prayer is translated as following:

God is Great (Allaho Akbar), God is Great
God is Great, God is Great
I bear witness that there is no god but God
I bear witness that there is no god but God
I bear witness that Muhammad is the Messenger of God
I bear witness that Muhammad is the Messenger of God
Come to the prayer, come to the prayer
Come to success, come to success
God is Great, God is Great
There is no god but God

Muslims all over the world pray facing towards the Ka'ba, the House of God, which is a cubical stone structure located inside the compound of the Sacred Mosque (Masjid al-Haram) in Mecca, Saudi Arabia. Muslims believe that the Ka'ba was originally built by Prophet Adam as a place dedicated for the worship of One God, and that later it was rebuilt by Prophet Abraham and his son Ishmael.

Facing towards the Ka'ba doesn't mean that Muslims worship the Ka'ba or any object there. It only provides a common direction or Qibla for all Muslims on a worldwide basis to face towards, and symbolizes unity of purpose, spiritual focus and direction. The inside of the Ka'ba itself is almost empty.

A unique feature of Islam is that it allows its adherents to perform worship anywhere on earth, so long as they can face towards the Ka'ba. Performance of Salat is not restricted to a mosque, the Muslim house of worship, but it can be offered individually or in a group, indoors or outdoors, at home or in the workplace, in a church, synagogue, or any other place, provided that the location is clean and quiet.

When praying outside a mosque, Muslims usually use a prayer mat to ensure a clean prayer space and some degree of comfort when kneeling on the ground.

Salat is the most important of all the formal acts of Muslim worship. Performance of Salat also requires one to be dressed properly in clean clothes and be in a state of ritual purity. The purification of the body is achieved by ritual washing known as Wu'du. It involves washing of hands, face, arms and feet.

The purpose of Wu'du is not only to literally cleanse parts of the body of dirt and dust but also to put oneself in a pure state of mind in preparation to go in front of God and worship Him. Salat is ideally performed after purging from one's mind and heart all thoughts about the material world and focusing on God.

The worshiper is expected to perform his/her worship with sincerity, humility, and love of God in the heart, and with the realization that he/she is in the presence of God Almighty. The standard themes of the prayer are the glorification and praise of God, expression of gratitude and humility, and supplication.

The act of Salat is performed in two to four cycles of specific movements with words of prayer. Each cycle is called a Raka' in Arabic. Each Raka' involves prayer and recitation from the Qur'an while standing, bowing, kneeling, prostrating, and sitting.

Each of these movements begins with the recitation of the phrase Allaho Akbar (God is Great). A Raka' takes a few minutes to complete, and each Raka' is started with the recitation of the opening chapter of the Qur'an, called Al-Fatiha. No prayer is valid without the recitation of Al-Fatiha. The translation of Al-Fatiha is as following:

In the Name of God, Most Beneficent, Most Merciful
Praise be to God the Owner and Sustainer of the worlds
Most Beneficent, Most Merciful
Master of the Day of Judgment
Thou alone do we worship and from Thou alone do we seek help

Show us the straight path
The path of those on whom Thou have bestowed Thy Grace
Not (the path) of those who have earned Thy Wrath
Nor of those who have gone astray.
(Qur'an 1: 1–7)

Additional verses from the Qur'an are also recited in the standing position of Salat. After recitation, a Muslim bows to God. This act is called Ruku' and it is performed by touching both knees with hands. In this position, one glorifies God by repeating three or more times "Glory to God, Most High."

Next step is prostration or Sujud. In Sujud, the worshiper does not kiss the ground, as is erroneously depicted in Western movies. Instead, he falls to his knees, places his hands on the ground, and brings his forehead and nose gently down to touch the ground between his hands. A Muslim assumes this position to demonstrate his servitude, utter humility, and helplessness to God, and to seek God's help, guidance, and forgiveness. It is important to note that a true Muslim will refuse to prostrate in front of anyone or anything, except God Almighty.

While in Sujud, the worshiper repeats three times: "Glory to God, Most High." Then he sits up and repeats the Sujud one more time to complete one cycle, or Raka', of prayer. The worshiper then stands up to repeat the entire cycle.

At the end of the second cycle the worshiper sits on his knees and recites salutation on Prophet Muhammad and testification: "I witness that there is no god but God and Muhammad is His servant and His Messenger." Then blessings on Prophets Abraham and Muhammad and their families are invoked and the prayer is concluded by turning the head to the left and the right and reciting the peace greetings: "Peace be upon you all and mercy of God."

While Muslims are allowed to pray by themselves, it is

preferable to attend a congregational prayer, preferably performed in a mosque. The experience of praying in a congregation, where everyone is making the same movements, creates a
great sense of brotherhood and unity of purpose.

A typical mosque is usually a simple building with a dome
in the center and at least one minaret. Some mosques have several domes and several minarets, such as the grand mosque in
Medina, Saudi Arabia. A typical mosque also has a niche called
Mihrab and a small staircase called Minbar (MIN-bar) in the
main prayer hall. The Mihrab is a niche in one of the walls of the
mosque. It faces towards Mecca, and marks the direction (Qibla)
towards the Ka'ba in Mecca. The prayer leader (the Imam)
stands inside or facing it while leading the prayer. The Minbar is
used by the Imam to deliver his sermon (Khutba).

The congregational prayer in a mosque is the most impressive religious sight that comes to view in Muslim lands. Scores
and even hundreds of Muslims stand shoulder to shoulder and
bow and prostrate together in the direction of Mecca. A leader
called an Imam leads the congregational prayer. Outside of the
mosque, any Muslim male at least 12 years old can lead a congregational prayer, as long as he can recite the Qur'an in Arabic. The prayer must be performed in Arabic, regardless of the
native language of the worshippers.

Women can lead a congregational prayer of women only. Typically, in a congregational prayer, men stand in straight horizon-
tal lines behind the Imam, and women behind the men. Women
pray behind the men out of a concern for modesty because the
Muslim prayer involves bending the entire body until the forehead touches the floor.

On Fridays, Muslims are required to attend a special mid-day
congregational prayer known as the Friday prayer. This prayer
can be compared to the Sunday mass for the Christians. It is different from other daily prayers in that in this prayer the Imam

delivers a sermon (Khutba) before the prayer. Muslims are commanded in the Qur'an to stop work during the time for the Friday prayer, which is between 1 and 2:30 pm local time, and perform the special prayer. They can resume their businesses or work after the prayer. Expecting the Muslims to work during this time on a Friday would be similar to expecting the practicing Christians to work on Sunday.

Although Friday is a special day of the week for the Muslims, it cannot be compared to Saturday as the Day of Sabbath for Jews, because the Muslims are allowed to go back to work after they have performed their special Friday prayer and worship.

There are two other occasions for special congregational prayers. These are at the occasion of the Muslim celebrations of Eid-ul-Fitr and Eid-ul-Adha. Eid-ul-Fitr is the first day after the completion of Ramadan, the month of fasting. Eid-ul-Adha marks the completion of the pilgrimage to Mecca. It is also the day of celebration for Muslims to commemorate Abraham's willingness to sacrifice his son at the command of God. At both occasions, Muslims attend special congregational prayers held after sunrise. It is preferable to hold this prayer outside the mosque in an open area, although it can also be held inside a mosque. The prayer precedes a Khutba. The purpose of the prayers is to give thanks.

For the Friday prayer, The Imam starts the Khutba with the glorification and praise of God. He then recites a portion of the Qur'an, explains its meanings, and invokes blessings of God upon Prophet Muhammad. Then he may talk about the affairs and problems of the community and give Islamic advice or Qur'anic teachings on how to solve them. The Khutba is concluded with prayer to God Almighty for the forgiveness, guidance, and success of the Muslims and their victory in struggle against tyranny, injustice, oppression, and persecution all over the world. The congregation listens to the Khutba without interruption. The end of the Khutba is followed by a call for prayer. The members of the congregation make meticulous lines behind the Imam and offer their prayer to God Almighty in the most earnest and humble way possible.

Like other houses of worship, mosques welcome visitors. For those who would like to visit a local mosque, it is best to make arrangements in advance. Some mosques have special open houses throughout the year. A non-Muslim visitor should dress modestly. Shirts and long pants are fine for men. Women should cover their hair with a scarf and wear clothing that covers arms and legs. After entering the building, but before entering the prayer area of the mosque, everyone is expected to remove their shoes. Muslims may stop in washrooms to perform Wu'du or ritual cleaning of face, hands, and feet, but visitors are not required to do this. Non-Muslims are not expected to join the lines of praying men and women, but they can sit in chairs placed along the sides of the room and watch quietly.

The prayer is to glorify, praise, and thank Almighty God for His blessings, and to ask for His Guidance and His Mercy. It is not to ask Him to grant our material needs, because He grants us what we need anyway. Rather, it is for our overall physical and spiritual wellness. A Muslim prays to God directly without the assistance of an intermediary and without elaborate rituals. The prayer keeps one constantly aware of one's duty to God, to himself, to other humans, and to other creatures of God. The ritual of washing (ablution) for the prayer five times a day keeps Muslims physically and spiritually clean. Prayer is an external expression of a Muslims' earnestness and devotion to his/her religion.

THE THIRD PILLAR OF ISLAM: PAYMENT OF THE ZAKAT

The Zakat is an obligatory act ordained by God Almighty in the Qur'an to be performed by every adult Muslim. It is one of the five pillars of Islam, and a form of charity obligatory for Muslims. It is levied on specific type of assets according to Islamic law (Sharia), and involves the payment of a certain portion of one's accumulated assets to the rightful recipients as an act of love of God. It translates into an expression of obedience and gratitude to God.

Zakat is paid once every year at a rate ranging between 2.5 and 20% of accumulated assets, not merely a percentage of income. The assets are calculated after deducting liabilities, including taxes. The rate at which Zakat is paid varies with the type of asset and the difficulty with which the asset has been acquired, evaluated by a built-in system of equity and justice. For cash savings, stocks, bonds, gold and silver, and business inventory, Zakat is 2.5%. On produce of land: if it is only irrigated by rain, it is 10%, because you are not spending as much effort or investment. It is 5% if you are using equipment to irrigate it. If someone finds a treasure or hits a mine, Zakat is 20%. More information on calculation of Zakat can be obtained online.

Zakat is not a tax. People try their best to avoid paying taxes, or pay them reluctantly. Zakat is paid as an act of worship to please God, and therefore is paid enthusiastically, not reluctantly. Muslims are encouraged to pay more than what is due. While there is a minimum, there is no maximum.

Zakat is different from charity. Charity is voluntary and can be paid in any amount and to anyone, or not paid at all. Zakat, on the other hand, must be paid in a predetermined amount, and to those who are needy and meet certain qualifications. Muslims are not prohibited from paying charity to non-Muslim individuals or organizations, but Zakat is paid to Muslims only. For example: the most deserving include the poor and the needy who do not ask for help because their dignity does not allow them; wayfarers stranded in foreign lands; employees appointed by Islamic states to collect Zakat; those who have converted to Islam and are experiencing financial difficulty; and those who are in debt as a result of a disaster. Zakat money can also be used to free slaves or prisoners of war by way of ransom, and in support of projects that are designed to propagate Islam and educate people about it.

Performance of Salat and payment of Zakat have appeared together in the Qur'an many times, indicating the importance of these two acts of worship in Islam. The fact that Zakat is an article of faith emphasizes that it is not enough to have the right beliefs and perform one's prayers; one must also fulfill one's obligations to fellow believers. Belief, acts of worship, and social justice are all harmoniously integrated in Islam.

In Islam, it is not forbidden to accumulate wealth, provided it is through honest and honorable means. It is a part of the Islamic tradition, however, to be generous and share your wealth with needy individuals. The payment of Zakat has particular significance in societies without state welfare systems. It provides an opportunity for those who are blessed with wealth to share the blessing with those who have little. Islam introduced this state welfare system in the seventh century. If the Zakat is practiced in its true spirit, there should be no poor and no need for a state welfare system in the Islamic societies.

It is primarily an individual's responsibility to calculate and pay Zakat, but in some Muslim countries, the government collects and redistributes the Zakat funds among qualified recipients. Individuals have the incentive to pay Zakat on their own accord because the Qur'an warns that failure to pay Zakat will earn the wrath of God and His punishment on the Day of Judgment. The Qur'an provides a terrifying description of what results from miserliness and lack of thankfulness to God; conversely, there are many passages in the Qur'an that describe a generous reward for those who pay Zakat and spend in the way of God.

Muslims do not only pay Zakat because it is required, but also for the numerous benefits it provides. Because Zakat is an act of giving for love of God, it purifies the heart of the giver from spiritual diseases such as selfishness, greed, miserliness, and materialism. While the term Zakat has been variously translated as a religious tax, an almsgiving, as charity, and so on, its literal meaning is "to purify." The Zakat literally "purifies" a Muslim's wealth. Zakat also purifies the heart of the deserving recipient from jealousy and hatred for those who possess wealth. Sharing through Zakat increases mutual concern, love, and fellowship.

The institution of Zakat also provides benefits on a social level. It provides a mechanism to purify a society from social injustice, class struggle, a sense of deprivation, and a lack of concern for others. Feelings of injustice and deprivation can give rise to a variety of subversive ideologies. Sharing of the wealth through the payment of Zakat helps to minimize or eliminate such social problems.

Muslims also give Zakat out of a belief that whatever material and spiritual resources humans have, God almighty has endowed us with them out of His Benevolence. After all, God is the real owner of everything–we are only His trustees on earth. The wealth and resources He has given us are no more than a test for us. Therefore, we must thank God for His Benevolence and share these resources with those who do not have them.

FASTING DURING RAMADAN—THE FOURTH PILLAR OF ISLAM

Muslims are required to practice self-discipline by fasting (Sawm) for an entire month each year. Muslims fast during Ramadan, the ninth month in the Islamic calendar. The Islamic calendar is a lunar calendar, which is eleven days shorter than the solar calendar. Due to this discrepancy, Ramadan occurs eleven days earlier each year, allowing people to experience Ramadan in all seasons of the year.

The month of Ramadan is a very special time for the Muslims.

The revelation of the Qur'an to Prophet Muhammad was initiated during Ramadan. The Qur'an was first revealed to him on an odd night, called the Night of Power, during the last ten days of Ramadan. Each year, Muslims give thanks and celebrate this day for the revelation of the sacred text of the Qur'an. They set aside the trials and tribulations of everyday life in order to create a special season of peace, harmony, compassion, tolerance, and sacrifice.

Ramadan is a time to draw closer to God and dedicate lives, hearts, and motivations to Him. Fasting sensitizes people to compassion for others. It makes one appreciate the suffering of the poor and the hungry, and it infuses piety and God-consciousness in those who fast. Fasting also teaches discipline and inculcates a feeling of community amongst Muslims.

The rules of fasting are stringent. From just before dawn until sunset, Muslims are required to abstain from eating, drinking, and sexual activity. Nothing should enter the body, not even cigarette smoke. Those who intend to fast wake up before sunrise for a meal called "Suhur," which must be finished before the sunrise. The fast is broken at sunset with a meal called "Iftar." Families and friends make a special effort to break their fast together.

After breaking the fast, Muslims offer their evening prayer. After the night prayer, special congregational prayers are held in mosques during the month of Ramadan in which a Hafiz (one who has memorized the entire Qur'an by heart) recites a portion of the Qur'an each night. The Qur'an is usually recited in its entirety during this month.

Some people are exempt from fasting. The elderly, children below the age of puberty, the sick, the travelers, and pregnant or nursing women are not required to fast if doing so will put them at risk. In some cases, the fast must be made up later, such as the case with women when they menstruate. For those who are too old, weak, or sick and are not able to make up the fast, the poor must be fed a meal for each day of missed fast.

The completion of the month of Ramadan is celebrated on the day of Eid-ul-fitr (the celebration of the feast of fast breaking). It is one of the two most important religious holidays for the Muslims and a very joyous celebration. On this day there is a special congregational prayer, followed by visiting with friends and relatives to share food and exchange gifts.

THE FIFTH PILLAR OF ISLAM: THE HAJJ

Hajj means a journey with a special religious purpose, or a pilgrimage. Muslims are required to undertake pilgrimage to the Ka'ba at least once in their lifetime, provided one is physically able and can afford the travel expenses. The Ka'ba is a cubicle structure known as the House of God. Draped with a black cloth embellished with Qur'anic verses embroidered in gold, it is located inside the compound of the Sacred Mosque (Bait al-Haram) in Mecca, Saudi Arabia. According to Islamic tradition, it built originally by Adam, as the first house of worship for One God. Later, Abraham, his son Ishmael, and wife Hagar rebuilt it.

The travel for Hajj is only undertaken during the twelfth month of the Islamic calendar. The Hajj season starts two months after the end of Ramadan. Each year during Hajj season, more than two million Muslims representing a tremendous diversity of cultures, travel to Mecca to form a single community of believers (Ummah) and live their faith.

Before entering the boundary of the Ka'ba, the pilgrims enter in a state of purity by discarding normal dress, which symbolizes social status, and instead donning two plain white sheets of cloth (symbolic of the dress we will wear in the grave) and sandals. Every man wears the same two sheets of cloth whether he is a prince or a pauper. This uniform dress code is an outward expression of ritual purity and symbolizes equality and humility before God, as well as unity as fellow believers.

Pilgrims experience an overpowering sense of community in the company of millions of others who are dressed in identical fashion and are performing the same rituals. The national, cultural, and socio-economic distinctions among them disappear, and they are truly one undivided community (Ummah) standing united in the worship of God. Women wear plain, simple dresses that covers the entire body except the face and the hands. Their dress does not have to be white.

Hajj is performed with a sense of devotion, beginning with the appropriate intention. As the pilgrims approach Mecca, they chant: "I am here, O Lord, I am here. There is no associate with You. I am here. Surely, the praise and blessings are for You, as well as the kingdom." During the performance of Hajj, the pilgrims are not allowed to use improper speech or actions.

There are a number of rituals that must be undertaken to complete the Hajj on entering the precincts of the Ka'ba. It takes about a week to perform all the required rituals, which are done in Mecca and the surrounding areas. The rituals of Hajj symbolize and commemorate the struggles undertaken by Abraham, his wife Hagar and their son Ishmael in submitting their wills to God. The main rituals of the Hajj include:

- Circumambulating Ka'ba in the footsteps of Prophets Abraham and Muhammad. The pilgrims go around the Ka'ba counterclockwise seven times. The circumambulation symbolizes their entry before the divine presence and simulates the circumambulation of the Throne of God by the angels in the Heavens.
- Jogging between two hills, Safa and Marwa, to commemorate Hagar's frantic search for water for herself and her son Ishmael.
- Traveling to the Plain of Arafat.

- Symbolic rejection of Satan by throwing stones at three pillars that stand at the sites where Satan met Abraham and Ishmael and tried in vain to tempt them to disobey God.
- Sacrificing an animal, to commemorate Abraham's willingness to sacrifice his only son in obedience to God's command. At the command of God, an angel brought a ram to substitute for the son.

As the pilgrims sacrifice their animals and share the meal, Muslims all over the world do the same thing as they celebrate the greatest feast of the year, Eid-ul-Adha (feast of the sacrifice) on the tenth day of the twelfth month of the Islamic calendar. After performance of the Hajj, many Muslims travel to the city of Medina to visit the grave of Prophet Muhammad.

IMPORTANCE OF THE FIVE PILLARS OF ISLAM

The five pillars of Islam, Shahadah, Salat, Zakat, Sawm, and Hajj are the external expression of a Muslim's internal beliefs. These are essential elements of worship that are shared by all Muslims. Performance of these acts of worship trains Muslims to put their faith into action, to serve and obey God, and to seek His mercy, guidance, and forgiveness.

Performance of Salat teaches the Muslims to humble themselves before their Creator and to glorify Him, to appreciate the equality of people before God, and to strengthens bonds of brotherhood amongst them. Payment of Zakat, on the other hand, teaches them the virtue of sharing and sacrifice. Fasting (Sawm) allows Muslims to develop self-control of their base desires for food, sex, and materialism. It also provides for them an opportunity to appreciate the hardship suffered by those who are less fortunate, and inculcates in them the virtues of giving to others and sharing their fortunes with them. Finally, the Hajj creates an opportunity for Muslims to perform pilgrimage to the sacred sanctuary in Mecca in obedience to God's Command, and meet Muslims from all over the world.

While these five formal acts of worship are performed by all Muslims, irrespective of their nationality, ethnic background, or affiliation with a given school of Islamic jurisprudence or sect, there are also voluntary religious practices which some Muslims perform. These depend on their association with different traditions, schools of jurisprudence, or sects. Some of these practices are highly regarded as valid forms of worship, while others are viewed as controversial. This is due to the great diversity within the Muslim Ummah, particularly with regard to the interpretation of events in Islamic history and the interpretation of Islamic jurisprudence.

For example: recitation of the Qur'an in private homes as well as in public places is considered by most Muslims as a source of blessing, and is quite common in most Muslim communities. In some communities, the Qur'an is recited in a melodious way when people gather for a funeral. Similarly, Qur'an is recited at other ceremonies that have religious significance, such as weddings, circumcision, and even graduation ceremonies.

Some Muslims express their love for God and Prophet Muhammad by singing poetry called Na'at. Glorification and praise of God and salutations for Prophet Muhammad are the common themes. No musical instrument is used. Those who follow the Sufi tradition of Islam also make use of chanting and singing to express their love for God and Prophet Muhammad. Some Sufi Muslims use music and melodious group singing called qawwali in their tradition. Occasionally, the combination of the poetry and music in the qawwali creates a state of ecstasy for the audience. Some individuals experience an overpowering emotion and mental exaltation, sometimes leading to dancing or a state of trance.

THE QUR'AN

MUSLIMS BELIEVE THAT the Qur'an is the last revealed word of God. The Qur'an (sometimes written as Koran) in Arabic means "something that is recited over and over." It is a book of divine revelation, comprising the eternal literal word of God, preserved in the Arabic language in which it was revealed. It defines the Will of God for all of humanity.

Muslims believe that the Qur'an is a complete record of the exact words and verses revealed by God through the Archangel Gabriel to Prophet Muhammad. As soon as the revelation was brought to Prophet Muhammad, he appointed scribes to write down its words and verses. The revealed verses were also committed to memory by several of Prophet Muhammad's companions and followers. Memorizing the Qur'an is a tradition in the Muslim world, going back to the time of Prophet Muhammad, and it is still practiced widely.

Under the supervision of Prophet Muhammad, the compilation of these verses became the Qur'an. The order of verses and 114 chapters was commanded by divine revelation and dictated by Prophet Muhammad before he died. The Qur'an was revealed to Prophet Muhammad one or more verses at a time, taking 23 years for the entire Qur'an to be revealed. Prophet

Muhammad was commanded by God to bring the message to mankind, and he brought it exactly as it was revealed to him. He did not add or remove a single word, as God Almighty had warned him against the slightest alteration in the message. In this respect, the Qur'an states:

"Say (O Muhammad): It is not for me to change it of my own accord.
I only follow that which is inspired in me.
Lo! if I disobey my Lord I fear the retribution of an awful Day.
Say: If God had so Willed, I should not have recited it to you,
nor would He have made it known to you."
(Qur'an 10: 15).

After the death of Prophet Muhammad, the first complete handwritten copy of the Qur'an, the Mus'haf, an official standardized version, was compiled by Abu Bakr and placed in the trust of Hafsa, the Prophet's wife. Later, at the order of Uthman, the third Caliph, seven copies of the Mus'haf were prepared and sent to different parts of the Islamic world. One of these is preserved in the Tashkent Museum. It is identical to the text presently in use all over the world.

The Qur'an teaches faith in One God Who creates and sustains all of creation. The theme and underlying message is the relationship between God and His creatures. It provides guidelines for a just society, equitable economic principles, proper human conduct, and peace and harmony in everyday life. The Qur'an also defines rules for prayer and other religious rituals; it establishes norms governing marriage and divorce, relations between man and woman, and the way to raise righteous children. It teaches virtues of honesty, justice, truthfulness, and fair dealing. Its teachings are of benefit to all cultures in all ages.

The Qur'an calls upon mankind to obey God, abstain from committing sins, and to live a pure life. It warns that many had strayed away from God's message, and admonishes mankind to return to the path of God, as revealed one final time to Prophet Muhammad. The Qur'an warns of God's final judgment, and describes scenes from the heaven and the hell. For Muslims, the Qur'an is the prime source of legislation and practice of faith. Its 114 chapters cover everything from the nature of God to laws governing the mundane affairs of man.

The Qur'an is not a new version of the Hebrew and Christian Scriptures. On the contrary, it corrects the distortions incorporated in these scriptures. It is not correct to call it the Bible of Islam, as some non-Muslim scholars have done.1 It is not a scripture, per se, as it is the direct Word of God revealed to Prophet Muhammad. It also has the distinction to be the last divine book. As there will be no more revelation, mankind will have to find guidance through the Qur'an until the Day of Judgment.

The Old and New Testaments do not take the form of God speaking directly to man; they merely report historical events as they happened. In the Qur'an, God speaks directly and powerfully to mankind, telling them about Himself and His laws, giving them guidance.

Muslims believe that the Qur'an is of divine authorship, and it is the eternal, literal Word of God preserved in Arabic, the language in which it was originally revealed. Scholars of Islam point out several factors that show that Prophet Muhammad served only as its conduit:

- Prophet Muhammad himself was unlettered and could not read or write;
- the Qur'an is devoid of contradictions, a quality that distinguishes it from the Christian and Hebrew scriptures;
- it is a masterpiece of Arabic language and poetry;
- there are many scientific facts contained in the Qur'an that have only recently been understood through advanced

research and sophisticated equipment, and thus were unknown to Prophet Muhammad and his Companions.[13]

The Qur'an is not a book focused on the life history of Prophet Muhammad, although it commands the believers to use Prophet Muhammad's person and way of life as a model. To those who may insinuate that Prophet Muhammad invented or authored it, God challenges them to try to 'invent' something similar to it:

> *"If they (the disbelievers) say that he (Muhammad)*
> *has invented it (the Qur'an); then Say:*
> *Then produce ten Surahs (chapters) the like thereof, invented,*
> *and call on everyone you can besides God, if you are truthful.*
> *And if they do not respond to you,*
> *then know that it is revealed only in the knowledge of God;*
> *and that there is no God except Him.*
> *Will you then become one of those who are Muslims?"*
> (Qur'an 11:13)

The Qur'an outlines quite a few scientific phenomena. For example, it tells us that at one time in the creation the whole universe was a 'smoke' material, and earth and heavens (the sun, the moon, the stars, planets, galaxies, etc) had common origin from this same 'smoke' material (Qur'an 21:30, and 41;11).

Another phenomena mentioned in the Qur'an that was not known during the time of Prophet Muhammad is the recently discovered fact that mountains have underlying roots that are shaped like pegs (Qur'an 78:6-7). The Qur'an also reveals that in the place where two seas meet, there is a barrier between them (Qur'an 55:19-20). It is now well known that when the Mediterranean Sea water enters the Atlantic Ocean over the Gibralter sill, it moves several hundred kilometers into the Atlantic at a depth of 1 km with its own warmer temperature and higher salinity. There is a sort of barrier between them that they do not transgress despite tides, large waves, strong currents.

Additional scientific facts mentioned in the Qur'an include the existence of darkness in the deep seas and oceans, and the existence of a set of internal waves below the surface of the oceans (Qur'an 24:40). Scientists have discovered internal waves existing at the interfaces between layers of different densities. Similarly, the Qur'an gives a description of how clouds, rain, and hail form (Qur'an 24:43).

The discussion of embryonic development in the Qur'an is particularly significant. In relatively few verses, the Qur'an comprehensively discusses human embryonic and fetal development, from the time the gametes commingle through organogenesis. In verses 12 to 14 of Chapter 23, the Qur'an describes human embryonic development and the attachment of the embryo to the uterus in different stages: first in the manner of a leech, and later like a clot of blood and a chewed substance. No such distinct and complete record of human development is known to have previously existed.

Prophet Muhammad also mentioned a specific timetable for the main embryological development in forty days. Such descriptions in the Qur'an and the sayings of Prophet Muhammad cannot be based on scientific knowledge available in the 7th century. The only conclusion is that these descriptions were revelations to Prophet Muhammad from God.

Reputable non-Muslim scientists from Canada, the USA, and other countries have acknowledged that the profound pronouncements (Qur'anic verses) stated by Prophet Muhammad more than 14 centuries ago were too scientifically accurate to be a matter of coincidence. They seem to have no problem accepting that these were divine revelations.[13]

The Qur'an challenges those who doubt that it is a revelation from God to produce a chapter like it, and even call their supporters and helpers to aid them in this challenge (Qur'an 2:23-24). Ever since the Qur'an was revealed fourteen centuries ago, no one has been able to produce a single chapter comparable to the chapters of the Qur'an in beauty, eloquence, splendor, wisdom, authenticity of information, and perfection. The smallest chapter (Chapter 108) is only ten words, yet no one has ever been able to meet this challenge. During the time of Prophet Muhammad, some disbelieving Arabs tried to meet this challenge to prove that Muhammad was not a true prophet. They failed, despite the fact that the Qur'an was revealed in their own language and dialect.

An astonishing fact about the Qur'an is that it has remained completely unchanged over the last fourteen hundred years; in the Qur'an, God claims that it will remain unchanged until the last hour, no matter how much effort anybody puts into changing or altering it. This is because God Himself has taken the responsibility of preserving the Qur'an. This is stated in the Qur'an:

"Surely, We have revealed this reminder and Lo,
We verily are its Guardian"
(Qur'an 15:9).

For Muslims, the presence of God can be experienced here and now through the very sounds and syllables of the Arabic Qur'an. Thus, only Arabic is used in prayer—even though the vast majority of Muslims are non-Arabs and many do not understand the language. To hear those words recited, and to take them into yourself through prayer is to experience the presence of God with great intimacy. The recitation reinforces the miracle of hearing the actual words of God expressed in human voice, and people have converted to Islam just upon hearing the Qur'an recited.

When the Arab people heard the Qur'an recited for the first

time, they were wonderstruck and shocked. They were sure that a language of such extraordinary beauty could come only from God. As a result, many converted instantly.

In her book A History of God, Karen Armstrong[10] describes how Omar ibn al-Khattab, a devoted idol worshiper and a hostile enemy of Prophet Muhammad, converted to Islam on hearing the Qur'an. One day he set out to assassinate the Prophet. Along the way someone told him that his sister and her husband had secretly become Muslims. Angrily he went to his sister's house and heard the Qur'an recited from outside the house. He stormed in and struck his sister, who started to bleed. Omar picked up a piece of the manuscript and started to read it. He was so moved by the verses he read that he instantly converted to Islam.

Karen Armstrong also states that without this power of the Qur'an it would have been extremely unlikely for Islam to have taken roots. She adds that it took Prophet Muhammad only 23 years to transform Arabs from idol worshippers to monotheists; whereas, it took ancient Israelites more than 700 years to break with old religious allegiances and accept monotheism.

The superb style of the Qur'an has a tremendous effect on the one who recites it. It leaves a soothing effect on the mind of the one who recites, even if he does not fully understand the meaning. It changes the pattern of life for those who believe and practice its teachings. Chanting of the Qur'an in Arabic is an art form whose style can be directly traced back to the Prophet and can only be mastered under scholars of recitation. Those who recite are held in great esteem. Many Muslims experience profound aesthetic pleasure and inspiration from listening to the rhyming recitation of the Qur'an. Muslims also believe in the healing power of the Qur'an, and even some non-Muslim scholars have recognized it.[11]

Like Jews, Muslims do not throw away anything that has the name of God written on it. As Muslims consider the Qur'an holy

word of God, they respect and honor it to the point that they do
not even touch it before cleaning themselves. It has the Name
and Attributes of God Almighty repeatedly mentioned in it and
is, therefore, so sacred that it is beyond description.

In view of this degree of reverence, Muslims are shocked and
deeply hurt when they hear about the desecration and burning
of the Qur'an. People who have insulted the Qur'an[14, 15, 16] have
done so out of foolishness, ignorance, and hate. At the Dove
Outreach Center (church) in Gainsville, Florida, where Christian Minister Terry Jones had threatened to burn the Qur'an and
then backed down, a copy of the Qur'an was finally burned on
March 20, 2011. As expected, it fueled anti-American sentiment,
and generated violent demonstrations in Afghanistan, where
mobs of thousands of protestors attacked UN compound killing
seven foreign U.N. employees. Four Afghans also died. The top
UN envoy in Afghanistan, Steffan de Mistura, called the Qur'an
burning an 'insane gesture.' Regardless of the insanity of burning the Qur'an, it was wrong to kill the UN workers in retalia-
tion for this horrible act.

Muslims recite passages from the Qur'an in their daily
prayers. Rhythmic and poetic recitation of the verses serves as an
introduction to community events, from weddings and funerals
to seminars and business dinners. Muslims all over the world
recite the Qur'an and memorize its portions in Arabic, whether
they understand it or not. They also pray in Arabic, regardless
of their local language.

Millions of Muslims, known as Hafiz (or "preservers") have
memorized the text of the Qur'an from the beginning to end,
and can recite any part of it from the memory. Therefore, even if
all the Qur'ans in the world today were destroyed, the original
Arabic text would still remain and would be reproduced into
text from the memory of the "preservers."

The Qur'an was revealed in Arabic language, and it is not

possible to translate it into any other language without losing the meaning and essence. Therefore, any translation is neither a Qur'an nor a version of the Qur'an. It cannot be called a Qur'an, but only an approximate translation of the meaning of the Qur'an. The Qur'an exists only in Arabic.

While we can come to know its teachings in translation, the Qur'an loses the beauty and impact that it has in Arabic. A translation sounds like a different book altogether, even to a Muslim. It is meant to be chanted aloud. The sound of the recitation is an essential part of its effect. It commands the reciter:

"And chant the Qur'an in a measured tone."
(Qur'an 73:4)

The Qur'an is not meant to be read merely as a reference book for the acquisition of information, and it must not be read in haste. It says much more than what a literal reading can possibly capture.

A major problem is the interpretation of the Qur'an and application of God's words to changed historical circumstances. Although there are generally agreed upon principles developed by scholars of Tafseer (exegesis), a fundamentalist may interpret a verse one way, and a more liberal Muslim may interpret it in a different way. As a result, anyone with an agenda may feel free to cite the Qur'an in his support. Disputes of Qur'anic interpretations are settled by Muslim jurists learned in the Sharia (Islamic jurisprudence) and Tafseer.

It should be noted that the Qur'an can only be interpreted by qualified jurists, and the jurists may differ. It is not up to a common Muslim to interpret it any way he wants without proper qualification. Islam does not teach that 'everybody has their own valid interpretation.'

7

THE SUNNAH:
THE OTHER SACRED SOURCE
OF INSTRUCTION IN ISLAM

IN ISLAM, NO aspect of life is outside the realm of religion, whether it is personal, public, social, economic, or political. When looking for guidance, Muslims try to follow the teachings of the Qur'an.

However, some of the verses or the Qur'an are beyond the understanding of common man and needed to be interpreted, which Prophet Muhammad did. For example, the Qur'an commands that the Muslims perform their daily prayer or Salat, but it does not explain how to perform it. This was done by Prophet Muhammad, who said "perform your prayer (Salat) as you have seen me performing." His method of prayer is recorded in Hadith.

While the Qur'an is the direct Word of God, Hadith is Prophet Muhammad's own sayings. A Hadith is an example of what he said at a given time in the course of normal life. For example: according to one Hadith recorded in the Bukhari collection, he said: "Obtaining of knowledge is a duty on every Muslim, male and female."

Prophet Muhammad's mission was not only limited to the transmission of the words and verses of the Qur'an, but also included their explanation and exemplification. He put the laws that God revealed into practice for the various conditions of ordinary human life, and perfectly lived up to the revelation. He followed the teachings of the Qur'an so closely that his wife Aisha called him the physical manifestation of the Qur'an—the walking Qur'an.

Prophet Muhammad's character was so refined and so magnificent that the Qur'an has declared him as a model of the best character for mankind and a person with the most sublime character:

*"Ye have indeed in the Messenger
of God a beautiful pattern of conduct
for any one whose hope is in God and the Final Day,
and who engages much in the remembrance of God."*
(Qur'an 33:21)

*"And you (O Muhammad) are most certainly of exalted
and most sublime character."*
(Qur'an 68:4)

As such, Muslims consider him as an excellent role model to follow and they try to emulate his character.

During the life of Prophet Muhammad the Muslims followed his example in putting into practice the teachings of the Qur'an in all aspects of life. In order to put the teachings of the Qur'an into practice, anything he did, approved, instructed, or forbade the Muslims to do is called the Sunnah (tradition) of Prophet Muhammad.

After the Prophet's death, his companions and family members shared their recollection of the things that Prophet

Muhammad said, did, approved or disapproved of while he was among them. Each recording of these prophetic traditions (Sunnah) is called a Hadith. Hadith is an Arabic word, which means "report."

Each Hadith has a chain of transmission giving an account of who said what to whom, and it eventually ends up with Prophet Muhammad or one of his companions. Although there are several Hadith collections, two in particular are considered especially authoritative by Sunni Muslims: those compiled by Ismail al-Bukhari and Muslim Ibn al-Hajjaj.

After the Qur'an, the Hadith is the most sacred source of inspiration and instruction for Muslims. They try to follow the Sunnah of Prophet Muhammad in all aspects of their life. He was and still is the model for the Muslim ideal to be emulated by all Muslims. The wide range of subjects discussed in the Hadith gives an indication of the importance of the role Prophet Muhammad played as a model for Muslims.

A few examples of the sayings (Hadith) of Prophet Muhammad[17] are as following:

"All created beings belong to the family of God, so the most loved one of God is he who shows the most kindness to His family."

"The best person among the people is the one who benefits others."

"None of you truly believes until he wishes for his brother what he wishes for himself."

"A person who is not kind to the children and respectful of the elders, is not one of us."

"The most perfect amongst believers in faith is he who is the best in manners and the kindest to his spouse."

"The Most-Beneficent (God) showers His mercy upon those who show mercy to others. So show mercy to earthly creatures, so that the One Who is in the Heaven should show mercy to you."

"The things which will make the majority of people enter Paradise are the fear of God and good manners."

"Strictly avoid envy, because envy consumes the good deeds as the fire consumes the wood."

"Powerful is not he who knocks (the other) down. Indeed, powerful is he who controls himself in a fit of anger."

"Verily, when the people see an evil (in the society), but make no effort to change it, God may inflict His punishment upon all of them."

"Verily, God forbids you to disobey your mothers."

"He is not a believer who eats to his fill but his neighbor goes hungry."

"Neither the deceitful nor the miser will enter Paradise nor he who mistreats those under his supervision."

"Let him who believes in God and the Last Day either speak good or keep silent, and let him who believes in God and the Last Day be generous to his neighbor, and let him who believes in God and the Last Day be generous to his guest"

"Fear God wherever you are; whenever you commit a bad deed, follow it up with a good deed; and behave towards people with courtesy."

"To act justly between two people is a charity; to help a man with his mount, lifting him onto it or hoisting up his belongings onto it is a charity; every step you take going towards prayer is a charity; and removing a harmful thing from the path is a charity."

"Whoever of you sees an evil action, let him change it with his hand; and if he is not able to do so, then with his tongue; and if he is not able to do so, then with his heart—and that is the weakest of faith."

"God Almighty has said: O son of Adam! so long as you call upon Me and ask Me, I shall forgive you for what you have done, and I shall not mind. O son of Adam! were your sins to reach the clouds in the sky and were you then to ask Me forgiveness, I would forgive you. O son of Adam! were you to come to Me with sins nearly as great as the earth and were you then to face Me, ascribing no partners to Me, I would grant you forgiveness nearly as great as it (the earth)."

A man came to Prophet Muhammad and said: "Counsel me." He said: "Do not become angry." The man repeated his question several times, and he got the same answer.

8

THE LIFE AND MISSION OF MUHAMMAD, THE MESSENGER OF GOD

WRITINGS ABOUT THE life of Prophet Muhammad are called Seerah. Most non-Muslims are not familiar with the character, teachings, and life history of Prophet Muhammad, and this leads to misunderstanding about him. Much has been written about him, and his life history is available in great detail. Such detail is not available about any other comparable religious personality.

Prophet Muhammad was born in the year 570 in Makkah (Mecca), Saudi Arabia, among people who had drifted from God's way. The world was completely different from the one we live in. There is no resemblance between the environment of the year 570 and that of today. People of Arabia of that time were mostly uneducated, knowledge was meager, outlook was narrow, they were steeped in extremes of ignorance and superstition, and communication was primitive and limited. There was growing division between the rich and the poor, and injustice was prevalent in the society.

It was an age of darkness all over the world, and Arabia was a land where this layer of darkness was even thicker. Arabia was insulated from the cultural influences of Byzantium, Persia, and Egypt, by an ocean of sand, and stood almost cut off from the rest of the world. Arab traders had to travel a long distance for months at a time to carry their good to and from these countries. They could hardly acquire any bits of knowledge during their travels.

There was not a single institution in the whole of Arabia, nor were there any libraries. The only books, that were available, were hand-written and rare treasures. No one seemed to be interested in the advancement of knowledge. A few who could read were not educated enough to be in any way involved in the existing arts and sciences. They did, however, possess some very good qualities, and were known for courage, honesty, hospitality, generosity, and fulfillment of a promise. They also had a highly developed language, Arabic, which could express the finest qualities of human thought and feelings in the most remarkable manner, especially in poetry. But their knowledge was very limited.

It was a land without a government, and every tribe claimed authority and considered itself an independent unit. There was no law except a primitive law of a tribal society. Murder of the innocent, revenge, abduction for ransom or slavery, stealing, and other crimes were common in the society, and people took pleasure in drinking, gambling, looting and plunder. They felt no shame in being seen naked by others, and the women even performed circumambulation of the Ka'bah sometimes completely naked. Life, property, and honor were always at stake. They buried their daughters alive because it was considered dishonorable to have a daughter. Different tribes were always ready to go to war for trivial reasons. The society was not based on differentiation between pure and impure, lawful and unlawful, or civil and uncivil.

They had become animistic polytheists, and worshiped stones, trees, idols, stars, and spirits among other things. They knew that they were descendents of Abraham and Ishmael, but they knew nothings about the teachings of those Prophets about God whom they worshiped. In fact, all around the world, the true religion had been forgotten or distorted. In such an ignorant society and among such uncivilized people, Prophet Muhammad grew up to be a man of God.

The Prophet's father had died before his birth and his mother died when he was only six years old. As a result, he was raised in an extended family—first by his grandfather and later by his uncle, who were from the Bani Hashem clan of the honored tribe of Quraysh and Custodians of the Ka'bah. Prophet Muhammad was raised unlettered, and was unable to read or write. In his boyhood, he tended flocks of sheep and goats in the company of Bedouin youth. Consequently, he was deprived of even the minimum training and upbringing which an Arab child of those times normally received. He never had a chance to sit in the company of learned men, for such men were non-existent in Arabia at that time.

When he was 25 years old, he started working for a businesswoman named Khadija, a 40 year old widow. She was so impressed with his high morals and honesty that she proposed to him for marriage. He accepted the offer, and they were married. She believed in him when nobody else did and she always comforted him in his difficult times. Their marriage was monogamous and a happy, and they had six children. They remained married for 24 years until Khadija died.

Prophet Muhammad did have a few opportunities to travel out of his country, but those travels were business trips undertaken by Arab caravans. If he met any learned men during his travels, they could not be assumed to have had such an impact upon him to change him so profoundly that there remained no likeness between him and the society he was born and raised in. Nor could such random meetings be considered sufficient to transform an unlettered Bedouin into a person with such a sublime and perfect human character; a leader not only for that age and those people, but for the world at large and for all time to come.

In terms of his character, the Prophet was known to be a person of caring and friendly disposition, sensitive to suffering of others. He was different from the people among whom he was born and with whom he spent his childhood and early life. Even his worst enemies never accused him of ever telling a lie throughout his entire life. Because of his truthfulness, the whole nation called him Al Sadiq (the truthful one), and because of his sense of justice and honor, he was given the title of Al Ameen (the trustworthy one) by his people. Although he was born to people who regarded alcohol and gambling as virtues, he never touched alcohol nor indulged in gambling.

His people were uncultured and uncivilized, but he was blessed with the highest culture and most refined characteristics. He was surrounded by crude and hard-hearted people, but his own heart was flowing with kindness and mercy for everyone. He was helpful to the orphans and the widows, and hospitable to travelers. He was especially kind to children, elderly people, and to his neighbors. He was raised in an idolatrous society, but he regarded nothing worthy of worship except One True God.

The superstitions and unjust ways of the people made Prophet Muhammad very unhappy. He was discomforted with the darkness and ignorance, corruption, immorality, idolatry, and chaos of the society he was living in. He used to retreat into a cave in a mountain to spend long hours in seclusion, meditation, and communion with his Creator, reflecting on the purpose of man's life. He longed to bring the people to the way of God, not unlike Prophets of old.

When Prophet Muhammad was forty years old, God's Divine Light shone in its full resplendence on him and the Prophet was honored by God to be His last Messenger to mankind. One day, when Prophet Muhammad was praying in the cave of Hira, near Mecca, Archangel Gabriel visited him. This first sight of the angel was overwhelming for the Prophet. The angel spoke to him, reciting to him words of God Himself.

His first command to the Prophet was "Recite." To that Prophet Muhammad answered: "I cannot recite." The angel took him and squeezed him vehemently, let him go, and repeated the command "Recite," to which Prophet Muhammad again answered: "I cannot recite." This process was repeated three times. After the third time, he ordered the Prophet:

> "Recite in the name of thy Lord Who created,
> He created man from a clot of blood.
> Recite! And your Lord is the Most Gracious Who teaches by the pen;
> He taught man what he knew not"
> (Qur'an 96:1-5)

The Prophet recited and from his lips came the first verses of the Qur'an, regarded by 1.5 billion Muslims around the world as the eternal Words of God Himself. After this first encounter with Gabriel, Prophet Muhammad was terrified; he rushed home where his wife consoled and comforted him. Soon afterwards, he was commanded in the revelations of the Qur'an to invite people to belief in the One and only God, the Creator and Sustainer of all the worlds, and the Master of the Day of Judgment.

These early revelations received by Prophet Muhammad were calls for religious and social reforms. They emphasized social justice (rights of women, widows, and orphans), corrected distortions to God's revelations in Judaism and Christianity, and warned that most people had strayed away from the original message of God brought by His Prophets.

The revelations of the Qur'an exhorted people to shun evil, do good, and love one another. They told them that real religion

was the removal of want and suffering of others and selfless service to fellow man. The religious rituals were of no use if they
did not inculcate in man the virtue to become righteous and
work for the good of others:

> *"Have you observed him who belies the religion?*
> *That is he who repels the orphan,*
> *and urges not the feeding of the needy.*
> *Ah! woe unto worshipers who are heedless of their prayer;*
> *who would be seen (at worship), yet refrain from works of kindness."*
> (Qur'an 107: 1-7).

Prophet Muhammad was commanded by God to call people
to the way of the Lord with wisdom and good speech and to
reason with them in ways most gracious. When he called mankind to the worship of One God, he was not looking for personal
benefit. He preached that there is only One God worthy of worship, and the idols that they worshipped were nothing but simply pieces of wood and stone.

He preached that mankind should praise, glorify and worship
the One God, Who is the only Reality; seek only His help and
guidance; to leave the idols, as they were of no use. He preached
that God is Great, He created us and sustains us, and so we must
submit to Him. Our entire strength lies in submission to the Will
of God (in Islam), so we should accept whatever He sends to us.

Thomas Carlyl[18] gives us a colorful picture of what Prophet
Muhammad might have said to the idol worshipers of Mecca:

"Idolatry is nothing: these wooden idols of yours, ye rub them
with oil and wax, and flies stick on them, these are wood, I tell
you! They can do nothing for you; they are an impotent blasphe-
mous presence; a horror and abomination, if ye knew them. God
alone is; God alone has power; He made us, He can kill us and
keep us alive . . . Understand that His Will is the best for you . . ."

Muslims believe that Prophet Muhammad was sent as Messenger of God to all mankind, and the message he has brought from God Almighty, the Qur'an, is the truth. This is stated in the following verses of the Qur'an:

"Proclaim (O Muhammad): O Mankind!
Behold! I am the Messenger of Allah to you all—
(the Messenger) of Him
to Whom belongs the sovereignty of the heavens and the earth.
There is no god except Him, He brings to life and He causes to die.
Therefore, believe in God and His Messenger,
the unlettered Prophet, who believes in God and in His Words;
and follow him, so as to become one of those who are rightly guided."
(Qur'an 7:158)

"O mankind! Behold!
The Messenger has come to you with the Truth from your Lord.
Therefore, believe; it is better for you."
(Qur'an 4:170)

The Prophet's mission was to bring good news and warning to mankind:

"O Prophet! Lo!
we have sent you as a witness and a bringer of good tidings
and a warner, and as a summoner to God by His permission,
and as a lamp that gives light."
(Qur'an 33:45-46)

"And We have not sent you (O Muhammad)
except as a bringer of good news
and a warner to all mankind, but most of mankind know not."
(Qur'an 34:28)

The Qur'an also reminds us that Prophet Muhammad was sent as the messenger of God not just to Arabs, but to all mankind, including the People of the Book (the Jews and the Christians):

"O People of the Book!
Now has Our messenger come to you to make things plain
after an interval of the messengers, otherwise you would say:
There came not to us a messenger of good news nor a warner.
So now a messenger of good news and a warner has come to you;
and God is able to do all things."
(Qur'an 5:19)

By sending Prophet Muhammad with the Truth, God has bestowed a great favor upon humanity:

"God has shown grace to the believers
by sending to them a Messenger
from among themselves, who recites to them His revelations,
and sanctifies them, and teaches them the Scripture and wisdom,
although before he came to them, they were in flagrant error."
(Qur'an 3:164)

In his preaching, Prophet Muhammad taught against discrimination based on skin color, caste, race, and nationality. He taught that all human beings were created equal in the sight of God, and the best person in the sight of God was the one whose deeds were the best. The leaders of Mecca, however, had vested interests in preserving the socioeconomic status quo and were in no mood to listen to the prophet. They felt threatened from his preaching because of several reasons:

- The message of monotheism threatened polytheistic beliefs.

- they were afraid that the pilgrims who came to Mecca from all over for the worship of its idols would not come anymore, and that would cause them great loss in revenue;
- the Qur'an's teaching of ethical and moral values would put a control on their unethical way of life; and
- its message of justice and equality in the sight of God. The people of Mecca did not want to practice social justice because their society was based on class distinctions.

As a result, they opposed the Prophet and his followers, often violently. They called him a magician, a soothsayer, a liar, a madman and a poet. These allegations greatly hurt him, but God consoled and reassured him and sent down the following verses:

"Therefore, praise thy Lord (O Muhammad),
by the grace of God you are neither a soothsayer
nor art thou one possessed;
or as they say - a poet, for whom we may expect
some calamity by Time."
(Qur'an 52: 29-30)

"Thou art not, by the grace of the Lord, a madman."
(Qur'an 68: 2)

"That is indeed the speech of an illustrious Messenger.
It is not the speech of a poet —little is it that you believe (O mankind).
Nor is it the word of a soothsayer —
little admonition is it that ye receive (O mankind).
It is a revelation from the Lord of the Worlds."
(Qur'an 69: 40–43)

The treatment of Prophet Muhammad by many of his people was not much different from that of the earlier Prophets. They insulted and ridiculed him for preaching about only one God, while they had many gods. When that did not stop the preaching, they violently attacked, terrorized and tortured him and his followers, imposing social boycotts and economic sanctions against them. Some of the followers were even tortured to death for their belief. The leaders of Mecca planned and made attempts to kill the Prophet himself. Thirteen attempts were made on his life, but God saved him each time.

After a decade of preaching, the persecution became so fierce and so intolerable that in the year 622 God gave the command to Prophet Muhammad and his small group of followers to emigrate. This emigration from Mecca to the city of Medina, 260 miles to the north, marks the beginning of the Islamic or Hijrah calendar to be codified later during the Caliphate of Omar ibn al-Khattab.

In Medina, the Muslims found safety and a nurturing haven. The Muslim community grew to establish the foundation of the first Islamic state that was ruled under law of God. In Medina, Prophet Muhammad preached about One God, appealed for individual transformation of character, and introduced revolutionary changes on a societal level. These included raising the status of women to position of having equitable, though different, rights and responsibilities with men; steps towards the abolishment of slavery; prohibition of all kind of intoxicants, usury, and gambling; putting an end to exploitation of the poor and weak by the rich and powerful; and the establishment of a welfare State.

During his life in Medina, Prophet Muhammad performed a variety of functions. In addition to being the Messenger of God, he was the head of the nascent Islamic state, a political leader, a judge, a teacher, an Imam, a preacher, and the commander-in-chief of the army. Because of his leadership and arbitration skills, he was able to create peace among the warring tribes of

Medina and create a functional federation of Arab and Jewish tribes. Rules were developed to protect the rights of each community, later known as The Charter of Medina. It assured peace and security to Arabs and Jews as long as they followed the rules laid down in the Charter. It was called 'the first written constitution in the world.'

Despite all these responsibilities, he continued to live a life as simple as he had lived in Mecca. He was known for dealing with justice and fairness, treating even his enemies with mercy and compassion. Because of his just and kind treatment, people loved him and were ready to follow him. After several years, the Prophet and his followers returned to Mecca in triumph, where they forgave their enemies and rededicated the Ka'ba, the house of God, to the worship of the One God.

Prophet Muhammad died at the age of 63 years. His mission was the culmination and completion of all of God's Prophets and Messengers to mankind. There will be no more authentic Prophet after him until the Day of Judgment. For this reason he is called the Seal of the Prophets.

Before the Prophet died, the greater part of Arabia had accepted Islam, and within a century of his death, Islam had spread to Spain in the West and as far as China in the East. Islam had brought millions of people together to create a new world order. Among the reasons for the rapid and peaceful spread of Islam was the truth and clarity of its doctrine. Islam calls for faith in only One God, Who is the only One worthy of worship.

One aspect of Prophet Muhammad's life that has received much attention is his several marriages. It must be pointed out that for 24 years during the prime of his life, from the age of 25 to 49 years, he had only one wife, Khadija. They were happily married and had six children. Khadija died at the age of 65 when Prophet Muhammad was 49 years old. It was after her death that Prophet Muhammad started to marry again. He married several times and all of his wives were widows or divorcees, except for Aisha.

He did not marry multiple wives because of lust or materialistic gains. Even his most determined enemies of that time never accused him for committing lustful activities. Some of his marriages were contracted to forge or strengthen political alliances, while others were marriages to widows of his companions who had died in battlefield. Five of his wives, Khadija bit Khuwailid, Sawda bint Zam'a, Hafsa bint Umar, and Umm Salama bint Abi Umayya had been widows before he married them; and Zainab bint Jahsh and Umm Habiba Ramla bint Abu Sufyan were divorced. Marrying the widows and divorced women was done to provide protection to them in a society that otherwise afforded them very little protection.[3]

Prophet Muhammad was not the first Prophet to have more than one wives. Biblical prophets before him were known to have several wives. Abraham, Jacob, David, Solomon and many other prophets had more than one wives, and some had concubines. Similarly, during the time of Prophet Muhammad polygamy was a common cultural practice of the Arabs and other civilizations of that time, i.e. Chinese, Persian etc. His marriages were in accordance with the tradition and culture of that time. (For more on polygamy in Islam, see Chapter 16 –The Status of Women in Islam).

CHARACTER OF PROPHET MUHAMMAD

Prophet Muhammad lived up to the highest ideals of the Qur'an and his life exemplified the virtues mentioned in it. When his wife Aisha was asked about his morals, she answered: "His morals are the Qur'an." The Qur'an also tells us that he lived his life in complete accord with the Will of God.

Unlike the inhabitants of the desert, who are harsh and rough in manner, Prophet Muhammad was courteous, polite, and considerate in his dealings with people. For this reason he was very effective in communicating with the people and spreading the message of Islam. This is also pointed out in the Qur'an:

> "It is by the Mercy of God that you (O Muhammad)
> treat them gently
> (with kindness and mercy), for if you had been severe
> or harsh-hearted,
> they would have been dispersed from around you"
> (Qur'an 3:159).

He was sent as a mercy to all nations, and his compassion extended to friends and foes alike. His advice to his followers, according to one Hadith, was: "If you love your Creator, then love your fellow creatures first."[17]

When he was being persecuted in the city of Taa'if, his companion asked him to curse his persecutors. He replied: "I have not been sent to curse but as a mercy to humanity." Then he prayed for his persecutors: "O Lord! Guide these people, for they know not."

A very well known example of his compassion and mercy was at the conquest of Mecca. He declared general amnesty and forgiveness for the entire city, including the Pagans and their leaders who had killed, tortured, and starved his companions, relentlessly conspired to kill Prophet Muhammad himself, and had tried their best to annihilate his religion.

He declared to them: "This day I have no reproof against you." He won the hearts of his enemies through kindness and forgiveness. A study of his life's history reveals that he was the greatest support to the poor and the oppressed. He strove all his life to rescue mankind from corruption and sins, and to lead them to the One God.

His compassion and mercy was not limited to humans, it also extended to animals. He was a man who once kneeled down to tilt a pot of water for a thirsty cat to finish drinking, and in order to avoid unnecessary fatigue for an animal, he had forbidden his companions to carry on conversation on horseback while standing still.

He was blessed with the best of conduct and God Almighty assigned him the role of a model in conduct in the following verses of the Qur'an:

"Verily in the Messenger of Allah you have
a good example (of conduct)
for him who looks to Allah and the Last day,
and remembers Allah a lot."
(Qur'an: 33:21)

"And you (O Muhammad) are on an exalted
(standard of) character."
(Qur'an 68:4)

There are many stories about his excellent character. Once he saw an old woman who was rushing along with a bag that seemed to be too heavy for her. Prophet Muhammad offered to help her with her load. She did not know who he was, but agreed to benefit from his help. As they were walking, the Prophet asked her what was her hurry. She said she has heard about a madman in the city of Mecca and she wanted to leave town because of him; she advised him to leave town as well. He asked her who it was, and she said his name was Muhammad. Prophet Muhammad then said with a smile: "That is me." She was so impressed with his politeness and help that she decided to accept his faith.

If we compare Prophet Muhammad's life before his mission

as a Prophet and his life after he began his mission, we will come to the conclusion that it would be impossible to think that he was a false prophet. In fact, he was materially much better off before prophet-hood was conferred upon him.

Commenting on the simple life lived by Prophet Muhammad, Thomas Carlyle[18] states:

"Mahomet (Prophet Muhammad) himself, after all that can be said about him, was not a sensual man. We shall err widely if we consider this man as a common voluptuary, intent mainly on base enjoyments, - nay on enjoyments of any kind. His household was of the frugalest; his common diet barley-bread and water: sometimes for months there was not a fire once lighted on his hearth. They record with pride that he would mend his own shoes, patch his own cloak. A poor, hard-toiling, ill-provided man; careless of what vulgar men toil for. Not a bad man, I should say; something better in him than hunger of any sort . . . or these wild Arab men would not have reverenced him so."

Prophet Muhammad's wife Aisha is reported to have said that they would sight three moons without lighting a fire (to cook a meal). They lived on dates and water. Sometimes their neighbors sent camel milk for them. He slept on no soft bed, but on a palm mat.[19]

During the early days of his mission he was rejected, ridiculed, persecuted, and tortured. Attempts were made to kill him by the idol worshippers of Mecca. Despite a life of hardship and suffering, he kept calling people to the worship of One God.

The leaders of Mecca offered to make him their king and the richest man if he would stop calling people to the worship of One God. Such an offer would be tempting to someone pursuing worldly benefits, and most certainly to a fake Prophet. Prophet Muhammad refused their offer and continued his mission.

Despite his responsibilities as a Prophet, a community leader, a judge, and a teacher, Prophet Muhammad used to do household chores himself. He used to milk his goats and sheep, mend his clothes, repair his shoes, and help with other housework. His life was an amazing model of dignified simplicity.

Usually the desire to wield power and status go hand in hand with lavish life-style, abundant food, fancy clothing, big palaces, armed guards, and indisputable authority. Prophet Muhammad had none of these. He lived a simple and humble life even when he became triumphant over his adversaries and met success in his mission.

In the later days of his life, when Muslims were victorious after eighteen years of his prophetic mission, the greater part of the Arabian Peninsula was Muslim. The state treasury was at his disposal, and almost all of the people of Medina, the city where he lived, had become wealthy. Even in those days, Prophet Muhammad lived a hard life until he died.

When he died, the only things he left behind were a few coins, a part of which went to satisfy a debt and the rest was given to a needy person who came to his house for charity. The clothes in which he breathed his last breath had patches.[19]

MIRACLES PERFORMED BY PROPHET MUHAMMAD

The truthfulness and authenticity of Islam has never relied heavily upon miracles performed by Prophet Muhammad. The central miracle of the truthfulness of Islam is the Qur'an. Looking to the figure of the prophet Jesus draws an interesting contrast. When the non-believers asked Prophet Muhammad to show them miracles, the response of the Qur'an was that miracles of God are all around them—they only need to open their eyes to see them.

Yet Prophet Muhammad did perform several miracles during his life, just as Abraham, Moses, Jesus, and other Prophets did. In fact, miracles were associated with Prophet Muhammad from the time before his birth until his death. Martin Lings, in his book titled *Muhammad—His Life Based on the Earliest Sources*, has described several miracles performed by Prophet Muhammad.[20]

One of the earliest miracles associated with Prophet Muhammad was as a 12-year old boy traveling with his uncle Abu Talib to Syria. A Christian monk known as Bahira lived in a cell near Bosra, in Syria. He was accustomed to seeing caravans, including those from Mecca, stop near his cell. When the caravan carrying the boy Muhammad approached his cell, Bahira was struck by something he had never seen before: a low cloud moving slowly above the caravan, remaining between the sun and one of the travelers in the caravan.

As soon as they halted, the cloud stopped moving, remaining stationary over the tree under which the caravan took shelter. The tree lowered its branches over them to provide additional shade. Bahira realized that these observations were related to a great spiritual presence in the caravan, so he entertained the group with food. He determined that the cloud and the tree provided shade specifically for the boy Muhammad. Bahira observed that the character and behavior of Muhammad matched with what had been described in his religious books, and he saw the Seal of Prophethood, a mark between the shoulders on Muhammad's back, and concluded that he had signs of a Prophet.

A similar miracle was observed when Prophet Muhammad was 25 years of age. This time, his wife's slave Maysarah observed that two angels were shading Prophet Muhammad from the heat of the sun. He told this to Khadija, who later married Muhammad. Khadija had a cousin, Warqa bin Naufal, who had converted to Christianity. He was a priest and had studied in the scriptures that a Prophet would arise among his people. When Khadija told him the story of the two angles, Warqa told her that Muhammad was the Prophet foretold in his books.

On another occasion, a shepherd was pasturing a flock of

sheep when Prophet Muhammad and his friend Abu Bakr passed by. Prophet Muhammad asked the shepherd if he could give them some milk to drink. The shepherd said he could not; the flock belonged to somebody else.

Prophet Muhammad asked him if he had an ewe that had not yet mated with a ram. The shepherd brought one to him. The Prophet put his hand to her udder and prayed. The udder swelled with milk. Abu Bakr brought a cup and the Prophet milked her into it. They all drank and when he said to the udder: 'Dry', it dried up. The shepherd was so impressed that he converted to Islam.

Martin Lings describes another miracle of Prophet Muhammad, which took place on a night of the full moon, not too long after it had risen. The full moon was seen above Mount Hira. A group of disbelievers approached Prophet Muhammad and asked him to split the moon if he was indeed the Messenger of God.

The Prophet said "bear ye witness" and pointed to the moon, which split into two parts that drew away from each other until there was one half moon shining brightly on either side of the mountain. The believers rejoiced at the miracle and several persons who hesitated to become Muslim, entered Islam. The nonbelievers who had demanded the miracle, however, rejected it, calling it an act of magic.

The eventual victory of the Muslims in Arabia is also something of a miracle. When the idol worshippers of Mecca made life impossible for Prophet Muhammad and his small group of followers in the initial stages of Islam, the Muslims decided to migrate to the oasis of Yathrib (later it came to be known as Medina), where they were eventually able to establish an embryonic Islamic State.

They had to defend their tiny state and their religion against overwhelming numbers of disbelievers all over Arabia—Prophet Muhammad and his followers were continuously fighting battles against the disbelievers. The Prophet and his followers won most of the battles, despite smaller numbers and inferior arms as compared with their enemies. Many miracles have been associated with these battles, in which Muslims received Divine help and were victorious despite smaller numbers and inferior arms.

The battle of Badr is a particularly good example of an unlikely, but miraculous, victory of the Muslims. During this first battle, the poorly-armed Muslims, numbering only 313, defeated one thousand well-armed Meccan troops in hand-to-hand combat. This was a stunning miracle of God for the Muslims and gave them the needed assurance that they were indeed on the side of the truth.

Many other miracles in this battle have been described by Martin Lings.[20] For example, at one point when the battle was most intense, a sword broke in the hand of a Muslim, named Ukkasha. He made his way to Prophet Muhammad and asked for another sword. Since there was already a shortage of weapons, the Prophet gave him a wooden club, saying: "Use this to fight with, Ukkasha." Ukkasha took the club and upon brandishing it, the club became a shining sword. He fought with that miraculous sword the rest of the battle and all the Prophet's subsequent battles.

Many miracles of the Prophet were recorded during the Battle of the Trench. The Muslims dug a trench around the city of Medina to keep away the overwhelming numbers of the attacking Meccan army that had surrounded the city. Muslims had to work long hours to dig the trench. They had a shortage of food, which caused them to suffer from pangs of hunger. Seeing Prophet Muhammad's exceeding leanness, one of his followers, a man named Jabir, invited him to have supper with him.

He had only a small quantity of barley and an ewe, which he sacrificed for the supper. Although Jabir had invited only the Prophet, the Prophet told one person to call out an invitation to everyone to go to the house of Jabir for supper with the Messenger of God. Jabir panicked and went on ahead to warn his wife. When the meal was placed in front of the Prophet, he blessed it, uttered the Name of God over it, and started to eat. Ten persons sat down with the Prophet to eat, and when they had all eaten their fill, they rose and left, making room for ten more, and so it went on until all workers at the trench had satisfied their hunger, and there still remained some meat and bread.

In another miracle, a girl entered the camp one day during the Battle of the Trench with something in her hand. Prophet Muhammad called her to him and asked her what was she carrying. She said she was carrying dates for her father. He asked her to give the dates to him, and threw them on a garment that was spread out. He asked those who were with him to eat from those dates for lunch. They started to eat and the dates kept increasing in numbers. After everyone had eaten, the dates were overflowing from the edges of the garment.

Once, the Prophet was traveling north with his companions from Medina towards Tabuk. It was hot and they were thirsty. The Prophet told his companions that the next day they would come upon a spring of water. When they reached the spring, however, it had only a trickle of water—not for the entire army to satiate their thirst.

The Prophet directed his companions to scoop up whatever water they could in the hollows of their hands and transfer it into a skin. When enough water had been collected, he washed his hands and face with that water and poured it over a rock that covered the mouth of the spring, passing his hands over it and praying for water. Water gushed forth from the spring and it continued to flow even after all those present had satisfied their thirst. He turned to one of his companions and said: "O Mu'adh, it may be that you will live to see this place as a valley of gardens." And it came to pass as he had said.[20]

Miracles of Prophet Muhammad did not come to an end after his transition from this life to the next. He continues to show miracles. One well-known miracle of Prophet Muhammad, called the Miracle of the Burda, took place during the 13th century. It involved an Egyptian sufi poet, Imam Sharaf ad-Din al-Busiri, who suffered a stroke and was paralyzed. With half of his body unable to move, he became invalid. During his paralysis, he composed a poem, called Qasida tul Burda or just Burda, in praise and honor of Prophet Muhammad. He used to sing the Burda often and, seeking intercession of the Prophet through the Burda, called upon God to heal him.

One day, after praying to God to heal him, he fell asleep. He saw Prophet Muhammad in his dream, and recited the Burda to him. The Prophet touched the paralyzed part of his body and threw his cloak (Burda in Arabic) over him. Upon waking, Imam al-Busiri found himself miraculously healed, and his paralysis was gone. Prior to this he had not told anyone about his composition of the poem, so nobody knew about it. On recovering from paralysis, he was very happy and decided to go for a walk outside the house.

On his way, he met a person who said to him, "I want you to give me a copy of the poem you have composed." Al-Busiri asked, "Which one?" He said, "The one you composed during your illness." The man then recited the opening lines of the Burda, and said: "By God, I heard it in a vision last night recited in the presence of the Messenger of God, upon him and his family be blessings and peace. It greatly pleased the Prophet, and I saw him thrust his cloak on the one who wrote it."

Imam al-Busiri gave the man a copy of the Burda, and thereafter the news of this miracle was spread everywhere. The Burda is highly venerated in the Islamic world and recited in spiritual gatherings.

WHY SO MANY NON-MUSLIM WRITERS HAVE ADMIRED
PROPHET MUHAMMAD?

Many non-Muslim historians, writers, and scholars have written extensively about the impressive personality and character of Prophet Muhammad. For example, Professor K. S. Ramakrishna Rao,[19] an Indian professor of philosophy and a non-Muslim, in his book *Muhammad-The Prophet of Islam*, calls Prophet Muhammad the perfect model for human life. He states that all contemporaries of Muhammad, both friends and foes, Muslims and non-Muslims, acknowledged his qualities of spotless honesty, noble virtues, absolute sincerity, and trustworthiness in all spheres of human activity.

Professor Rao stated that the objective of Prophet Muhammad's mission was to educate and serve mankind and to purify and elevate it to a higher (spiritual) level. His thinking, his speech, and his actions were all directed towards the good of humanity. In his dealings with people, he was so fair and just that even those who did not accept his message accepted him as arbitrator in their personal disputes.

In comparison with some of the previous Prophets and Messengers of God who did not attract too many followers during their lifetime, Prophet Muhammad attracted thousands, although his mission lasted only 23 years. At the last pilgrimage (Hajj), he was accompanied by 144,000 Muslims.

Most of his companions were noble, intelligent, educated men and women, who knew him most intimately. They must have been convinced of the truth of his mission and the genuineness of his divine inspiration; if they had perceived any sign of deception or fraud in him, the Prophet's mission of spiritual awakening and social reform would have failed during his lifetime. His companions believed, trusted, obeyed, and honored him even under the most excruciating torture, severe mental agony, and under conditions that put their lives in great danger. They suffered all kinds of persecution for his sake but remained faithful to him.

It cannot be denied that Prophet Muhammad was able to discipline unruly Arabs, who were given to tribal warfare, and teach them to worship God Almighty. He resorted to battle purely in self-defense and only when efforts at peaceful resolution and conciliation had failed. He went to battle only when no alternative was available, but he changed the whole strategy of the battlefield. In an age of barbarism, the battlefield was humanized, rules were introduced, and strict instructions were given to the soldiers not to kill women, children, or old men; not to mutilate; not to molest those engaged in worship; and not to destroy vegetation.

Prophet Muhammad's own treatment of his bitterest enemies was the noblest example for his followers. When he conquered Mecca, he had the power to do whatever he could to the people of Mecca. These people had rejected his mission, had tortured him and his followers, driven them into exile, and had unrelentingly persecuted and boycotted them even when they had taken refuge in the city of Medina. That city now lay at the feet of Prophet Muhammad, and by the rules of war, he could have justly avenged all the cruelties inflicted on him and his people. Instead of taking revenge, he forgave his enemies and declared: "This day, there is no reproof against you and you are all free." By doing so, he demonstrated a practical example of the maxim: "Love your enemies."

Professor Rao has also noted that among the greatest contributions of Prophet Muhammad to the social elevation of mankind were his teaching of the principles of a universal brotherhood and equality of mankind. Professor Rao said that all great religions have also preached the same principles, but the teachings of Prophet Muhammad were unique in that he had put this theory into actual practice.

Giving an example of Prophet Muhammad's practice of human equality and social justice, Professor Rao mentions appointment of Bilal, a negro slave, to the high office of the first Muazzen of Islam. As the Muazzen, Bilal climbed on the roof of the Ka'ba, the holiest place in Islam, to call people for prayer, immediately elevating Bilal's social status to a level where the noblest and purest among the Arabs honored and respected him.

Professor Rao has quoted Mahatma Gandhi[21] who said that the Europeans in South Africa feared the arrival of Islam; even though Islam had civilized Spain, took the torch of light to Morocco, taught equality of races, and preached to the world the gospel of brotherhood. Gandhi indicated that the real reason for this fear was Islam's teaching of human brotherhood and equality of the races.

In his book *The World's Religions*, Huston Smith,[22] has described Prophet Muhammad as a person who was sweet and gentle in disposition, had a pure heart, and was loved by his companions. Smith noted that the Prophet's own bereavements sensitized him to human suffering, and he always extended a helping hand to others, especially the poor and the weak. The Prophet's noble character and qualities of truthfulness and honesty won him the titles of "The Truthful" (As-Sadiq) and "The Trustworthy" (Al-Ameen) from the people of Mecca.

Thomas Carlyle[18] has said that Prophet Muhammad was a man of justice, truth, and fidelity; true in what he did, spoke or thought; and his companions named him Al-Ameen. He was silent when there was nothing to be said, and when there was need to speak, he spoke pertinently, wisely and sincerely. He was good-natured and cordial in his disposition. He was serious, yet he had a sense of humor.

Smith1 also recognized Prophet Muhammad's modesty. The idol-worshipping people of Mecca wanted Prophet Muhammad to perform miracles to prove that he was a genuine prophet. He responded to them by saying that he was only a preacher and had been sent with a message from God Almighty. He told them that he was not sent to work wonders and perform miracles, and that if there was a need for signs to be seen, then there were signs of greatness of God that could be seen everywhere, if only they had their eyes open. He told them they did not need miracles to see signs of greatness of God.

Stanley Lane-Poole,[23] a well known historian, sums up the character of Prophet Muhammad as the one who was the messenger of one God, who tolerated the hatred of his enemies, and who loved children, never passing a group of children without a smile and a kind word.

Alphonse De LaMartaine,[24] one of the greatest poets of France, writing about Prophet Muhammad, stated that no other man had set himself a more splendid aim than Prophet Muhammad, whose mission was to remove superstitions which had been interposed between man and God, and to restore the rational and sacred idea of the worship of One God.

In *Historie de la Turquie*, De Lamartaine states about Prophet Muhammad: "He preferred migration to fighting his own people. But when oppression went beyond the pale of tolerance, he took up his sword in self-defense. Those who believe religion can be spread by force are fools."

De LaMartaine also stated that no one had ever undertaken a task so utterly beyond human capability with such small means as Prophet Muhammad had. He noted that no one in the history of great men could compare with (Prophet) Muhammad, who with very little means and resources achieved astounding results.

The most famous men in history created armies and empires only, which often crumbled away in their lifetime. Prophet Muhammad taught something more enduring that influenced

millions of men and created a spiritual nationality based on the
teachings of a book (the Qur'an) which blends together peoples
of many cultures and races.

According to De LaMartaine, Prophet Muhammad's life was
evidence of a firm conviction to restore rational belief in the
unity of God. His simple way of living, his devotion in worship,
his struggle to eliminate superstitions of his people, his courage in defying the anger of the idol worshippers, his firmness in
enduring abuse for thirteen years in Mecca, his forbearance in
victory, and his struggle for the success of the Divine Message
that he was delivering are all examples.

Based on these observations, De LaMartaine stated, Prophet
Muhammad was by far the most remarkable man that ever lived
on this earth. He preached a religion, founded a state, built a
nation, laid down a moral code, and instituted numerous social
and political reforms. He established a powerful and dynamic
society to practice and represent his teachings, and profoundly
affected human thought and behavior for all times to come.

In his book *Heroes, Hero-Worship, and the Heroic in History,*[18]
Thomas Carlyle stated:

"Our current hypothesis about Mahomet [Prophet Muham-
mad] that he was a scheming imposter, a falsehood incarnate,
that his religion is a mere mass of quackery and fatuity, begins
really to be now untenable to anyone. The lies (Western slander)
which well-meaning zeal has heaped round this man ((Muhammad) are disgraceful to ourselves only."

Carlyle stated that the charge of the skeptics that Muhammad was a false prophet and Islam a false religion is nonsense.
If Muhammad was a false prophet, millions of people would not
have followed him and if Islam was a false religion, it would not
be still around after more than fourteen centuries. He suggested
that the imposter hypothesis must be dismissed.

Carlyle noted how Prophet Muhammad was a man with

a noble mission: uniting humanity to the worship of One and Only God, and teaching mankind the way to honest and upright living based on Divine commands. By uniting humanity under One God, he effectively created the first League of Nations.

Commenting on Prophet Muhammad's mission of uniting humanity, Professor Hurgronje[25] stated that the League of Nations founded by the Prophet of Islam created a splendid example of international unity and human brotherhood for all nations to follow. He said that no nation of the world could show a parallel to what Islam had done towards the realization of the idea of the League of Nations.

According to Dr. William Draper,[26] Prophet Muhammad's title as the Messenger of God was justified based on the fact that he exercised the greatest influence upon the human race, was the religious head of many empires, and guided the daily life of one-fifth of the human race.

Sir George Bernard Shaw[27] stated that he had studied Prophet Muhammad's life and found him to be a wonderful man. He suggested that Prophet Muhammad should be called the Savior of Humanity. He also stated that if a man like Prophet Muhammad were to assume the leadership of the modern world, he would succeed in solving its problems in a way that would bring it the much needed peace and happiness.

In his book Muhammad at Mecca, W. Montgomery Watt,[28] wrote that Prophet Muhammad's readiness to undergo persecution for his beliefs, the high moral character of the men who believed in him and looked up to him as a leader, and the greatness of his ultimate achievement are all proof of his fundamental integrity. He stated that skeptics called Prophet Muhammad an impostor because out of all the great men in history, he was the most poorly appreciated in the West.

Watt added that despite the criticism of Prophet Muhammad by the modern Westerners, Muhammad's standards were higher than those of his time. In his day and generation, he was a social, as well as moral, reformer. He created a new system of social security and a new family structure, both of which were a great improvement on the old systems. He also took the best of the moral values of the Bedouins and introduced them to the settled communities. In addition, he established a religious and social framework for the lives of many races of men.

Edward Gibbon and Simon Ockley[29] wrote in *History of the Saracen Empire* that the greatest success of Prophet Muhammad's life was a result of the sheer moral force and the simplicity of the declaration of faith that says: "I witness that there is no one worthy of worship except God and Mohammad is the Messenger of God." They also stated that in Islam, the intellectual image of the Deity has never been degraded by any visible idol, and the reverence of the Prophet has never transgressed the limits of human virtues.

In a Reader's Digest article titled *Islam: The Misunderstood Religion*, James Michener,[30] has stated that like almost every major Prophet before him, Prophet Muhammad limited himself to serving as the transmitter of God's word. When the Archangel Gabriel appeared to him the first time and commanded him: "Recite," the Prophet responded: "I cannot recite." As he received the divine message, he began to teach it to mankind. He was profoundly practical in everything, and he was successful in his mission because he taught by putting the message to practice. The message soon revolutionized a large segment of the human population.

Michener also described that when Prophet Muhammad's baby son Ibrahim died, an eclipse occurred and some people spread rumors of God's personal condolence. When Prophet Muhammad heard the rumors, he immediately denounced them, and declared: "An eclipse is a phenomenon of nature. It is foolish to attribute such things to the death or birth of a human being."

Commenting on the character of Prophet Muhammad in his book, *Mahomet and His Successors*, Washington Irving[31] has given a description of how Prophet Muhammad lived a simple life. Irving noted that the Prophet ate little, observed fasting, and was scrupulous about personal cleanliness. He did not indulge in fancy dresses, and did not wear nor approve for his male followers the wearing of silk and gold. He wore cotton or wool garments, which sometimes had patches.

In his dealings with people, Prophet Muhammad was kind, tolerant, and just. He treated friends and strangers, the rich and poor, the powerful and weak, all with equity, and was loved by the common people for the courtesy with which he treated them and listened to their problems. His servant Anas served him from many years and reported that the Prophet never scolded him even though he spoiled things for him many times.

Irving described that if Prophet Muhammad had been selfish in his purpose that all of the successes and battlefield victories would have made him arrogant and vainglorious. However, even in the time of his greatest power, he maintained the same simplicity in his manners and appearance as in the days of his hardship and difficulty. If he was struggling for any kind of supremacy, it was the supremacy of the faith. With respect to the authority that came with his position, he used it with responsibility and humility, and did not try to perpetuate it in his family.

Prophet Muhammad renounced the material comforts of this life, kept himself occupied in prayer, and in times of trial he put his trust in God. The wealth that came from his victories he spent helping the poor and in works that helped to promote the faith. Irving has quoted Omar ibn al Harith, one of the companions of Prophet Muhammad, saying that Prophet Muhammad did not leave behind any gold or silver coins or slaves. The only things he left at the time of his death were his mule and his arms.

Reverend Bosworth-Smith[32] wrote in *Muhammed and*

Muhammedanism that Prophet Muhammad was the head of a state as well as religious authority. In a way, the Prophet was Caesar and Pope in one, but without Caesar's legions and the Pope's pretensions, and without a standing army, a bodyguard, a palace, or fixed revenue. He further stated that if any man could say that he ruled by a divine right, it was Prophet Muhammad; he had all the power without its instruments, supports, or the dressings of power.

Michael Hart,[33] in his book on ranking the people who contributed towards the benefit and uplift of mankind wrote:

"My choice of Muhammad to lead the list of the world's most influential persons may surprise some readers and may be questioned by others, but he was the only man in history who was supremely successful on both the religious and secular levels. It is probable that the relative influence of Muhammad on Islam has been larger than the combined influence of Jesus Christ and St. Paul on Christianity . . . It is this unparalleled combination of secular and religious influence which I feel entitles (Prophet) Muhammad to be considered the most influential single figure in human history."

REFERENCES TO PROPHET MUHAMMAD IN THE BIBLE

The Qur'an teaches that one of the missions of Jesus was to inform people about the coming of a final Prophet after him. The Muslims believe it refers to none other than Prophet Muhammad. There are numerous references to him in the Bible, a few of which are listed below.

In John 16: 12,13, Jesus is reported to have said: *"I have yet many things to say unto you, but ye cannot bear them now. Howbeit when he, the Spirit of truth, is come, he will guide you into all truth, for he shall not speak of himself but whatsoever he shall hear, that shall he speak, and he will shew you things to come."*

The Muslims believe that 'Spirit of Truth' refers to Prophet Muhammad, because he was known in his community to be a truthful person and the community had conferred the title of As-Sadiq on him. (As-Sadiq is an Arabic word for the truthful). Whatever revelations (verses of the Qur'an) he received from God, he conveyed them to people without any addition or subtraction.

The Qur'an also states that Prophet Muhammad was mentioned by name in the original Gospel given to Jesus:

And when Jesus son of Mary said: O Children of Israel! Behold!
I am the Messenger of God unto you,
confirming that which was revealed before me in the Torah,
and bringing good tidings of a messenger who cometh after me,
whose name is Ahmad
(one of the Prophet Muhammad's names, meaning the Praised one).
But when he hath come unto them with clear proofs,
they say: This is only magic.
(Qur'an 61:6)

In Deuteronomy 18:18, addressing Moses, God said:

"I will raise them up a Prophet from among their brethren,
like unto thee,
and will put my words in his mouth;
and he shall speak unto them all that I shall command him."

Muslims believe that this refers to Prophet Muhammad who was like Moses in many respects. He came from the brothers of the Israelites, i.e. the Ishmaelites, and God put His words into his mouth and he declared exactly the words he received from God. In fact, there were hardly any two prophets who were so much alike as Moses and Muhammad.

Rev. James L. Dow in Collins Gem Dictionary of the Bible Says: "The only man of history, who can be compared even remotely to him (Moses) is Mahomet (Prophet Muhammad)." There are several reasons for this. First, both had natural births (from union of a mother and a father), were married, accepted as leaders of their people and Prophets of God, were given a comprehensive law and code of life, molded the national character of their people, encountered their enemies, migrated, were victorious in their missions during their earthly life, and died natural deaths.

Second, the words of God were truly put into Prophet Muhammad's mouth. God sent Angel Gabriel to teach Prophet Muhammad the exact words of God (the Qur'an) and commanded him to recite them to his followers as he had heard them. The words were, therefore, not his own. They did not come from his own thoughts but were put into his mouth by the Angel Gabriel.

Third, in Deuteronomy 18:18 this prophesy also mentions that the Prophet will speak in the name of God. We find that each one of the 114 chapters of the Qur'an (except chapter 9, in which the name of God is mentioned in the text) begins with: "*In the name of God, Most Gracious, Most Merciful.*"

Another reference in the Bible to the coming of Prophet Muhammad is in Gospel of John (John 1:19-21). It indicates that the Jews were waiting for the fulfillment of three distinct prophecies. The first was about the coming of Christ, the second about the coming of Elias, and the third about the coming of a Prophet. So they asked these questions from John the Baptist:

"Who art thou? And he confessed, and denied not; but confessed,
I am not the Christ. And they asked him,
What then? Art thou Elias?
And he saith, I am not. Art thou the prophet?
And he answered, No."

Muslims believe the prophet referred to is Prophet Muhammad. The Bible also mentions the coming of "The Comforter" after Jesus. For example in John 14:16, and 16:7, respectively, Jesus is reported to have said:

> "And I will pray the Father, and he shall give you
> another Comforter,
> that he may abide with you forever."

> "It is expedient for you that I go away, for if I go not away, the Comforter will not come unto you, but if I depart, I will send him unto you."

The Church interprets "The Comforter" as the Holy Spirit, but if the Holy Spirit was already present during Jesus' ministry, then its coming was not a future event. The Muslims believe "The Comforter" referred to is Prophet Muhammad, who is called in the Qur'an *"a mercy to the peoples."* (Qur'an 21:107).

In Genesis 49: 1-10, the Bible refers to a prophecy made by Jacob just before his death: *"And Jacob called unto his sons, and said, Gather yourselves together that I may tell you that which shall befall you in the last days. Gather yourselves together, and hear, ye sons of Jacob, and hearken unto Israel your father. . . . The scepter shall not depart from Judah, nor a lawgiver from between his feet, until Shiloh come; and unto him shall the gathering of the people be."*

According to Islamic tradition, the mysterious Shiloh is Prophet Muhammad, to whom would be transferred, "in the latter days," the spiritual authority which until then had remained with the Jews, with Jesus being the last Prophet of the line of Judah.

Also, Isaiah 42: 1-13 describes the servant of God. Prophet Muhammad is called "the servant and messenger of God" in the Islamic declaration of faith. In Isaiah 42:4, the Bible says:

"He shall not fail nor be discouraged,
till he have set judgment in the earth,
and the isles shall wait for his law."

Prophet Muhammad patiently pursued his mission on earth, was not discouraged, but was successful in establishing Islam during his lifetime. The law referred to is the Qur'an.

Isaiah 42:11 states that this awaited one is a descendent of "Kedar." According to Genesis 25:13, Kedar was the second son of Ishmael, an ancestor of Prophet Muhammad. Isaiah 42:10 talks about the messenger singing "a new song." Muslims believe this refers to the Qur'an, which is in Arabic, a new language. Qur'an is poetical, and its recitation is like singing. These and many other references in the Bible clearly give indications of the coming of Muhammad as the awaited Prophet.

9

THE RELATION OF ISLAM TO JUDAISM, CHRISTIANITY

ISLAM TEACHES RESPECT for all religions, and the Qur'an teaches that God has raised Prophets in every nation to guide the people to the path of truth and righteousness. We know about some of the Prophets, but we don't know about many. The Qur'an teaches:

"There is not a nation but a warner hath passed among them."
(Qur'an 35:24)

"And for every nation there is a Messenger."
(Qur'an 10:47)

"Verily, We sent Messengers before thee (O Muhammad),
among them are those of whom We have told thee,
and some of whom We have not told thee."
(Qur'an 40:78)

"Mankind are one community,
and so God sent (unto all nations) Prophets

as bearers of good tidings and as warners,
and revealed therewith the Scripture with the truth
that it might judge between mankind
concerning that wherein they differed."
(Qur'an 2:213)

Being the loving Creator and Sustainer of all the worlds, God cannot become partial and choose one nation to the exclusion of all others for revealing His message. Therefore, ideally, a Muslim will respect people of all religions. However, Muslims feel closer to Jews and Christians because the three religions Judaism, Christianity and Islam have a common origin in Prophet Abraham, and all three belong to the same monotheistic family of religions. Moses and Jesus were descendents of Abraham's son Isaac, and Prophet Muhammad was descendent of his son Ishmael. Thus, the three religions find a common spiritual and biological lineage in Prophet Abraham.

Islam grants both Judaism and Christianity an honored place and special respect; the Qur'an gives a special title to their followers, calling them the People of the Book, because they are following a book or scripture given to them by God. Many of the stories and characters found in the Jewish and Christian scriptures are also in the Qur'an. Stories of Adam, Noah and the flood, Joseph's dreams, Moses and Pharaoh, Jesus, and the Jews are all in the Qur'an.

Because of the common Abrahamic origin of Islam, Judaism, and Christianity, the three faiths have common belief systems. Both Qur'an and Bible teach the eternality of God, and that God is without beginning and without end. He is not bound by laws of nature; He does not have a form or shape; He is the sole Creator of all things, Sovereign, Omnipotent, Omniscient, and Omnipresent. He is in control of all things and carries out His Will.

Christians and Jews will be surprised to learn that Muslims respect and revere all Prophets of Judaism and Christianity including Abraham, Moses, David, Solomon, Jesus, John the Baptist, and others and God's revealed books (in their original forms and original languages), including books given to Abraham, Moses (Torah), David (Psalms), and Jesus (Gospel of Jesus). Muslims and Christians both believe in Angels, in resurrection, accountability on the Day of Judgment and in Heaven and Hell.

Muslims do not see Judaism and Christianity as some alien religions they should tolerate; they consider Islam, Judaism, and Christianity as a family of truly revealed religions from God. In this, Islam is unique—for no other religion in the world has made belief in the truth of other religions a necessary condition of its own faith. Muslims have been commanded in the Qur'an to believe in all Prophets as true and righteous Prophets of God. Therefore, they have respect, reverence, and love for all of them, and can never speak disrespectfully about them.

"Say (O Muslims): We believe in God and that which is revealed
unto us
and that which was revealed unto Abraham,
and Ishmael, and Isaac, and Jacob, and the tribes,
and that which Moses and Jesus received,
and that which the Prophets (of every nation) received from their
Lord.
We make no distinction between any of them,
and unto Him we have surrendered."
(Qur'an 2:136)

The Qur'an teaches the Muslims that of all the people on earth, Christians will be closest to them in affection. This is based on their commonly shared values of the love of God and humility:

*"And thou wilt find the nearest of them in affection to Muslims
(to be) those who say: We are Christians.
That is because there are among them priests and monks
and because they (the Christians) are not arrogant."*
(Qur'an 5:82)

Both Christianity and Islam claim to be revealed religions. Jesus Christ declared that the Message he was delivering was not his but God's: *"For I have not spoken of myself; but the Father which sent me, He gave me a commandment, what I should say, and what I should speak"* (John 12:49).

According to John 8:40, Jesus described himself as *"a man that hath told you the truth, which I have heard of God."* In the same way, it is claimed in the Qur'an that the revelation which came to Prophet Muhammad was from God:

*"And lo! It (the Qur'an) is a revelation of the Lord of the worlds,
which the True spirit hath brought down upon thy heart (O
Muhammad),
that thou mayest be one of the warners."*
(Qur'an 26:192-194)

Christians and Muslims believe in the virgin birth of Jesus and revere and honor Mary and her son Jesus. Both religions teach their followers living a life of high morality and ethical conduct, and repentance for willful disobedience to divine commands. Both teach the importance of seeking the Will of God in all aspects of life. In their teachings, both Christianity and Islam emphasize the message of universal peace and love:

"And the servants of God Most Gracious are those
who walk on earth with humility, and when the ignorant
ones address them, they say: "Peace!"
(Qur'an 25:63)

"Blessed are the peacemakers: for they shall be called
the children of God."
(Matthew 5:9)

Christians and Muslims both believe that the world will come to an end, and Jesus will return in the Last Days. Both believe in resurrection after death and God's Judgment for their conduct in the life on earth and answer for their deeds. Both also believe in Eternal afterlife in Paradise or Hell.

Jews and Christians will find that some teachings of the Bible and the Qur'an are similar. This is because they are from the same source, God the Almighty, not because of plagiarism. However, they will also find differences. A major reason for these differences is that the scriptures originally given to Moses (Torah) and Jesus (Gospel of Jesus) have been altered and corrupted by human hand. Muslims accept the authenticity and truth of the original unaltered Torah and the original Gospel of Jesus as they were revealed in their original languages by God. However, these scriptures are not present in their original form any more, and the teachings of Moses and Jesus are not available in their original purity anymore.

The books of the New Testament as we have them presently are not the same as the original Gospel of Jesus. Muslims respect these texts, but are wary of them, because they cannot know for certain which verses are direct revelations from God and which have been composed or altered by human editors. Muslims can accept the Bible as containing the inspired word of God, but they cannot accept the notion that all the narrative and editorial work was inspired because God was guiding the human workers on the text.

It is well known that the Bible has suffered changes throughout the ages. Both the Hebrew Bible and the New Testament contain many conflicting verses. Even in its recent history, Bible has been repeatedly altered. As a result, there are several versions of the Bible. Even scholars of the Bible charged with revising the Holy Bible have admitted that the scriptures have undergone significant variations, additions, or omissions, the text has suffered in transmission, and none of the versions of the Bible provide a satisfactory restoration.[34]

Some of the changes in the Bible, at least in the English versions, have included deliberate changes of words and phrases because these words and phrases in English language were claimed to have lost their meaning with the passage of time. So the words and phrases were changed "in the interest of consistency, clarity, or accuracy of translation."[34]

Professor Bart Ehrman,[35] Chairman of Religious Studies at the University of North Carolina at Chapel Hill in his book Misquoting Jesus gives examples of how some passages now found in the New Testament were not found in earlier manuscripts. One example he gives is the passage on the famous story of the woman taken in adultery, found in the Gospel of John, Chapter 8. Professor Ehrman states that this passage was neither originally in the Gospel of John nor in any of the other gospels. It was added by later scribes.

Another example involves the last twelve verses of Gospel of Mark, Chapter 16. These passages give an account of Jesus upbraiding his disciples for failing to believe that he was alive (after his life on earth), and then commands them to proclaim that those who believe and are baptized, will be saved and those who do not, will be condemned. The last two verses claim that those who believe will be able to cast out demons, speak new tongues, take up snakes in their hands, and drink poisons without getting harmed.

Professor Ehrman points out that these passages were not present in the two oldest and best manuscripts of Mark's Gospel. He presents evidence that these are additions to the Gospel of Mark, and concludes that these passages represent "two out of thousands of places" in which the manuscripts of the New Testament were changed by the scribes.

Since God's revelations to Moses and Jesus do not exist today in their originally revealed form, Muslims follow the subsequent, final, and preserved revelation of God, i.e. the Holy Qur'an. Its original text in Arabic (the language it was revealed in) has remained unchanged since the time it was revealed. The Qur'an points out that human hands have introduced alterations in the revelations given to Moses and Jesus and rectifies these alterations.

Islamic teachings differ from Christianity on some key issues. For example, Islam teaches that Jesus was a Prophet of God and honors him as such. He was sent to bring the Children of Israel back to the true religion from which they had deviated. Muslims do not believe in the trinity or that Jesus was God incarnated or that he was son of God. Nevertheless, they love, respect and revere Jesus as an honored Prophet of God Almighty.

Muslims also reject the belief that God or Jesus atoned for the sins of mankind by his purported death on the cross. God is all merciful, so He would not allow an innocent person to suffer for the sins committed by other people. God did not send Jesus as expiator of sins of people, because it would mean man could commit sins and crimes without hesitation. God is the source and fountainhead of justice. It is, therefore, not possible that He should make any man a ransom for the sins of all mankind.

God is almighty—there is no need for Him to require assistance from anyone. He alone possesses the full power to save mankind and to keep them from committing sins and crimes.

He has the power to forgive the sins of mankind without requiring atonement by another.

Islam teaches that each person is responsible for his or her own actions, and on the Day of Judgment every individual will be resurrected and will have to answer God for his actions in this life. Consequently, an ideal Muslim is always striving to be righteous in his words and deeds.

In Islam, there is no one person or group on earth who represents God exclusively. There is no religious hierarchy in Islam, no equivalent of Pope, no priesthood, monasticism, celibacy, confession, and no baptism. Every person is directly answerable to God Himself without any intermediary. The Qur'an teaches that God is "nearer to him (man) than his jugular vein,"(Qur'an: 50:16) and He (directly) answers the prayers of the supplicant when he prays to Him. (Qur'an 2:186)

Islam also differs from Christianity on the idea of original sin. Islam rejects the concept of the original sin, i.e., that because of the sin committed by Adam, people are born in a state of sin and are doomed to go to hell unless their sins are expiated by an acceptance of Jesus. The following verses of the Qur'an teach us that Adam and Eve both committed the sin, but repented and prayed to God for forgiveness. God accepted their prayers and forgave their sin:

> *"Our Lord! We have wronged ourselves.*
> *If Thou forgive us not and have not mercy on us,*
> *surely we shall certainly be of the losers."*
> (Qur'an 7:23)

> *"Then Adam received appropriate words from his Lord and repented,*
> *and God accepted his repentance.*
> *Surely He is the Acceptor of Repentance, the Merciful."*
> (Qur'an 2:37)

According to Islamic teachings, God created man in the best possible form:

"Surely, we have created humanity in the best of moulds."
(Qur'an 94:4)

The fundamental nature (fitra) of humans at birth is good, they are born pure and without any sins. They are blessed with dignity and honor, and are entitled to self-respect. However, they may lose hope of going to Heaven for their own sins when they are old enough to be guilty of deliberate wrong doing, and may even be "abased to be the lowest of the low."(Qur'an 95:5). Conversely, a Muslim can attain Heaven by his belief in God, good deeds and, above all, God's mercy.

Despite theological differences with followers of other religions, Islam does not teach hatred towards non-Muslims. Muslims are enjoined in the Qur'an to respect all human beings, especially Christians and Jews who, along with the Muslims, are honored to belong to the 'People of the Book.' Muslims are taught to reach out to the Christians and Jews with wisdom and understanding. The Qur'an exhorts Muslims to interact with the Christians and Jews and come to a some kind of understanding with them to establish common goals:

Say: "O people of the Scripture (Christians and Jews)!
Let us get together on what is common between us and you:
that we shall worship none but God,
that we shall not associate any partners with Him,
that we shall not take from among ourselves any lords besides God."
If they reject your invitation, then tell them:
"Bear witness that we are Muslims (who have surrendered to God)."
(Qur'an 3:64)

"Rest assured that Believers (Muslims), Jews,
Christians, and Sabians
– whoever believes in God and the Last Day and performs good deeds,
will be rewarded by their Lord,
and no fear shall come upon them neither shall they grieve."
(Qur'an 2:62)

It is obvious that the Qur'an teaches the Muslims to be kind and considerate when dealing with people of other faiths. Muslims believe in Jesus and Moses as honored Prophets of God and love, honor, and respect them as they love, honor, and respect Prophet Muhammad.

"And dispute ye not with the People of the Book,
except with means better (than mere disputation),
unless it be with those of them who inflict wrong (and injury);
but say: "We believe in the Revelation which has come down to us
and in that which came down to you;
our God and your God is One;
and it is to Him we bow (in Islam)."
(Qur'an 29:46)

Islam teaches its followers tolerance for adherents of the other religions, and Prophet Muhammad admonished his followers to treat well the non-Muslim minorities living among them, especially the Jews and the Christians. There are many examples where he himself demonstrated his good relations with the Jews and Christians of his time. For example, when a delegation of Christians from Najran visited him, he welcomed them and offered them to stay in his mosque and offer their prayer therein.

In another example of his high regard for the Christians, in the early days of Islam, when persecution became unbearable for the Muslims in Mecca, Prophet Muhammad advised them to immigrate to Abyssinia, a Christian country, and stay there until it was safe for them to return.

When the Prophet migrated to Medina, Jews of Medina were at first friendly towards him, and Prophet Muhammad entered into a covenant with them and Arab tribes of Medina. This covenant came to be known as the Charter of Medina. It guaranteed religious freedom and rights of Muslims, Jews and others.

Muslims, Jews and Christians lived and worked together in perfect harmony and peace in Baghdad during the 6th, 9th, and 10th centuries, and the scholars from among them worked together to translate and improve upon Greek philosophy and science. Scholars from the three faiths also worked together in Muslim Spain, where their fruitful collaboration helped in ushering in the European Renaissance.

There are many examples in the history where Muslims and Christians worked together in peace and harmony. Under the Nordic rule in Sicily, for example, the first translation of Arab philosophy was accomplished which would have profound effect and influence on the works of Albert the Great and the famous Christian scholar Thomas Aquinas. St. Francis of Assisi visited the Mamluk Sultan of Egypt during the height of the Crusades. In 16th century the Mughal emperor Akbar the Great of India, a Muslim, sponsored dialogues between Muslim and Christian scholars.

It is also important to remember that when Jews were persecuted by Christians in Europe during the Middle Ages they found peace, harmony, and acceptance among the Muslims in Spain. In fact, this era of the Jewish history is known as 'the golden age.' And when the lives of the Jews of Spain were threatened by agents of Reconquista in Spain, the Muslim ruler of the Ottoman empire dispatched his navy to rescue the Jews and bring them to parts of Ottoman empire, where they found peace and safety. There are many examples in the history of Muslims, Christians and Jews living and working together in harmony.

10

ISLAM TEACHES GREAT RESPECT AND HONOR FOR JESUS AND MARY

Islam teaches that Mary was chosen by God over all women of creation and so Islam grants Mary a very special place in the entire human race from the beginning to the end of time. The Qur'an states that God chose Mary, purified her and raised her above all other women of the creation:

> *"And when the angels said:*
> *O Mary! Lo! God hath chosen thee and made thee pure,*
> *and hath preferred thee above (all) the women of creation.*
> *O Mary! Be obedient to thy Lord, prostrate thyself*
> *and bow down with those who bow down (in worship)."*
> Qur'an (3:42-43)

Mary appears much more often in the Qur'an than she does in the New Testament, and more biographical information about her is given in the Qur'an than in the New Testament. She is the only woman mentioned in the Qur'an by name, and one of the chapters of the Qur'an (Chapter 19) is named after her.

The Qur'an also teaches that Mary was a human, and miraculously conceived Jesus when she was a virgin. Muslims do not consider her the mother of God. The Qur'an teaches that God Almighty did not beget, nor was He begotten:

> *Say (O Muhammad); "He is God, the One; God, the eternally besought of all.*
> *He begetteth not, nor was He begotten.*
> *And there is none comparable unto Him."*
> Qur'an (112:1–4)

Muslims have great respect for Mary, and she is greatly loved and revered in Muslim societies as a pious woman and the mother of Jesus (pbuh), but she is not venerated or worshipped in any manner. Muslims express their love for Mary by naming their daughters after her. The commonly used Muslim names after Mary are Maria, Maaria, Maryam, Maryum and Muryum.

WHAT DOES THE QUR'AN SAY ABOUT THE BIRTH OF JESUS?

The Qur'an teaches that Jesus was miraculously born of the virgin Mary. In Chapter 19, named after Mary, the Qur'an gives us vivid description of the miraculous birth of Jesus:

> *"Relate in the Book the story of Mary,*
> *when she withdrew from her family to a place in the east.*
> *She screened herself from her people.*
> *Then We sent to her Our Spirit,*
> *and it appeared before her as a man in all respects.*
> *She said: I seek the refuge of God Most Gracious from thee.*
> *Do not come near me if you have fear of God.*

He said: Nay, I am only a Messenger from thy Lord,
(to announce) the gift of a holy son.
She said: How shall I have a son when no man has touched me,
and I am not unchaste?
He said: So (it will be): Thy Lord saith, that is easy for Me:
and (We wish) to appoint him as a sign unto mankind
and a mercy from Us.
It is a matter (so) ordained.
So she conceived him, and she retired with him to a remote place.
And the pangs of childbirth drove her to the trunk of a palm tree.
She cried (in her anguish) - Ah! would that I had died before this!
Would that I had been a thing forgotten and out of sight!
But a voice cried to her from under the palm tree:
Grieve not! For thy Lord hath provided a rivulet beneath thee;
and shake towards thyself the trunk of the palm tree.
It will let fall fresh ripe dates upon thee.
So eat and drink and be consoled.
And if thou dost see any one, say:
I have vowed to fast to (God) Most Gracious,
and this day will I enter into no talk with any human being.
At length she brought the baby to her people,
carrying him (in her arms).
They said: O Mary! Truly an amazing thing hast thou brought!
O sister of Aaron! Thy father was not a man of evil,
nor thy mother a woman unchaste!
But she pointed to the baby.
They said: How can we talk to one who is a child in the cradle?
Then he (Jesus) said: I am indeed a servant of God:
He hath given me revelation and made me a Messenger.
And He hath made me blessed wherever I be,
and hath enjoined on me prayer and charity as long as I live.
He hath made me kind to my mother, and not arrogant, unblest.
So, Peace is on me the day I was born, the day that I die,

and the day I shall be raised up to life (again).
Such was Jesus the son of Mary
(Qur'an 19:16–34)."

More about what Jesus said is described in another chapter in the Qur'an. In one of the many miracles of Jesus mentioned in the Quran, but not in the New Testament, Jesus is speaking to people as a newborn in the cradle and saying that he will be sent as a Messenger of God to the Children of Israel and he will be performing miracles with the permission of God:

(And remember) when the angels said: "O Mary! Lo!
God giveth thee glad tidings of a word from Him,
whose name is the Messiah, Jesus, son of Mary,
illustrious in the world and in the Hereafter,
and one of those brought near (unto God).
He will speak unto mankind in his cradle and in his manhood,
and he is of the righteous.
She said: "My Lord! How can I have a child when no mortal hath
touched me?
He said: So (it will be). "God Creates what He wills.
If He decrees a thing, He says to it only: "Be!" And it is.
And God will teach him the Book and Wisdom, the Law (Torah) and
the Gospel,
and appoint him as an apostle to the children of Israel,
(with this message): I have come to you,
with a sign from your Lord, in that
I make for you out of clay, as it were, the figure of a bird, and breath
into it,
and it becomes a bird by God's leave:
and I heal those born blind and the lepers,
and I raise the dead by God's leave . . .
So fear God's displeasure and obey me.

It is God Who is my Lord and your Lord; then worship Him.
This is a way that is straight."
(Qur'an 3:45–51)

THE HONORED STATUS OF JESUS IN ISLAM

One cannot be a true Muslim if he/she does not love, respect and revere Jesus. Muslims never refer to Jesus simply as "Jesus", but add the phrase peace be upon him (or pbuh), as they do for all Prophets. This practice is in accordance with Islamic teaching. Acceptance of Jesus by Muslims as a prophet of God is a fundamental article of faith in Islam. Jesus (Eesa in Arabic) is mentioned thirty five times in the Qur'an.

The Qur'anic account of Jesus and his teachings have some similarities and differences. Some of the major differences are that, according to the Qur'an, Jesus never claimed to be God. For this reason, although Muslims believe in the virgin conception and birth of Jesus, they do not believe that Jesus is the son of God or part of the Trinity of Father, Son and Holy Ghost, as the Christians do. Additionally, the Qur'an narrates that Jesus was neither killed nor crucified, but God took him up to Himself (in a manner similar to what happened to Elijah). Muslims believe that Jesus did not die on the cross, nor was he subsequently resurrected (Qur'an 3:55, 4:157).

Muslims consider Jesus as one of the Messengers of God sent to the Children of Israel and revere him just as they revere the other Messengers and Prophets of God to mankind including Abraham, Moses and Muhammad. They also believe that Jesus prophesied in his Gospel the coming after him of Prophet Muhammad. Muslims have deep love for Jesus, and they express it by naming their children after him.

The Qur'an teaches that God sent Jesus, like several other Prophets before him to the Children of Israel, to guide them back to the straight path. This is mentioned in different verses in the Qur'an, for example:

> *"And We caused Jesus, son of Mary, to follow in their footsteps*
> *confirming that which was (revealed) before him,*
> *and We bestowed on him the Gospel wherein is guidance and light,*
> *confirming that which was (revealed) before it in the Torah —*
> *a guidance and an admonition unto those who ward off (evil).*
> *Let the People of the Gospel judge by that which*
> *God hath revealed therein.*
> *Whoso judgeth not by that which God hath revealed*
> *such are evil-doers."*
> (Qur'an 5:46–47)

These and other verses in the Qur'an teach us that Jesus was given the Gospel (God's Good News), and that Muslims believe in the Gospel of Jesus. Presently, however, the Gospel of Jesus does not exist in its original pure form. Although some parts of the Gospel of Jesus may still be present in the New Testament, a lot of other material has been mixed in, and it is difficult to discern which part of the Bible is the original scripture revealed by God and which is not.

In addition to the Divinely revealed Gospel of Jesus, there existed several other books and apocryphal manuscripts during the three centuries after Jesus, but there was no 'official' Bible. In 325 AD the Roman Emperor Constantine convened the First Council of Nicaea and ordered the composition of an official Bible. It included some of the books and manuscripts in circulation at that time, including the four Gospels, but left out several other manuscripts and books. As a result, the scriptures revealed by God did not reach mankind in their pure form.[35]

Jesus performed miracles by God's Will. He healed the blind, cured the lepers, and brought the dead back to life. He performed miracles even with simple things, such as bringing food for his disciples miraculously from heaven. The Qur'an testifies that Jesus performed miracles by God's permission (Qur'an 5:112–115). However, it does not mean that he was God or the son of God.

The key attributes of God are that He is Eternal, Independent, Omnipresent, Omniscient, Omnipotent, All knowing, All wise, All good, Immortal, and exempt from suffering pain, fear, hunger, sorrow, and fatigue. There are so many verses in the New Testament where Jesus has denied having any of these divine attributes. For example, in Matthew 12:18 he said he was servant of God, in Matthew 28:18, John 5:26 he said all the authority and power given to him was from God, and in John 5:19 he said he could do nothing of his own accord. He thanked God (John 11:41), always did things to please God (John 8:29), obeyed God's commandments (John 15:10), and begged God to save him (Matthew 26:39). All these indicate human weaknesses, of which God is free.

Moreover, the Bible refers to God the Father as the One and Only God (1 Corinthians 8:6), that God the Father is greater than all, including Jesus (John 10:29 and 14:28), and Jesus taught his followers to pray to God the Father (Matthew 11:25).

The Old Testament is full of verses of stunning boldness and clarity wherein God says "*I am God Almighty*" or "*I am the Lord Your God*" (Genesis 35:11, Leviticus 11:44, Exodus 20:1, Exodus 6:2, Exodus 6:6, Exodus 6:7, Judges 6:10). We would expect the New Testament to be full of verses where Jesus said "I am God." However, no such verse exists in Gospels or anywhere else in the New Testament. In fact, Jesus is never reported to have called himself God.

The claim that Jesus is God because Jesus was called the Son of God, does not hold much merit. The term "Son of God" was used as a metaphor in the Old Testament to indicate closeness to God, and it has been used for several individuals in the Old Testament. For example, according to Exodus 4:22, Jacob is son of God and his firstborn; in 2 Samuel 7:13–14, Solomon is son of God; in Jeremiah 31:9, again Ephraim (Jacob) is God's firstborn; and in Luke 3:8, Adam is son of God. In fact in many verses of the Bible, common people have been called sons of God (Deuteronomy 14:1, Romans 8:14, John 1:12 and 3:1–2; Job 1:6, 2:1, and 38:7; and Philippians 2:15).

11

WHAT DO SO MANY
NON-MUSLIM WRITERS
ADMIRE ABOUT ISLAM

MANY NON-MUSLIM WRITERS have admired Islam, its teachings, and its civilization. Bertrand Russel[36], in his book *History of Western Philosophy*, has stated that even though the people in the West may believe that civilization means only the Western civilization, during 699 to 1000 A.D., when Western Europe was in the dark ages, the brilliant civilization of Islam flourished from India to Spain.

In his *book Islam—A Concise Introduction*, Professor Huston Smith[1] has quoted Bernard Lewis who has stated in Atlanta Monthly (September 1990 issue) that there is something in the religious culture of Islam which inspires a dignity and courtesy towards others in even the humblest peasant or peddler, and this characteristic is never exceeded and rarely equaled in other civilizations.

Professor Smith[1] has said that Islam brought a remarkable moral change in the climate of Arabia. He pointed out that before (Prophet) Muhammad there were practically no rules for inter-tribal warfare, there was great social injustice and economic disparity between the rich and the poor, women were regarded more as possessions than humans, it was common to kill infant girls, and gambling and drunkenness were prevalent in the society. However, within a half century Islam changed all that in the society.

Islam's teachings of social justice and interpersonal relations include the teachings of all of the prophets who came before, including the teachings of Jesus. Islam completed and systematized the laws of morality taught by all previous prophets, and put them in the form of a legal compendium—the Qur'an.

The distinctive feature of Islam is not just its ideal but the detailed procedures and methodology of how to put the ideal into practice. Professor Smith[1] has quoted Amir Ali who said in his book "Spirit of Islam," that the Qur'an and Hadith together offer such detailed procedures for implementing the laws of morality that Islam can be called the most socially explicit of the Semitic religions.

Stoddard[37] has called the rise of Islam the most amazing event in the history of mankind. Arising in a desert inhabited by a nomad people unknown for any significant achievement and against all odds, Islam overthrew long established religions, conquered well-established empires, and spread fast with miraculous ease. In a few years its flag was flying from the Pyrenees to the Himalayas and from the desert of Central Asia to the desert of Central Africa - over half of the known earth at that time.

Stoddard has stated that whereas other religions spread with the aid of their powerful rulers such as Asoka, Constantine, and Cyrus, each using his mighty force in the service of his religion, there was no such monarch to help Islam.

Commenting on the extinction of racism from Islamic culture, A. J. Toynbee[38] has said that one of the outstanding achievements of Islam is the eradication of racism from the society. He said that the contemporary world is badly in need of the Islamic virtue of racial harmonization.

H. A. R. Gibb[39] has admired Islam's teaching of equality, and its magnificent tradition of inter-racial understanding and cooperation. He has stated that no other society has attained such a success in uniting a variety of races at all level of society. He said that Islam has the power to reconcile the apparently irreconcilable elements of race and tradition, and it offers a solution to Europe in its inter-racial problem with the people.

Speaking on the Islamic teaching of the equality of people before God, Sarojini Naidu,[40] a famous poetess of India said: "Islam was the first religion which preached and practiced democracy." She described that the concepts of democracy and equality before God were put into practice by the Muslims when they responded to the call for the prayer (Salat); the worshippers embody the democracy of Islam when the peasant and the king kneel together side by side and proclaim: "God is Great."

Ms. Naidu, a non-Muslim, was most impressed with what she called 'indivisible unity of Islam that makes a man instinctively a brother." She said that the sense of justice was one of the most wonderful ideals of Islam, and the dynamic principles and ethics of life about which she read in the Qur'an, were practical for the daily conduct of life and suitable for the whole World.

In his book *Islam and Christianity Today* Montgomery Watt[41] stated that he believed there was Divine truth in the Qur'an from which Westerners could learn, and that Islam had the potential to offer the basic framework for the one religion of the future.

Edward Montet[42] wrote in *La Propagande Chretienne et ses Adversaris Musulmans* that Islam is a religion that is quite rationalistic, and the Qur'an has taught the dogma of the unity of God "with a grandeur, majesty, invariable purity, and conviction which is hard to be found surpassed outside the pale of Islam." He also said that the creed of Islam is "so precise, so simple and stripped of theological complexities, and consequently so easy to understand by a common man that it possess a marvelous power of winning its way into the consciousness of men."

In his book *Short History of the Arabs*, the historian Phillip Hitti[43] has written that during the entire first part of the Middle Ages no other people made as important a contribution to human progress as the Arabs. He wrote that for centuries, Arabic remained the language of learning, culture, and intellectual progress for the civilized world (with the exception of the Far East) From the 9th to the 12th centuries there were more philosophical, medical, historical, religious, astronomical and geographical works written in Arabic than in any other human language."

In his book *History of Intellectual Development of Europe*, Dr. William Draper[26] stated that during the rule of Abbasid dynasty in the Islamic Empire, learned Christians and Jews were not only held in high esteem but were also appointed to posts of great responsibility, and were promoted to the high ranking government jobs. During the rule of Caliph Haroon al-Rashid, it did not matter to which country a learned person belonged or what was his faith and belief; the only thing that mattered was his excellence in the field of learning.

Cooperation and good relation among Jewish, Christian and Muslim communities in the Muslim lands have also been mentioned by Professor John Kaltner[2], who wrote that during the Muslim rule in Spain and many other places, Jews and Christians lived and worked side by side with Muslims, and all three communities benefited from the experience. This cooperation has also been dramatically depicted in a documentary film Cities of Light—The Rise and Fall of Islamic Spain, produced by the Unity Production Foundation (UPF).

In *The Genuine Islam*, Sir George Bernard Shaw[27] stated that if any religion had the chance of ruling over England or Europe in the next century, it would be Islam. He declared that it was the only religion, which seemed to have the assimilating capacity for the changing world, and appealed to people of every age. He predicted that Islam would be as acceptable to the Europe of the future as it was beginning to be acceptable to the Europe of his day.

It can be summed up that many non-Muslim writers have admired Islam for a variety of reasons. Islam has taught social justice, equality of people before God, and inter-racial cooperation and understanding. It has systematized the laws of morality and the Qur'an and Hadith have given detailed procedures for the practical implementation of these laws. The creed of islam is simple, precise, and free from theological complexities and mysteries, and its language, Arabic, remained for four centuries the language of learning, culture, and intellectual progress.

12

ISLAM WAS NOT SPREAD BY THE SWORD

THERE IS A general misunderstanding in the West that Islam was spread by the use of force. As Professor John Kaltner[2] has stated in his book *Islam — What Non-Muslims Should Know*, such an approach would go against the Muslim view of religious faith that is reflected in an important verse of the Qur'an that says:

> *"let there be no compulsion in (the matter) of religion."*
> (Qur'an 2:256)

Islam must come from inner conviction and free choice, and not from outside force. Additionally, the Qur'an teaches that mankind having different faiths is the will of God:

> *"If it had been the will of your Lord*
> *that all the people of the world should be believers,*
> *all the people of the earth would have believed!*
> *Would you then compel mankind against their will to believe?"*
> (Qur'an 10:99)

During the first thirteen years of Islam in Mecca, the idol worshippers of Mecca tried very hard to wipe out the then small community of Muslims. They tortured them, persecuted them, economically and socially boycotted them, and forced them to abandon their families, homes, and businesses and go into exile. The Muslims went about their daily lives despite the persecution, and did not try to fight back. Even after the Muslims migrated from Mecca to the city of Medina, their Meccan enemies continued to threaten them. For their survival and for the survival of their religion, the Muslims were then allowed by divine command to defend themselves and their faith. They had no choice but to fight back by the use of arms.

There is no question that Islam spread fast, but it did so primarily because it conquered hearts. Among the reasons for the rapid and mostly peaceful spread of Islam was the simplicity of its doctrine. Indeed, according to Edward Montet,[42] the creed of Islam (the Shahada) is so precise, so simple and easy to understand by a common man that it possess a tremendous power of winning its way into the hearts of the people.

Additionally, many early Muslims set such splendid examples by their good behavior that people around them became attracted towards the belief that produced such remarkable people. As a result, many embraced the pure teaching of Islam. This is still happening in the present day; many people convert to Islam by seeing examples of good Muslim character.

Islam is the fastest growing religion in the world, and no one is using force to convert the non-Muslims. One of many examples, which attest to Islam's non-violent expansion, is the conversion of the Indonesians. No Muslim army ever set foot in Indonesia, the world's largest Muslim nation. Traders, teachers and merchants established Islam there.

However, it would be incorrect to say that no Muslim army ever invaded a non-Muslim territory to conquer it. There are examples of Muslim armies invading non-Muslim territories for plunder, but such examples are exceptions and not the rule. They are not aligned with the teachings of Islam. In many cases where Muslim armies entered non-Muslim territories, they did so at the behest of the local population to liberate them from tyrannical rule.

In many cases where Muslim armies conquered a territory, local populations were given a number of options. They were first educated about the Islamic faith and invited to join it. If they chose to become Muslims, they were accepted as full members of the Muslim nation or Ummah, were granted all rights that other Muslims enjoyed, and were treated as equals. A second option was that they could keep their faith as long as they paid a special tax called *jizya*. This placed them in the category of the protected minority, and gave them freedom of religion to worship as they wished.[1]

They also did not have to enlist in the army, nor did they have to pay the Zakat, which was generally mandatory for Muslims. Only in the event that neither of these two options was taken, was military action taken. But this last option was rarely implemented. Most non-Muslims, however, chose to either convert or accept the rank of protected minority. This option was especially appealing to Christians and Jews because Muslim authorities allowed them to govern their own people according to their religious traditions and laws.

The way Muslims treated religious minorities is quite different from how other powers treated them. For example, the people of some conquered nations, such as the Persian and the Byzantine Empires, hated their oppressive rulers. According to Professor John Kaltner[2], the Byzantine Empire often made life very difficult for those who came under its rule. Therefore, many non-Muslims fared better under Islam than they did under the Byzantine Christians.

In some cases, the non-Muslim inhabitants of conquered lands surrendered to invading Muslim armies almost without a fight. In fact, they welcomed the Muslims as deliverers. Giving an example of this, Professor Hugh Salzberg[44] writes in his book *From Caveman to Chemist* that when the Muslim armies reached Alexandria, Egypt, the dissident residents of this impregnable port city, with a large garrison backed by a naval fleet, refused to fight a handful of Muslim soldiers who rode in from the desert.

Many non-Muslim writers have rejected the allegation that Islam was spread at the point of a sword. De Lacy O'Leary[45] writes: "History makes it clear, however, that the legend of fanatical Muslims sweeping through the world and forcing Islam at the point of sword upon conquered races is one of the most fantastically absurd myths that historians have ever repeated."

Additionally, James Michener,[30] in his Reader's Digest article titled *The Misunderstood Religion,* states: "No other religion in history spread so rapidly as Islam. The West has widely believed that this surge of religion was made possible by the sword. But no modern scholar accepts this idea, and the Qur'an is explicit in the support of the freedom of conscience."

Similarly, Lawrence E. Browne[46] in his book *The Prospects of Islam,* writes: "Incidentally these well-established facts dispose of the idea so widely fostered in Christian writings that the Muslims, wherever they went, forced people to accept Islam at the point of the sword."

Finally, Thomas Carlyle[18] has also stated: "Much has been said of Mahomet's propagating his religion by the sword. It is no doubt far nobler (than) what we have to boast of the Christian Religion, that it propagated itself peaceably in the way of preaching and conviction. . . .We do not find, of the Christian Religion either, that it always disdained the sword, when once it had got one. Charlemagne's conversion of the Saxons was not by preaching."

There are examples in history where sword has been used to force people to convert to Christianity. For example, in 782 after a Saxon uprising at Verden, Charlemagne ordered the beheading of over 4500 Saxon prisoners for worshiping others than God. The only choice he offered those he conquered was to accept Christianity or meet God right away.

The Spanish Inquisition is another example of the forceful conversion to Christianity of Muslims and Jews. Jerald F. Dirks has described some detail about it in his book Muslims in *American History: A Forgotten Legacy*.[47] The Inquisition was authorized by Pope Sixtus IV, and initiated in 1483. Originally, it was conceived as a means to force Spanish Jews to either convert to Christianity or be expelled from Spain. The proceedings of the Inquisition were secret, and the accused had no right to legal counsel or appeal. Torture was used routinely to extract confessions, and there was no system of checks and balances.

In 1492, the Jews of Spain were told that they had to convert to Christianity and undergo baptism, or be forcibly expelled. While some Jews converted, at least outwardly, between 100,000 and 170,000 Jews refused to convert and were expelled. Approximately 13,000 were killed through torture and execution, and 2,000 more were publicly burned at the stake.[47]

Muslims came to rescue the Jews. When Sultan Bayazed II, the Muslim ruler of the Ottoman Empire, heard about the plight of the Jews of Spain, he dispatched his navy to evacuate the oppressed and persecuted Jews from Christian Spain. The evacuees were settled in Turkish towns, where they were allowed to practice their religion and their occupations in peace and safety. Most of the Jews in modern day Turkey are the descendants of those Spanish Jews who were rescued by Muslims.

Like the Jews, the Muslims of Spain were also given the choice of forced conversion to Christianity and baptism or expulsion. To inflict more damage on the Muslims, half a million priceless books and manuscripts of the great Islamic libraries of Granada were burned, and 2,000 Muslim women of Granada were sold into slavery at auction.

Seeing these inhuman cruelties, many Muslims outwardly converted to Christianity, but practiced their faith of Islam in private. Such people were termed Moriscos. The Inquisition made their life almost impossible for them. In order to discourage them from the practice of Islam, Muslims and Moriscos were forbidden to wear their traditional Muslim dresses, speak Arabic language, use Muslim (Arabic) names, or abstain from drinking alcohol and eating pork. They were also prohibited from keeping their doors or windows closed on Fridays, or recite Qur'an at funerals or weddings.

Violators were severely punished. Their properties were confiscated by the government and their wives and children were turned homeless. In fact, Islam was officially prohibited throughout Spain. In 1609, a royal decree was issued to expel all Moriscos from Spain. Dirks states that between 275,000 and 300,000 Moriscos were expelled from Spain as a result of this order; most took refuge in North Africa.[47]

It seems like Inquisition was contagious those days. Following the example of Spain, Portugal also sanctioned its own Portugese Inquisition, which was more vicious and lethal than the Spanish version.

From these few accounts, it can be seen that the Muslims have not only been falsely accused of spreading their faith by force, in reality many have been forced to convert to Christianity at the point of the sword.

13

THE CONTRIBUTIONS
OF ISLAM TO HUMAN
CIVILIZATION

AFTER THE DEATH of Prophet Muhammad in the year 622, Islam spread rapidly and within a few decades had extended into Asia, Africa, and parts of Europe. By the year 750, it had stretched from the Atlantic coast of Portugal to the western borders of China and included Spain, Portugal, all of North Africa, the Middle East, the Near East, and most of Central Asia.

In his book *How Islam Created the Modern World*, Mark Graham[48] states that the Muslim civilization during the Middle Ages (8th century to 13th century) was the greatest in size and technology that the world had ever seen. This enormous area contained all of the cultural and technological centers of the Middle East and the Mediterranean, except for Greece and Italy. This period in time is also called the Golden Age of Islam.

It is surprising to note that despite tremendous scientific and cultural achievements by the Muslims, their contribution to civilization is not commonly known or acknowledged. According to an article by Geneive Abdo published in the October 27, 2006 issue of the Washington Post, a public opinion survey showed that a majority of Americans saw "little" or "nothing" to admire in Islam or the Muslim world. Such an opinion indicates that the American public is not educated about the very significant contribution of Islam and Muslims to the civilization, especially to the Western world.

In reality, Western civilization would have been impossible without the works of Muslim scientists and philosophers during the Middle Ages such as al-Khwarizmi , Ibn Sina, and Ibn Rushd, who are known in the West by their Latinized name as Elkaurexmus, Avicenna, and Averroes, respectively. Most likely, the participants in Abdo's survey had never heard of these and other Muslim men whose work in astronomy, algebra, mathematics, physics, chemistry, medicine, surgery, optics, geography, cartography, and philosophy dominated medieval Europe for centuries.

Islam teaches great respect for knowledge, and instructs mankind to use its faculties of intelligence and observation in pursuit of knowledge. Indeed, learning is so important in Islam that the very first word of the Qur'an that was revealed by God to Prophet Muhammad was 'Read' (Qur'an 96:1). Muslims are commanded to seek more knowledge (Qur'an 20:114). Prophet Muhammad has emphasized the importance of knowledge in his sayings. For example, he said:

"Whoever follows a path in the pursuit of knowledge,
God will create a path to Paradise for him,"
"The ink of a scholar's pen is more precious than the blood
of a martyr," and
"The worship by a learned person is a thousand times better than the
worship by an ignorant person."

In view of such a high degree of respect for knowledge, throughout their history Muslims have tried to acquire, preserve, and promote knowledge. Unlike many other conquering armies, such as the Mongols, who destroyed the conquered lands and burned their libraries, the Muslim conquests did not result in the destruction of the conquered territories and their intellectual cultures. On the contrary, the developing Muslim civilization absorbed the heritage of ancient civilizations such as Egypt, Persia, and Greece, and preserved their knowledge in the libraries and with the scholars. It also led to the cross-fertilization of Eastern and Western ideas, and new thought with old.

The reader should appreciate the fact that Islam started with the Arabs, who had emerged in the seventh century from their peninsula with little culture of their own, apart from a highly developed art of poetry. Science among them was rudimentary or unknown. They had to acquire science, before they could transmit it to others. But they were keen to learn, and they learned rapidly.

The Empire of Islam was a huge economic and cultural free-trade area, and the greatly increased trade and travel between different regions of this vast empire stimulated the flow of information and knowledge everywhere. There was large-scale cultural and commercial exchange between different parts of the empire. Commerce and trade bustled nationally and internationally. North African merchants traveled to India and China and Arab businessmen traveled north to different parts of Europe. Navigational inventions facilitated travel and commerce.

It is sad to observe that with the exception of scanty references here and there, much of western literature almost completely ignores the achievements of the Muslims of the Middle Ages who contributed so much to the Western civilization. However, the truth is that Muslims were civilized when Europe was in its Dark Ages and steeped in ignorance and superstition. Europe learned a lot from Islam in almost all fields, and these included astronomy, mathematics, medicine, optics, chemistry, physics, art, architecture, poetry, philosophy, and rationalism. However, once the Western world got out of the Dark Ages and entered the modern age, it kept advancing with their knowledge; whereas, the Muslims stopped and consequently fell behind.

Jerald Dirks states that throughout their history in Spain (Andalusia), Muslims were a beacon of intellectual and cultural light in a Europe that was just coming out of the Dark Ages. They had achieved great advancement in the fields of agriculture, architecture, literature, and science, and their advancement later helped in ushering the European Renaissance.[47]

The Muslim Abbasid Caliph (king) Haroon al-Rashid (763–809) and later his son al-Ma'mun (786–833) ruled the Empire of Islam during later part of the 8th and the early part of the 9th century, with Baghdad as the capital of the empire. They were forward thinking rulers and were devoted to the pursuit of knowledge. Al-Ma'mun established The House of Wisdom (Arabic name: Bayt al-Hikmah), an unrivalled intellectual institution and research center for the study of humanities and sciences. They gathered the greatest Muslim as well as non-Muslim intellectuals and scholars, and ordered them to accumulate the greatest collection of knowledge in the world, review it and build upon it through their own research. It was this knowledge that later formed the foundation on which the groundwork for the European Renaissance was built.[48]

Al-Ma'mun, who reigned for 20 years from 813, appreciated the power of logic, reason, and rational thinking and understood the importance of the Greek philosophy. He gathered scholars from all over and ordered them to find all of the works of ancient Greece that they could find and translate them into Arabic. In addition to translators, The House of Wisdom was staffed with authors, poets and professionals in various fields of science and humanities. They included Muslims, Christians, Jews, and followers of other religions who were Arabs, Persians,

Turks, and people from a variety of ethnic backgrounds. Al-Ma'mun appointed Yahya bin Masawaih, a Nestorian Christian, as the head of The House of Wisdom.

The intellectuals met on a daily basis for reading, writing, translating, and discussing their works. The House of Wisdom luminaries included al-Kindi, inventor of decryption and musical theory; al-Khwarizmi, the father of algebra; Hunayn Ibn Ishaq, physician and translator, and others. They did not just translate, but also performed research, built upon the knowledge they acquired, and wrote volumes on their works. For example, Hunayn Ibn Ishaq wrote a textbook on ophthalmology.[48]

Scholars found and translated important works from Greek, Persian, Syriac, and Sanskrit, an old Indian language, into Arabic. Consequently, at one point in history Arabic became and remained for many centuries the most important scientific language of the world and the depository of much of the wisdom and the sciences of antiquity.

The works that were translated into Arabic included most of the important works of philosophical and scientific work of Aristotle, Plato, and Pythagoras as well as other major works of Greek astronomy, geometry, mathematics and medicine such as the Almagest of Ptolemy, and the Elements of Euclid. Also translated were the works of Hippocrates and Galen, classical treatise of Apollonius, and Archimedes, and works of other Greek Philosophers. This way Greek wisdom and philosophy passed to the empire of Islam. Muslims put this knowledge to work and revolutionized every known field of science, engineering, and technology, ushering in the Golden Age of Islam.

It is important to note that Muslim scholars not only translated the ancient works, but also further advanced them through their own research and passed them on to the West to fuel the Renaissance.

The genius of the medieval Muslims was their ability to

identify and adopt what they needed from the Persian, Hindu, Greek and other foreign cultures, and to modify and enhance their ideas to fit the practical, intellectual, and religious demands of their own times. Muslim empire's reach over three continents during its golden age enabled it to assimilate a variety of traditions and cultures. Muslims exercised a monopoly over knowledge for centuries until Europe entered its own age of discovery.[49]

During the later parts of the 8th century, Muslims were way ahead of Europe. When the Europeans were still using animal skins to write on, the Muslims were using paper, and had thousands of books in their bookstores and libraries. When the Europeans were bartering their goods in local markets, the Muslims were recording transactions with their international trading partners on paper. By the end of the 9th century, Islam was the most powerful and intellectually most advanced civilization in the world.

John Kaltner[2] has stated that during the golden age of Islam its influence and prominence were unrivalled, and Muslims made significant contributions and advancements in art, science, literature, architecture, and philosophy. They also excelled in astronomy, geography, languages, medicine, mathematics, and physics. In Spain and many other places, Muslims, Jews, and Christians benefited from the experience of living and working side by side.

Hugh Salzberg[44] writes that between 750 and 1150, the Islamic world reached a level of prosperity and cultural attainment not matched in the West until the late years of the Renaissance. Starting in the middle of the 7th century, for the next five centuries scientific activity remained predominantly Islamic. Christian and Jewish scientists were also active in the Islamic lands and followers of all three Abrahamic faith traditions collaborated in cultural, scientific, and technological advancement.

Many enlightened Muslim rulers (Caliphs) of 8th to 12th

Centuries were patrons of literature, science, and philosophy and had developed research institutes specializing in the study of Hellenistic science. They supported famous scholars and equipped universities with libraries where Muslim scholars translated the philosophical and scientific works available in other languages into Arabic.

One of the areas where the contribution of the Muslims has been greatest is mathematics. The Muslim contribution to mathematics has been extraordinarily rich. This immediately comes to light in the form of what we call the Arabic numerals 1-9, with the zero or cipher. Both of these last two expressions are simply Arabic sifr, or "empty," represented by the sign 0. This system has been a boon to calculations. Throughout the Middle Ages in Europe the numerical system was based on the Roman numerals, represented by letters I, V, X, L, C, D, and M, which stood for 1, 5, 10, 50, 100, 500, and 1000, respectively.[48]

It was cumbersome to work with large numbers using Roman numerals, but they were used in Europe until al-Khwarizmi's work on arithmetic first introduced the Hindu numerals (later known as Arabic numerals) to the West. Al-Khwarizmi's work also introduced the decimal positional number system to the Western world. As a whole, the system was not commonly used in the West until after Leonardo Fibonacci work called *Liber Abaci* was published in 1202. It was a treatise on various operations of arithmetic and algebra using Arabic numerals. From that time on, the Roman system was replaced.[50]

Abū Abdallāh Muhammad ibn Mūsā al-Khwārizmī (780-850) was one of the foremost mathematicians of all time. He was also an astronomer and geographer, and is considered to be the founder of algebra. It was from al-Khwarizmi's most famous book called Al-Kitab Al-Mukhtasar fi hisab al-jabr wa'l muqabala (the book on calculations by restoration and confrontation) that we derive the name "algebra," which is a European corruption for the word al-jabr. It literally means restoration, and involves transfer of negative quantities in an equation to the opposite side and changing the signs to positive.

The Arabic word muqabala, meaning confrontation, involves adjusting the negative and positive quantities in an equation and subsequently reducing them by cancellation of common factors. For example:

The equation $bx + 2q = x^2 + bx - q$
by al-jabr becomes $bx + 2q + q = x^2 + bx$
and by al-muqabala becomes $3q = x^2$

His book presented the first systematic solution of linear and quadratic equations. He devised a system of algebra so significant that it was used as the main textbook of mathematics in Europe, under the name *Liber Algorismi* for five centuries (1200 to 1600).[51] The term "algorithm" comes from al-Khwarizmi's name.[52] His most recognized work, and one that is so named after him, is the mathematical concept algorithm. Al-Khwarizmi was also a noted astronomer, and wrote books on astronomy and astronomical tables. His astronomical tables included values of trigonometric sine and tangent functions before trigonometry became a subject by itself. In addition, under his leadership, a group of geographers produced the first globe of the known world.

In addition to Al-Khwarizmi, many other Muslim mathematicians are known to have contributed significantly to various areas of mathematics. They include Al-Battani; Al-Biruni, who determined the circumference of the earth; Abu'l-Wafa Buzjani, famous for introducing the secant and cosecant for the first time in trigonometry; Al-Haytham (Latinized: Alhazen), who developed analytical geometry by establishing linkage between algebra and geometry; Abu Kamil Shuja; and Nasir al-Din al-Tusi, famous for Tusi couple concept and non-Euclidian geometry. He is also well known for his masterpiece book on trigonometry written in 1258. Its Arabic title was *Kitab ash-Shakl al-Qatta* and it was considered the highest achievement in trigonometry.[50] Another great Muslim mathematician was Omar Khayyam, famous for his poetry (Rubayat). He was known to have calculated solutions of equations of the third and fourth degrees.

Abu Abdallah Muhammad ibn Jabir al-Battani (858–929) (Latinized: Albategnius, Albategni or Albatenius) was also one of the greatest Muslim mathematicians and astronomers of history. One of his best-known achievements was the determination of the solar year as being 365 days, 5 hours, 46 minutes and 24 seconds long. He made corrections to the work of Ptolemy on the calculation of the orbit of the moon and certain planets. He also proved the possibility of annular solar eclipses, and determined with great accuracy the true orbit of ecliptic, the length of the tropical year and the seasons.

One of al-Battani's most important work is his zij, a set of astronomical tables known as al-Zīj al-Sābī. The zij is based on Ptolemy's theory, and it has influenced the works of great European astronomers Tycho Brahe, Johannes Kepler, and Nicholas Copernicus. Copernicus mentioned his indebtedness to Al-Battani and quoted him in his book *De Revolutionibus Orbium Coelesium.*

In Mathematics, Al-Battānī produced a number of trigonometrical relationships and developed formulas. He also came up with equations and compiled tables for calculating tangents and cotangents. In honor of his work, the Albategnius crater on the moon is named after him.

Abu Rayhan Muhammad ibn Ahmad al-Biruni (973–1048), known in Latin Alberonius, was an Uzbek Muslim Mathematician, astronomer, geologist, mineralogist, and geographer. He was contemporary of Avicenna and used to correspond with him. Al-Biruni was the first person in the Mideast to state that the earth orbits around the sun. He regarded the earth as a sphere and computed its circumference close to its modern values.[53]

Al-Biruni also calculated mass of elements and their densities. His measurements resulted in numerical values very close to modern determinations, and were not equaled in precision by European scientists until the 18th century. He did considerable work in math on triangulation method for determining longitude, trisecting angles, doubling a cube, etc. A book of location of chords in the circle describes his original mathematical methods and proofs.

Abul Wafa Ibn Muhammad Ibn Yahya Ibn Ismail al-Buzjani (940–997) was a great Muslim mathematician, and contributed important work in the fields of geometry and trigonometry. His contribution to trigonometry was extremely significant, and he developed the knowledge on the tangent. He calculated a table of tangents, and introduced the secant and cosecant for the first time. In fact a sizeable part of today's trigonometry can be traced back to him. He was the first to show the generality of the sine theorem relative to spherical triangles, and developed a new method of constructing sine tables with the value of sin 30' being correct to the eighth decimal place.

He wrote a large number of books on mathematics and other subjects. Apart from being a mathematician, Abul Wafa also contributed to astronomy. In this field, he researched the different movements of the moon, and discovered 'variation'. He was also one of the last Arabic translators and commentators of Greek works, and wrote commentaries on Euclid and Diophantos. In recognition of his contributions to science, a crater on the moon has been named after him.

Al-Hasan ibn al-Haytham (Alhazen) was a great Muslim physicist and optician. He disproved Euclid and Ptolemy's theories that light was emitted from the eye itself. He showed experimentally that humans saw objects by light reflecting off of them and entering the eye. He did a lot of research on optics and invented lenses. He wrote a book on optics called *Magnum Opus*. Without lenses there would have been no microscope, magnifying glasses or telescopes. The invention of the modern day camera is based on his observation of camera obscura or pinhole camera. In this he observed an inverted image from an object in the path of light entering a dark room through a pinhole.[54]

Muslims have played a very significant role in the study of astronomy. Muslim astronomers, especially in the 10th century, were actively engaged in research and celestial observations, and several observatories were built by the Arab rulers of that time for this purpose. One such observatory was built by Sultan Sharaf al-Dawlah in his palace in Baghdad in 982, where Abd al-Rahman al-Sufi and other astronomers were engaged in research and observation.

Al-Sufi also wrote an illustrated treatise, *Kitab al-Kawakib al-Thabit al-Musawwar*, that contained a catalog of stars based on his own observations, giving magnitudes and coordinates. It is the first star atlas to take cognizance of the nebula in Andromeda and is still of great importance today. During that time, even private Muslim citizens had observatories at their homes.

Muslim scientists also checked and sometimes found errors in the works of Greek scientists. For example, they found and revised errors in Ptolemy's great astronomical textbook *Almagest*. Muslim scientists also found errors in Ptolemy's calculation of the length of the solar month and in his measurement of the angle of the sun's course around the earth, known as the ecliptic, and corrected these calculations. Muslim scientists also introduced Muslim trigonometric functions into the Arabic translation of *Almagest*.

Ptolemy's model of the universe, as taught by Aristotle, had the celestial objects all move in uniform circular motions with the earth at their center. However, in order to account for the irregular movements of the celestial bodies, he shifted the theoretical axis of rotation away from the center of the universe. This introduced an error in the Almagest planetary motion that was not uniform.

Muslim philosophers, including Avicenna and Averroes took note of the errors in Almagest and tried to correct them by introducing a new model with a nest of hollow spheres all centered on the earth. Although the model did not work, it showed that these philosophers were using the scientific method in their research. Later, at the Maragha observatory in Iran, Nasir al-Din Tusi devised an ingenious approach to generate linear motion from the uniform rotations, in opposite direction of two spheres, called the Tusi Couple. It solved major shortcomings in Ptolemy's astronomy.[49]

Muslim astronomers, especially Ibn al-Shatir, later used Tusi's theorems to solve a variety of problems related to planetary movements. Although it was the genius of Copernicus who came up with the idea of sun being at the center of all planetary movements, by imposing uniform circular motion of planets around a single point, Ibn al-Shatir's work, made Copernicus's conceptual breakthrough that much easier.

Another Muslim scientist, Abu Ma'shar al-Balakhi (Latinized: Albumazar) was the first to explain the tides as influenced by the moon. Omar Khayyam, famous in the West for his poems (Rubaiyaat), was also a mathematician and an astronomer. He accurately calculated the length of the solar year. Al-Biruni studied the rotation of the earth on its axis centuries before Europeans did.

Muslims also excelled in the field of chemistry. Muslim chemical researchers were the first to organize chemical knowledge. They classified chemical reactions and chemical compounds on the basis of their physical properties. This was an important step towards the organization of chemistry as a science.[44] Muslim chemists modified the Greek theory of substances and worked with many more substances than the Greeks had known. In addition, they improved previously known chemical processes, especially those of distillation.

In the field of industrial chemistry, Muslim scientists described processes for steel, ink, and glass; for dying cloth and hair; and for water-proofing materials. They knew about alloys of metals, such as bronze and brass, and did not list them as metals. The most famous of the Muslim scientists who worked with chemistry were Al-Kindi, Al-Razi (Latin: Rhazes), Ibn-Sina (Avicenna), and Jabir Ibn-Hayyan.

Al-Kindi was a mathematician, but he also wrote books on music, optics, logic, astronomy, mathematics, meteorology, and chemistry. One of his books, Book on the Chemistry of Perfumes and Distillations, contained 107 recipes for preparation of aromatic oils and perfumes.

In medicine, Muslim scientists were far superior to both their ancient predecessors and their European contemporaries. Unlike the medieval Christian West, which tended to view illness and disease as divine punishment, the Muslim physicians looked for physical causes that could be treated as a part of their religious mission. [49]

Muslims made a very significant contribution to the science of medicine. For example, in 870, Abu Mansur invented plaster of Paris casts to immobilize fractures.[44] His pharmacopoeia included 585 drugs. Muslim pharmacists invented several types of drug formulations, such as pills, powders, syrups, plasters, and dressings.

Al-Razi was known as the greatest physician of his time. He was born in Iran in 851 and studied there at the University of Jundishahpur. He was later appointed as the Director of the Baghdad hospital.[48] He wrote a book titled Al-Hawi, which was an encyclopedia of medicine, and the most voluminous work ever written in Arabic. In Latin its title was *Liber Continens*, and it was used as the standard text book in European medical schools for five hundred years.

He also wrote *Kitab al-Mansuri* (Liber Almansoris), a compilation based largely on Greek medicine. According to Dunlop50, Latin translation of this book was used as a textbook at University of Padua well into the 16th century. His research covered gynecology, obstetrics, ophthalmology, and immunology. His research on smallpox and measles was known to be one of the most accurate works and was later translated and published in English by William A. Greenhill (London, 1848).

Al-Razi was not just a physician; he was a chemist, physicist, astronomer, mathematician, and a philosopher. He conducted research and wrote on physics and chemistry. His work in chemistry has been published in his book *Kitab al-Asrar*. Another famous Muslim medical researcher was Ali ibn al-Abbas al-Majusi (Latin: Haly Abbas d. 994). His book, known in Latin as *Liber Regius*, was used as a standard textbook in Europe for many years until it was superseded by Ibn Sina's world famous *Al-Qanun fil Tibb*.

In the history of medicine, the name of Abu Ali al-Husayn ibn Abd Allah ibn Sina (Avicenna, 980–1037) was even more famous than Al-Razi or any of the other Muslim medical scientists. He wrote more than one hundred books, one of which was a medical encyclopedia, The Canon of Medicine, known in Arabic as Al-Qanun fil Tibb. Its Latin translation was printed through 15 editions during the last 30 years of the 15th century, and it remained Europe's standard medical textbook for 500 years.[52]

Its pharmacopoeia contained 760 drugs. Avicenna's *Canon of Medicine* was an important contribution to the scientific method, which included clinical observations of various diseases. It also taught man how to use laws of nature to his own benefit, a characteristic that later defined the new world of Western science.

Avicenna is also credited with the idea that chemicals maintain their identity in a compound. This was in contrast to Aristotle's postulation that when substances react, each one loses its
identity.[44] In acknowledgement of their achievements, the portraits of Al-Razi and Ibn Sina adorn the great hall of the Faculty
of Medicine in the Paris University.

In medical research, Muslim scientists and physicians have
made a particular contribution in the field of ophthalmology.
They were also pioneers in invention of surgical equipment,
wound stitching materials, and excelled in surgical technique.
Around the year 1000, the famous Muslim surgeon Al Zahrawi
published a 1500 page illustrated encyclopedia of surgery that
was used in Europe as a medical reference for the next five centuries. He is credited with the first caesarean operation and
invention of the first pair of forceps.[54]

Dunlop has quoted an 18th century Spanish Jesuit Andres,
who stated that while the Christian schools of the mediae-
val Europe were engaged in teaching church singing, reading
and simple arithmetic, the Muslims sent out their scholars to
find good Latin and Greek books, established observatories to
study astronomy, traveled to study natural history, and founded
schools to teach sciences.[50]

Muslims were pioneers not only in medical and scientific research, but also in other areas of human health, such as
endowment of public hospitals, institution of traveling hospitals, in establishing a system of regular examinations of physicians and award of certificates to them to practice medicine, and
in institution of medical assistance to ailing prisoners.

The first public hospital for the cure of diseases in a hygienic
environment, was built in Baghdad in the year 805, during the
rule of Caliph Haroon ar-Rashid.[48] Revealing an early recognition of the presence of germs in the environment, the authorities
performed an experiment to select the least contaminated part

of the city to build the hospital. Raw meat was exposed to outdoor air at different locations in the city; the location where meat putrefied the slowest was selected for the hospital.[49]

Hospitals with wards and teaching centers were first established in 9th century Egypt. The first such hospital was Ahmad ibn Tulun Hospital, founded in 872 in Cairo. It provided free care for anyone who was in need of it. It was followed by public hospitals all over the Muslim empire from Spain and Morocco to Persia.

Islam teaches its followers of spiritual and physical purity and of the importance of cleanliness. Muslims are required to be clean and in a state of ritual purity before they can offer their 5-times a day mandatory prayers. Ritual ablution or washing of hands, face, and feet is required before the prayer.[49] The great Muslim engineer Al-Jaziri had made mechanical robots that delivered water in just enough quantity for a Muslim to perform his ritual washing for prayer.

In order to achieve thorough cleaning, soap was prepared by mixing an oil (usually olive oil) with an alkali. The mixture was boiled to the proper consistency and poured into molds to set as bars of soap. Muslim scientists also developed cosmetics. The famous surgeon Al-Zahrawi considered cosmetics a branch of medicine, and in his book on medicine called *al-Tasrif* he wrote a chapter on cosmetology called The Medicines of Beauty.[54]

Al-Zahrawi also researched the problems of hair, skin, teeth, and other parts of the body. He developed skin creams and nasal sprays, perfumes, deodorants, hair dyes and suntan lotions. Similarly, al-Kindi also wrote a book on perfumes, called Book of the Chemistry of Perfumes and Distillation. This book contains not only formulas for perfumes, but also the methods of preparation and the needed equipment.

Muslims consider personal hygiene and cleanliness so important that it is common among them to brush their teeth before performing their prayers, and before and after eating or sleeping. It should be of no surprise to the reader to learn that the Muslims invented tooth brushing. Prophet Muhammad was known to brush his teeth with a twig of Miswak (Salvadora persica). Modern day research has shown that it has antibiotic properties and prevents tooth decay.

One of the first things the Muslims did in Spain was to introduce good and clean water supply system — for drinking as well as for irrigation. They developed agriculture, introducing rice, cotton, sugarcane, and new fruit trees that included apricots, figs, pomegranates, oranges, lemons, peaches, and date palm trees. They also introduced land reforms and divided the land into smaller holdings.

Sophisticated instruments including the astrolabe, the quadrant, and navigational charts and maps were invented or developed by the Muslims; these instruments were later used in European voyages of discovery. Astrolabe was a metal star-map used in measuring the altitude of the sun, the moon, and the stars. It was also a very efficient clock and a global positioning device. It was used in astronomy, surveying, and navigation. The first Muslim to construct an astrolabe was Ibrahim bin Habib al-Fazari.[50] Mark Graham states that astrolabe was also used as late as 1492 by sailors accompanying Christopher Columbus.[48]

The astrolabe was used in calculating the true time of day, dates on the ecclesiastical calendar, measuring the height of a tower and depth of a well, determining geographic latitude, marking the direction of true north, determining the position of the sun, and measuring the regular movements of major stars and planets. Muslims and Christians could find their prayer times, and Muslims could determine the direction to Mecca to face for their prayer. The perfection of the astrolabe reflected the genius of Muslim science. It helped solve the problems in such fields as timekeeping, astronomy, astrology, and cartography.

Correct orientation of a Muslim towards the Ka'bah anywhere
in the vast Muslim empire necessitated interaction between faith
and science. Instead of using primitive methods for determining accurate geographic locales, Muslim scientists of the Middle
Ages used scientific techniques. For example, during the 11th
century Al-Biruni used spherical trigonometry to calculate accurate direction to the Ka'bah.[49]

In the field of engineering, Muslims invented all sorts of
machines and tools, as they needed devices to know the time
of the day for their daily prayers and for breaking the fast of
Ramadan. A 13th century Muslim engineer al-Jazari is known
for making clocks of a variety of designs and other mechanical
devices. He described fifty mechanical devices in his book called
The Book of Knowledge of Ingenious Mechanical Devices. The
big Elephant Clock in the Ibn Battuta Mall in Dubai is based on
al-Jazari's model.

Abbas ibn Farnas was the first person to make a flying
machine during the 9th century. He actually flew in it for a while
near Cordoba, Spain before falling to the ground. In 1633, a Turk
named Lagari Hasan Celebi invented the first manned rocket,
which he launched using 300 pounds of gunpowder as the fir-
ing fuel.

The Muslim invasion of Spain in 711 and its conquest led to
its transformation from a Christian backwater of Europe into
an undisputed cultural superpower. The raw materials for this
transformation came from the Muslim heartland. From the
eighth century to the twelfth, science, technology and know-
how emerging in the East flowed steadily westwards through
Egypt to the Muslims of North and West Africa and Muslim
Spain that bordered on Christian Europe. [49]

Among the technologies that were transferred by the Muslims to Spain via North Africa was agricultural technology. They
introduced new crops such as eggplant, watermelon, spinach,

sugarcane, rice, citrus plants including oranges, and many other food plants. Similarly, Arabs from Yemen who migrated to North Africa and Spain, brought with them technology of their well-established irrigation system, new crops, and other agricultural technologies that resulted in increased yields. In a way, they imported a green revolution of their era to the West.

Those familiar with applied research will appreciate the fact that successful transfer of technologies requires field tests under the new soil and environmental conditions. The Muslims brought all the needed technological expertise with them to Spain.

In certain areas, scientists of Muslim Spain made greater progress than Muslim scientists in the East, specifically in agriculture. They had developed a system for forecasting the weather conditions and could predict the coming of storms. Their scientific research was advanced, and their journals published research information on the topics of animal science, fertilizers, horticulture, soil, and water.

When the Christians took Spain, Sicily, and other territories from the Muslims in the 11th and 12th centuries, they could not maintain this green revolution. The agricultural advances disappeared under the new European landowners. The Christian farmers lacked the skills needed to cultivate the specialized crops and of the irrigation techniques and associated agronomic practices. Faced will deficiency of skill, the Christians farmers resorted to old-fashioned cultivation of familiar low value crops. Attempts made to reproduce Muslim technology usually failed or at best produced, would produce a low yield.[49]

Islam puts a great emphasis on education, and many institutions of higher education were established during the golden age of Islam. The first degree-granting university was established by a princess in Fez, Morocco in the year 841. It was named al-Qarawiyin University. The subjects of study included astronomy, arithmetic, logic, geography, medicine, theology, and law. At this university not only the education was free, the students were also given financial assistance for food and accommodation.54 Another old-time Islamic educational institution, the famous al-Azhar University in Cairo, was founded in 972, and it remains one of the renowned traditional universities of Islam today.

During the Muslim rule in Spain (al-Andalus) many schools offered free education. Many universities were opened, and rapidly, the population became educated. Seventy libraries were opened, the largest containing 500,000 books. Every year, 70,000 books were hand-copied.

Muslim civilization also developed great cultural and civic centers. This is particularly true of the Moors, whose Muslims civilization in Spain was the greatest in the world, outside of China. They ruled parts of Spain for nine centuries. According to Abercrombie,[52] during their ruling, the land enjoyed a degree of cultural achievement unsurpassed in the rest of Europe. In the major cities, music, literature, philosophy, mathematics, and medicine all flourished.

Arabic language was considered the medium of high culture, and of everyday life within and among the Muslim, Jewish, and Christian communities of al-Andalus. The Christian clergy complained that the use of Arabic posed a great threat to Latin, the language of the Catholic Church, as Christians were reading Arabic books and it was even common for them to correspond with their friends in Arabic.

Muslims developed a very tolerant society and introduced many social reforms in Spain. Slaves were either freed or given the choice to earn their freedom by work. The liberated non-Muslim slaves readily accepted Islam. Female slaves, on marrying Muslim citizens, automatically became free.

Muslim culture in Spain gave women more freedom than any

other society in Europe. Al-Andalus had many schools where women studied and earned diplomas. Women could work and earn their own salaries. Many women worked as lecturers, teaching law or theology, and as copyists, who copied books for customers. Availability of such jobs enabled women to support their families.

Another indication of Al-Andalusian Muslims society being tolerant was that people of all three monotheistic faiths: Muslims, Jews, and Christians worked together to forge the brilliant civilization that helped lead Europe out of the Dark Ages. In Toledo, scholars from around the world gathered to translate the works (long since lost in original), of Aristotle, Euclid, and Ptolemy into Latin. Muslims did not just preserve the scientific and mathematical knowledge of the Greeks; they translated it, put it to work, and improved it. It is from their work that modern science was born.

During the 10th century, Cordoba blossomed into the largest city in Western Europe, and stood with Baghdad and Constantinople as the great cultural centers of the world. It was a metropolis of half a million people, with 21 suburbs, 70 libraries, 300 public baths, 500 mosques, and miles of paved, lamp-lit streets. Cordoba had these amenities seven hundred years before London could boast of any form of public illumination.[48, 49]

In describing the elegance of Cordoba, Townson stated that while the rest of Europe was filthy and primitive, the Muslim capital of Cordoba was a wonderful city of patios, gardens, fountains, palaces, and pleasant houses.[51] New architectural designs, including the use of stucco and tiles, were introduced. The streets were paved with stone and hundreds of silver lamps decorated mosques. It was a center of scholarly learning for peoples from all over Europe.

Islamic architectural style is easily recognizable. The most commonly known Islamic architectural types are palaces, gardens, forts, tombs, and mosques. The earliest Islamic design was known for circular domes, big minarets, large courtyards, interior vaulted spaces, Arabic calligraphy, and the use of an arabesque pattern, which is characterized by repeating stylized decorative themes.

Repeating themes represent infinity and evoke the concept of God's infinite power. No human or animal forms are depicted in the motif, but stylized foliage is commonly used. Arabic calligraphy is used to enhance the interior of a building by copying verses of the Qur'an or other Islamic writings and geometrical designs. An early example of Islamic architecture can be seen in the Dome of Rock in Jerusalem, which was built in 691.

After the Muslim conquest of Persia in the 7th century, Islamic architects incorporated elements of Persian architecture into Islamic architecture, leading to new methods. For example, several innovations were introduced in dome building. The dome of Soltaniyeh mosque built in the 14th century in Zanjan, Iran is the third largest and tallest masonry dome ever built. It has played a significant role in Islamic architecture.

The distinct feature of Persian domes, which separates them from domes built by the Ottomans, Mughals and others, is the colorful tiles. Persians invented domes that were covered with tiles on their interior as well the exterior. This architectural style was perfected during the rule of the Safavid dynasty, when the *haft rangi* or seven-color style of tile burning was invented. This process enabled the Persian architects to apply more colors to each tile, creating richer and more attractive patterns. The dome of Masjed-e-Shah built in 1629 in Isphahan, Iran is one example of this method.

Other distinguishing features of Islamic architecture include columns, piers, and arches. The Muslims invented the Horseshoe arch in Spain and used it as a main architectural feature.

Islamic architecture in the Iberian Peninsula started with the construction of the Great Mosque of Cordoba beginning in 785. The mosque is famous for its striking interior arches. Moorish architecture reached its peak with the construction of the Alhambra, the magnificent fortress palace of Granada, with its breezy, open interior spaces adorned in red, blue, and gold. The walls are decorated with stylized flower motifs, calligraphic inscriptions, arabesque designs, and walls covered in glazed tiles. Moorish architecture has its roots deeply established in traditional Arab architecture. Islamic influence had a lasting impact on Spanish architecture, even after the Reconquesta.

A prominent example of architectural achievement during the Abbasid Caliphate is the original construction of the city of Baghdad, founded by Caliph al-Mansur on the west bank of the Tigris in 762. The construction of the fortress-capital—in the form of a perfect circle with a five-mile circumference, surrounded by a triple wall—was considered a fantastic achievement of that era. Such an architectural achievement had never been seen before. Later, it became the richest and most civilized city in the world.[50]

The architecture of the Turkish Ottoman Empire has its own distinct style. Many of the mosques were built by the great Ottoman Empire architect Mimar Sinan. For example, the Suleymaniye Mosque, considered the most beautiful mosque in Istanbul, is the second largest in the city after the Blue Mosque with its six minarets. Ottoman Emperor Suleyman the Magnificent ordered it to be built to rival the nearby Hagia Sophia, and it is set prominently on a hill. It was built in seven years, beginning in 1550, and is the largest and most complex masterpiece of Ottoman architecture.

Another example of Islamic architecture is the Mughal architecture of Muslims in India and Pakistan. The Mughal architecture of 16th century South Asia is a fusion of Arabic and Persian architecture. The Mughal emperor Akbar the Great constructed the royal city of Fatehpur Sikri, 26 miles west of Agra, in the late 16th century.

The most spectacular example of Mughal architecture is the Taj Mahal in Agra. It was built in 1648 by emperor Shah Jahan as a mausoleum in memory of his wife, Mumtaz Mahal. This monument made extensive use of precious and semiprecious stones as inlay and a vast quantity of white marble. It represents the pinnacle of Mughal Islamic architecture in India and is one of the Seven Wonders of the World. Other structures that show a great depth of Mughal architecture are the Shalimar Gardens and the Badshahi Masjid in Lahore, Pakistan.

The Shalimar Gardens were built in 1642 by the Mughal emperor Shah Jahan. Its architect was Khalilullah Khan. The Badshahi Masjid, which means the 'Royal Mosque', was built in 1674 by Mughal emperor Aurangzeb. It is one of Lahore's best known landmarks, and epitomizes the beauty and grandeur of the Mughal era.

Muslim architects have maintained their high achievement standards throughout Islamic history, and in the more recent times Islamic architecture has achieved a new level with the construction of buildings such as the King Abdulaziz International Airport's Hajj Terminal, designed for pilgrims on the Hajj in Saudi Arabia. The architect of this terminal is Bangladeshi architect Dr. Fazlur Rahman Khan, who received the prestigious Agha Khan Award for Architecture for "An Outstanding Contribution to Architecture for Muslims." Khan, who immigrated to United States, also designed Chicago's John Hancock Center in 1970, the One Shell Plaza in Houston in 1971, and the Sears Tower in Chicago in 1973. He was the inventor of the tube structure design used in all super-tall skyscrapers since the 1960s.

Turkish architect Vedat Dalokay built the King Faisal Mosque, Islamabad, Pakistan, named after King Faisal of Saudi Arabia. Completed in 1986, it is the fourth largest mosque in the world.

With no dome, its design is different from that of a traditional mosque. Each of its four minarets is 80 meters, which makes them the tallest in South Asia. The mosque represents an outstanding example of modern Islamic architecture, and Vedat Dalokay won the Agha Khan Award for Architecture for this project.

One of the most popular elements In Islamic art is the arabesque (as shown on the front cover of this book). Usually found decorating the walls in the mosques and Muslim homes and buildings, the arabesque is a design based on repeating geometric shapes, floral patterns, and in rare situations, animals, especially birds. To Muslims, these forms symbolize the infinite, extending beyond the material world. The Islamic arabesque art conveys spirituality, and is very different from the Christian art of iconography. Arabesque is a way of decorating mosques and Islamic buildings by using beautiful embellishing and repetitive geometric designs instead of pictures of humans and animals.

Islamic calligraphy is closely related to geometric Islamic art, and is used on the walls and ceilings of mosques and other Islamic buildings, as well as for decoration on pages of books. It is a visible expression of spirituality, and is considered one of the most venerated forms of Islamic art. It involves artistic writing of Qur'an verses and other Islamic writings.

A variety of scripts is used in Islamic calligraphy, including Kufic, Thuluth, Naksh, and Muhaqqaq. The modern trend of Islamic calligraphy was founded in Baghdad during the Abbasid caliphate of the 10th century. At that time, new scripts had taken shape from the earlier, informal writing and had gained in popularity. Through the works and teachings of masters in Baghdad, the art of calligraphy radiated to other Islamic cultural centers.

Considerable changes were introduced in Islamic calligraphy by master calligraphers of the Ottoman Empire. However,

Islamic calligraphy reached its peak in the late nineteenth century, and it is experiencing a revival today. The art continues to reign supreme in its ability to convey in the most profound way the message of the written Islamic texts.

Muslims have also demonstrated their musical talent. It was the Muslims, particularly al-Kindi, who introduced the notations for writing down music.[48,54] They also introduced new musical instruments to the Western world. Before Muslims came to Europe, they only had the harp and similar stringed instruments. Muslims introduced the lute (al-ud), the guitar, and the tambourine. Al Farabi invented an instrument called rababah, an ancestor of the violin family, and qanun, a table zither.[54] Mark Graham states that 'Muslim culture did more than teach Europeans philosophy and science. It taught them how to live with style and elegance.[48]

Abul-Hasan Ali ibn Nafi, nicknamed Ziryab, moved from Baghdad to Cordoba in 822 and took up a job in the court of Caliph Abd al-Rahman II. He was a master musician, fashion designer, and gourmet chef. From Baghdad, he brought several new ideas to introduce into European culture, including elegant cuisine, the concept of multicourse dinners, washable tablecloths, and use of crystal glasses in place of heavy metal goblets and gold cups. Ziryab is also known to have introduced Europe to fashion dresses, high heel shoes, cosmetic items such as underarm deodorant and toothpaste, new music, and the games of chess and polo, as well as a number of common household items.[48]

Other items known to have originated in the Muslim world include carpets and coffee. The import of carpets to Europe goes back to the 12th century. Readers may be surprised to learn that coffee was discovered and introduced to Europe by Muslims.[54]

Muslim theology and literature have also directly influenced the European history. There are many similarities between

Muslim accounts of 'Isra and Mi'raj' described by Ibn al-Arabi (1165–1240) in his book Al-Futuhat al-Makkiya, and The Divine Comedy by Dante (1265–1321), suggesting that Ibn al-Arabi's work may have provided themes later used in Dante's poem.[48]

Muslim philosopher al-Kindi had taught that research, logic, preparatory science, and a long period of instruction were needed for attaining knowledge. Latin scholars of the late Middle Ages discovered this recipe in Arabic texts. They found it to be very valuable and adopted it.

Philosophy put forward by the Arabs and the Greeks had enormous appeal to the medieval West. While it covered elements of the traditional Christian view, it also contained much new material, such as physical sciences, that was not covered by teaching of religion.

Jonathan Lyons states that the Muslims played a key role in establishing a natural philosophy in Europe. In terms of the Western worldview, they played the role of master architects. The new scientific worldview of the West was not just due to the 'recovery' of the classical wisdom by the medieval Romans, as most Western historians seem to suggest. Rather it was because of the enormous transfer of invaluable Muslim knowledge and technology directly to the Christian West.[49]

Muslims have contributed to the human civilization in many ways. London's Science Museum and New York's Hall of Science have held exhibitions of Muslim inventions; the Foundation for Science, Technology and Civilization, in Manchester, UK has published a book with the title *1001 Inventions–Muslim Heritage in Our World*. This book, edited by Professor Salim Al-Hassani, describes many Muslim inventions.[54]

Knowledge of Muslim science and technology was transferred to Western Europe in a variety of ways. Western scholars and tradesmen would share knowledge when they travelled to the lands that were under Muslim rule, such as Spain, Italy, and

Sicily, or land that bordered Muslim ruled territories, such as Catalonia. When Christian forces conquered Muslim lands, they were able to acquire Muslim works of knowledge in the form of libraries and manuscripts. Even the crusader armies played a role in transfer of Muslim knowledge to Europe. The returning crusaders brought back with them not only Muslim knowledge in manuscripts but also Muslims architects, artisans, and craftsmen.

During the Middle Ages, Al-Andalus, or Muslim Spain, was the scientific and cultural powerhouse of the Muslim civilization. It was from here that Muslim scientific and cultural knowledge spread to the neighboring European lands, whose breadth of knowledge was inferior to the Muslims. European scholars must have desired to learn from the Muslims about their science, philosophy, and culture.

Arabic became the principal language of the empire of Islam, and for Muslims and Christians alike. For any non-Muslims to learn about the science and philosophy of the Muslims, it was a necessity to learn Arabic; even the Spanish church found it necessary to translate their Scriptures and other religious works from Latin into Arabic. Many scholars of the Christian West went to Al-Andalus, Sicily, and other Muslim lands to study and learn about Muslim science, philosophy and culture. Many travelled to acquire Arabic manuscripts and translate them into Latin. For translation work, many Christians learned Arabic, while others hired Arabic speaking individuals to help them in translation work.

Dunlop states that the transmission of Muslim science to the West was made possible by the translations from Arabic into Latin. Without the scholars who travelled to Spain, Sicily, and elsewhere in search of Arabic manuscripts, the Latin versions which were so eagerly read from that time on would never have been made, for neither native Arabic speakers nor stay-at-home scholars and theologians were in a position to produce them.[50]

The transfer of the science and philosophy of the Muslims to the Western Europe started in the 10th century and reached its apex during the 12th and the 13th centuries. By the end of the 13th century, Muslim science and philosophy were taught at European institutions; European scholars had a variety of Muslim science and philosophy texts at their disposal.

One of the earliest scholars was Gerbert d'Aurillac, the future Pope Sylvester II (946–1003). He was one of the first Christians from the West to learn about Muslim science and technology. After his initial education in a French monastery, he was sent to Catalonia in 967 for advanced studies and stayed there for three years. Catalonia was a Christian outpost located at the border of Christian Europe and Muslim Spain; a lot of knowledge transfer from Muslim culture to Europe took place here. Andalusian Muslims travelling to Catalonia brought cultural trends, ideas and inventions, with them. Catalonia was one of the places where the Arab numerals, the Muslim astrolabe, and information about Muslim science and technology were transferred to the Christian West.

In Catalonia, Gerbert learned subjects that no one in the rest of Europe had even heard of, the most important being Arabic numbers. When he returned to his native France, he established schools where liberal arts were taught. He was the first person to bring Arabic numerals to Western Europe; he introduced the Arabic numbers 1 to 9 by using an abacus. This led to more common use of the abacus with Arabic numerals in the West in place of the prevailing Roman numerals.[50]

It took another two centuries for Arabic numerals to become an acceptable means of calculation in the West. The Roman system was not completely replaced until the publication of Leonardo Fibonacci's Liber Abaci in 1202. Gerbert also promoted Arabic knowledge of arithmetic, mathematics, and astronomy, and reintroduced the abacus and armillary sphere, which had been lost to Europe since the end of the Greco-Roman era. Even after his return to France, Gerbert continued his acquisition of Muslim knowledge of sciences. For example, in 984 he wrote to Lupitus in Catalonia to send him his Latin translation of Arabic manuscripts on astronomy.

In support of the claim that the transfer of the Muslim science to Western Europe occurred in the 10th century, Dunlop has drawn attention to the work of Harvard Professor Haskins. Haskins has mentioned that in the library of the monastery at Santa Maria of Ripoll in Catalonia, Latin manuscripts of 10th century had treatise on astrolabe and tables of stars with Arabic names.

John of Gorz was another source of transferring Muslim knowledge to the West during the 10th century. Appointed as an ambassador of the German Emperor Otto the Great to the court of Caliph Abd ar-Rahman III at Cordova in 950, he stayed in Spain for three years before returning to Lorraine. Dunlop quotes a reference of James Westfall Thompson who, in his book The Introduction of Arabic Science into Lorraine in the 10th Century, shows evidence of Arabic science in the schools of Lorraine, after John of Gorz returned from Spain in the second half of the 10th century.[50]

During the 10th century, the inferiority of Western scholarship was such that they were unable to translate texts of Muslim science and technology without making errors. For example, the earliest Latin translation of texts on the astrolabe had many errors; even the associated Arabic technical terminology was not translated correctly. The West was unable to produce its own coherent astrolabe texts until the mid-twelfth century. Lack of Latin terminology for some Arabic terms may have been a reason.

Although Latin translations of Muslim texts started during the 10th century, it was only after was Christians retook Toledo in 1085 that a burst of translations took place. Christian scholars came to Toledo from all over Europe to discover the great minds of Islamic civilization and to translate their work into Latin. Translation became an industry in Toledo, and was partly financed by the church. As a result of these translations, the names of Ibn Sina (Avicenna) and Ibn Rushd (Averroes) became popular in European universities.

The first piece of Muslim knowledge transferred to Europe was from Spain. It was on mathematics, astronomy, and menstruation. Medical knowledge was transferred later in the 11th century from Southern Italy, and its source was Constantine the African. Philosophical knowledge was next, transferred during the 12th century through the work of Dominicus Gundisalvi (in 1150).

In the 12th century, Gerard of Cremona and Gundisalvi transferred knowledge in mathematics, astronomy, medicine, alchemy, and philosophy. Italian scholars, Gerard of Cremona, and Plato of Trivoli went to Spain and translated Arabic texts into Latin and thereby contributed to the transfer of Muslim knowledge to Western Europe. In the 13th century, Michael Scot worked at Toledo and Sicily translating Arabic texts into Latin. This information comes from D. M. Dunlop,50 and it gives a summary of the transfer of Muslim knowledge to Western Europe from the 10th century through the 13th century.

Constantine the African (1020–1087) made considerable translations from Arabic to Latin. He was an Arabic speaking Christian trained in Muslim medical schools. He had travelled throughout the known world and had ended up in Salerno, Italy where he taught at the first medical university of Europe. His translations included works of al-Razi, Ibn Sina, Ali ibn al-Abbas al-Majusi (Haly Abbas) and other great Muslim scientists.

One of these texts was a medical book of Ali ibn al-Abbas al-Majusi, physician to the Caliph. Constantine the African began the translation of this book, and it was later completed by Stephen of Pisa.[48] This book explained ways to treat hemorrhoids, nasal polyps, cataracts, infections, and gynecological problems. Students graduating from the Salerno medical university wrote their own medical and surgical texts, incorporating the material they had learned from Islamic medicine. This process of advanced medical education helped pull European medicine out of the Dark Ages and sow the seed for Italian Renaissance.

It was not uncommon for the European scholars travelling to Muslim lands in search of knowledge to learn the Arabic language in order to gain a better understanding. For example, Adelard of Bath (1080–1152), known as the first English scientist, learnt Arabic and spent seven years in lands under Muslim rule to find Muslim knowledge and translate it from Arabic into Latin.

In order to understand the Muslim knowledge, Western scholars had to not only learn Arabic, but adopt a new way of looking at the world around them.[48] Muslim learning was different in that it was based on rational thought, experimentation, and personal experience, rather than blind acceptance of traditions and customs, as was the case in the West at that time. Muslim scientists of the Middle Ages were so superior that the West could not produce an equal until the later stages of the Renaissance, such as Copernicus in the sixteenth century.

Adelard was fascinated when he learned that Muslim scientific knowledge was based on experimentation, rational thought, and personal experience. After returning to England, he started to look at the world around him in a new way. He felt that while the Western world followed a halter of authority, Muslim knowledge was based on reason and logic; he realized that knowledge could liberate the Western world from the burdens of orthodoxy.

Among the places he visited was the medical school at Salerno, in southern Italy (then under Muslim rule), to learn about Muslim science of medicine. Among the texts he translated from Arabic to Latin were astronomical tables of al-Khwarizmi, Introduction to astrology of Abu Ma'shar (Albumazar), and Euclid's Elements. He also translated techniques for using the astrolabe, and texts on chemistry. Euclid's Elements became the textbook of mathematics for Western Europe, and remained so until the 16th century. It gives an excellent example of how Greek knowledge was retrieved by Muslims and transferred to Western Europe.

Adelard's other great revolutionary work was the Latin translation of al-Khwarizmi's star tables, the zij al-Sindhind (or the zij, as it is called for short), complementing his translation of Euclid's Elements from Arabic to Latin. Euclid's Elements had been translated from Greek to Arabic by al-Hajjaj during the reign of the Abbasid Caliph Haroon ar-Rashid in the 9th century. The star tables explained the movements of the sun, the moon, and the five visible planets. Several attempts had been made before Adelard to translate the zij, but all had failed.

In the West, Al-Khwarizmi's work was so challenging that new vocabulary had to be developed in order to comprehend the full scope and importance of the zij. It took a long time for Western scholars to fully appreciate the scientific knowledge it generated. In 1149, Adelard published his original treatise On the Use of the Astrolabe, which further revolutionized the way Western thinkers understood the universe around them. He highlighted the link between the new technology and Muslim scientific knowledge behind it.

Jonathan Lyons describes how Adelard believed that the dynamic knowledge of the Muslims had the potential to liberate the Western world from the burden of orthodoxy, and that it could lead them on a new course based on reason and rationalism. He was so impressed with the Muslim scholars from whom he had learned that he referred to them as "My Arab Masters." In his work On the Use of the Astrolabe, he proposed to the future King Henry II that the kingdom should recognize the authority of Arabs scientists and thinkers, and not that of the rigid (Christian) clergy.[49]

Adelard also translated Abu Ma'shar al-Balakhi's (Albumazar) The Introduction to Astrology from Arabic to Latin—an astrology encyclopedia written in 848 in Baghdad. Adelard's own Latin work Abbreviation of the Introduction to Astrology was published in the West in 1120, introducing Albumazar to the West as the supreme authority on astrology. [49]

Lyons bemoaned the fact that the names of Albumazar and other influential Muslim scholars have been forgotten. He indicated a tendency among Renaissance scholars and their successors to dismiss the contributions of the ideas of the Muslims to the Western world.

Nevertheless, he gave credit to Albumazar for his centuries of influence on the development of science and philosophy in medieval Europe. His work served as the first important conduit to the West for Aristotle's natural philosophy. Some, including Roger Bacon, the West's first true scientist, considered Albumazar, not Aristotle, to be the leading authority in natural science.[49]

The works translated into Arabic included not only Euclid's Elements, but also Ptolemy's Almagest, Indian texts on astronomy, and Aristotle's works on natural philosophy. In fact, Euclid's Elements was one of the first major Greek texts translated into Arabic by al-Hajjaj during the reign of the Abbasid Caliph Haroon al-Rashid. Thabit ibn Qurra made a later translation. These translations would set the stage for Greek knowledge to spread through the Islamic empire. It was three centuries later that Adelard translated the Arabic translation of Euclid's Elements into Latin.

From the twelfth century onwards, Western scholars fanned

out into the lands from which Muslims were retreating—especially Spain, Sicily, southern Italy, and the Latin East—searching for works on philosophy, arts, and sciences that the Muslims had left behind. Christian conquests of these lands opened the way to an intellectual wealth of the Muslim libraries. In order to benefit from the newly discovered materials, the Western scholars learned Arabic, and where they themselves were not well versed in Arabic, they hired translators to translate Arabic books into Latin. However, they faced many practical problems, as Latin lacked the vocabulary to keep up with the Arabs' scientific language.

Another Western scholar known for translation of texts of Muslim science into Latin was Stephen of Pisa. During the first part of the 12th century he travelled to Antioch, which had become an important center for translation of Arabic texts into Latin, and translated, among other works, a 10th century medical book written by Ali ibn al-Abbas al-Majusi (Haly Abbas). This book had been widely used as a textbook across the Muslim world. Even though Stephen himself was not a physician, he translated this Arabic medical book into Latin in 1127, thus creating a textbook for the Europeans.

During the 12th century, European scholars put major efforts towards new learning, leading them to recently conquered parts of Europe that had once been under Muslim rule and still had substantial Arabic-speaking populations. These areas included central Spain and Sicily; both had come under Christian rule in the eleventh century. The combination of Muslim scholars and Christian rulers in these areas made them intellectually attractive and politically accessible to Latin scholars.

A typical example is that of Gerard of Cremona (c. 1114–87). He travelled to Toledo, several years after its reconquest by Christians in 1085. Seeing an abundance of books in Arabic on every subject, and feeling sorry for the West for lack of access to such advanced knowledge, he decided to learn Arabic language thoroughly in order to translate the Arabic scientific and cultural works into Latin.

He translated more than seventy Arabic texts into Latin. Among these were Al-Razi's Liber Almansoris, Yahya bin Sarafiyun's Kitab al-Kunnish, and Ali bin Ridwan's Expositio Galeni, which was Arabic translation of Galen's Ars Parva. Gerard also translated many other texts on chemistry, astronomy, mathematics, optics, and other sciences, as well as Avicenna's Canon of Medicine and Ptolemy's Almagest. He had profound love for these books but he could not find them in Latin.

Another Western scholar who went to Toledo and Sicily and translated Muslim texts from Arabic to Latin was Michael Scot, who was born in Scotland late in the 12th century. He went to Toledo in 1217 to translate Muslim literature into Latin. Later, during the 1220s, he went to Sicily to the court of the Holy Roman Emperor Frederick II, where he became royal science advisor.

While in Toledo, Michael Scot translated the work of a Spanish Muslim astronomer Nur ad-Din Abu Is'haq al-Bitruji (Latin Alpetrageus) titled On the Sphere. This book was concerned with the criticism of Ptolemy's theory of eccentrics and epicycles to account for the observed movements of heavenly bodies, and with a development of Aristotle's view of homocentric spheres.

There were two other Muslim critics of Ptolemy's work mentioned by al-Bitruji, Abu Is'haq Ibrahim bin az-Zarqalah (Latinized Arzachel) (1029–1087) of Cordova and Abu Muhammad Jabir bin Afah al-Ishbili, who lived in Seville in the middle of the 12th century. Al-Bitruji's work was very important, and the Western scholars, including Roger Bacon, referred it to in the 13th century. It seems that Copernicus had also studied the work of Muslim scientists, as he has quoted Arzachel (az-Zarqalah) and Albategneus (al-Battani) in his book De Revolutionibus Orbium Coelestium.

At the royal court in Sicily, Michael Scot continued his translations of Muslim literature from Arabic into Latin, including Avicenna's work on biology and Averroes's work. The translation experience made him the leading public intellectual of his time, and he was considered a key figure in the intellectual and cultural development of the 13th century Europe.

Emperor Frederick II played an important role in the transmission of the Arab philosophy and sciences to the West. He also established a university at Naples in 1224, and it was at this university that the great Catholic thinker Thomas Aquinas (died in 1274) started his university career and learned about Muslim sciences. His writings from the 1250's indicate that he had studied the writings of both Avicenna and Averroes.

In his book, Jonathan Lyons mentions one of Michael Scot's students, Leonardo Fibonacci (1170–1250), known as the most talented western mathematician of the Middle Ages. He is best known for Latin work dealing with the use of the Arabic numbering system, first spelled out by al-Khwarizmi. Fibonacci realized that arithmetic became much simpler when Arabic numerals were used instead of the commonly used Roman numerals. He traveled to study under the leading Arab mathematicians of the time. After returning home, he wrote his Book of Calculation or Liber Abaci, which was published in 1202. In his book, he showed how using Arabic numerals and methods of Arabs, which he found very valuable, could solve a variety of problems.[49]

The other important works that Michael Scot translated from Arabic to Latin included Aristotle's zoological work Historia Animalium, which had been translated from Greek into Arabic in the ninth century by Yahya bin al-Bitriq (died 815). Michael Scot translated the Arabic text into Latin in 1220.

Abul Walid Ibn Rushd, known in the West as Averroes, is considered the greatest of the Muslim philosophers of all times.

He had written commentaries on Aristotle's De Coelo, Ethics, and others. Michael Scot translated these Arabic texts into Latin, and Dunlop has remarked that Michael Scot's contribution to knowledge through these translations of Averroes's commentaries were very significant.50 His explanation of Aristotle's philosophy were fundamental to the West's emerging understanding of science, nature, and metaphysics.

Averroes (1126–1198) was the son of a famous Muslim jurist of Cordoba. He was educated in medicine, religious law, and theology, served as the Qadi, or religious judge, of Seville from 1169 to 1172, and then appointed as chief justice of Cordoba. He was summoned by Sultan Abu Yaqub Yusuf, a ruler of al-Andalus, to study Aristotle's books and explain their aims for common man to grasp their meaning. Michael Scot later publicized his views on philosophy to the Western world. His rational approach to philosophy changed Western thought forever.

Michael Scot translated several Commentaries of Averroes, which were distributed to Italian universities, the University of Paris, and other European universities. This kind of transmission of Muslim knowledge shaped the new generation of the early modern scientists of the West.

The other scientific and philosophical Islamic works translated by Michael Scot from Latin into Arabic included al-Farabi's Ihsa al-Ulum, which came to be known as Divisio Philosophiae, Avicenna's Ash-Shifa, which came to be known as Abbreviatio Avicennae de Animalibus, and Averroes's De Substantia Orbis.

Two other names that need to be mentioned here are Albertus Magnus, a teacher of Thomas Aquinas, and Peter of Albano. Albertus Magnus is known for the Latin translation of the Arabic text on Aristotle's De Animalibus. Peter of Albano, born in Padua in 1250, is known for compilation of extensive amount of information on the transfer of Muslim science and philosophy in his book Concilliator of the Differences of the Philosophers and particularly the Medicals (published in 1303). Dunlop points out that the effect Peter of Albano's Muslim science and philosophy teaching was felt at Padua for several centuries.

There were many other European scholars who translated manuscripts of Muslim science and philosophy from Arabic into Latin. Dunlop has listed a number of them. In addition to Constantine Africanus, Gerard of Cremona, and Michael Scot, he adds the names of Hermann Alemannus, John Avendeath, Dominicus Gundisalvi, and John of Seville to the list of those who translated the works of al-Farabi, Avicenna, Averroes, al-Razi, Ali al-Abbas, Albumazar, and other Muslim scientists and philosophers into Latin.[50]

Constantine the African is credited with translating the Arabic texts on the works of Hippocrates and Galen, and Ishaq ibn Imran's work with Latin title of De Definisionibus. Hermann Alemannus translated al-Farabi's Compendium of Aristotle's Rhetoric, John Avendeath translated Avicenna's De Anima and De Coelo et Mundo, and Dominicus Gundisalvi translated Al-Farabi's De Ortu Scientiarum and Avicenna's The Metaphysics. John of Seville was known for the translation of Abu Ma'shar Balakhi (Albumazar)'s Introductorium, Masha'llah's Epistola de Rebus Eclipsis Lunae et Solis, and Abu al-Qabisi's work on judicious astrology called Leber Isagogicus De Planetarium Conjunctionibus.

Muslim intellectual heritage was translated from Arabic into Latin on a large scale, and for this, the translators came to Spain from France, Germany, England, Italy, Scotland, and other parts of Europe. This transfer of knowledge from the Greeks and Muslims shook Western scholars out of their narrow worldview. Philosophical questions about the nature of universe started to dominate Western learning, and Arabic terms and phrases started to become a part of Western scholarly literature.

The translations were rich in philosophy of Aristotle and

Muslims' advanced sciences, and they were exported to West's earliest universities during the early thirteenth century including Bologna, Padua, Paris, Salamanca, and Oxford. The European universities which were known for teaching philosophy of Averroes included the University of Padua in Italy and university at Salamanca in Spain.

The 13th century University of Padua had strength in medicine and philosophy. Philosophical education was based on the teachings of Averroes rather than Aristotle. During the 15th century the Averroist philosophy was absolute. Philosophy was associated with medicine and not theology, and it was taught by doctors with medical degrees rather than theologians. Avicenna held the same position in medicine that Averroes held in philosophy. Medical books of Avicenna were used as text books in European universities well into the 17th century.

Dunlop has stated that the Muslim science directly influenced European scientific development for seven hundred years, from the 10th to the 17th century, from the Dark Ages of Europe down to the Renaissance.[50]

Jonathan Lyons states that the Arabs unleashed science (by Arabs, he means the Muslims). At the time, Adelard wrote On the Use of the Astrolabe. Western geography taught that the world was flat and in the shape of a wheel. However, Adelard had learned from the Muslims, who learned from the ancient Greeks, that the earth was a sphere.

The compromise between the church and the discoveries of Western scientists, which Thomas Aquinas had developed under the influence of Muslim philosophers, still holds true to this day. Adelard of Bath, described how the Muslim philosophers had taught the West: "Of course God rules the universe, but we may and should enquire into the natural world. The Arabs teach us."[49]

It can be summed up from this chapter that Muslims have

contributed considerably to the human civilization in astronomy, mathematics, engineering, science, technology, architecture, philosophy, poetry, art, healthcare, city planning, agriculture, personal hygiene and beautification, culinary science, music, and many areas of life.

Many scientific and technological achievements and inventions of modern age are based on the discoveries made and of Muslim scientists of the Middle Ages. Many books on medicine, science, mathematics, astronomy, philosophy, and other subjects written by Muslims were used as textbooks in European universities for several centuries. Western historians report that the Muslim science directly influenced European scientific development for seven hundred years, from the 10th to the 17th century, and paved the way for European Renaissance.

14

MORAL AND ETHICAL VALUES TAUGHT BY ISLAM

ISLAM IS A simple, straightforward religion. If followed sincerely, Islam brings peace and tranquility to the human mind and soul, and elevates the hearts of those who submit to it. It gives them guidance in their affairs and strengthens them in difficult times. Muslims believe that the Qur'an contains what every soul requires for its tranquility and spiritual elevation. It is free from dogmatic tenets and mysteries. It contains noble percepts and inspiring passages with wisdom and practical advice for everyday life.

Islam conveys the message of peace and security to humanity. It leads humanity to a vast expanse of right guidance, and a path that is uniform and straight. It can satisfy the needs of every member of human family, and it can offer solutions to present day problems. Importantly, Islam does not call man to submit to it without thinking and reflection.

It invites men and women to think and reflect deeply and clearly and to weigh every Islamic belief on the scale of understanding and wisdom before accepting it. It opposes stagnation and deterioration in life. Islam encourages people to achieve advancement and development. It allows the individual to earn money and wealth and attain industrial and commercial development. Islam gives each person the right to wages and reward, as long as these are from lawful activities and are not ill gotten.

Many critics of Islam fall back on the 'bad life' of the people in Muslim countries, shutting their eyes to the fact that their vices are not due to the teachings of Islam but to the dire poverty, lack of education, and ignorance in which they live because of the physical and political conditions of their countries.

ISLAM TEACHES GOOD VIRTUES AND MORAL VALUES

Islam, like other religions and some non-religious cultures, teaches its adherents the acquisition of positive moral values as a good quality. It teaches that kindness (to humans, animals, and the environment), compassion, mercy, courage, patient perseverance, truthfulness, dignity, restraint, politeness, fidelity, justice, honesty, trust, and loyalty are all good qualities and moral values. An ideal Muslim is expected to be gentle, social, tolerant, and with an easy disposition. He is generous to the poor, the orphans, and the needy; kind to neighbors, friends, co-workers, relatives, and especially to his parents.

The Islamic emphasis on virtues is unparalleled and unsurpassed. The Qur'an and Hadith are full of instructions to Muslims on moral conduct in their daily life. A few selected examples of Islamic moral values are given below with references from the Qur'an and Hadith.

The religion teaches moderation and temperance in all things, which requires restraint. Islam places importance on living a balanced life, from a physical as well as a spiritual perspective. The purpose of this life is to test us, and that in being tested we grow spiritually.

Muslims are taught to be grateful in times of plenty, faithful and patient in adversity, and to accept God's will, whatever it may be. In everyday life, each righteous act of a true Muslim is counted as an act of worship towards God, if done with the right intention. This concept leads to a harmonious and balanced life. For example, Islam teaches that a person who supports his family using money earned through permissible means is in fact performing an act of worship.

Ideally, Muslims should strive to remain conscious of God all the time, through all the normal activities of life. At the same time, they should not wish to withdraw from normal life. A true Muslim would wish every action and thought to be permeated with the remembrance of God. This is because Muslims believe that we are always in the presence of God; even if we cannot see Him, He sees us and is with us no matter where we are. Islam teaches Muslims to remember that they will return to God when their time in this world is done. Since we do not know when that moment will be, we must consider every second of our lives as a gift from God, and not our right.

HUMANS ARE VICEGERENTS OF GOD ON EARTH

Islam teaches Muslims to behave in a particular way because they believe humans are God's vicegerents on earth. Indeed, Muslims believe that God's purpose for creating mankind is to be His vicegerent on earth. Adam and Eve were created to play this role of vicegerency and were equipped with knowledge of things to do their job. Then they were tested, and were forbidden to eat from a certain tree. They fell victim to persuasions of Satan and committed sin by eating from the forbidden tree. Immediately after sinning they repented, sought God's forgiveness, and were forgiven. It was after they were forgiven and redeemed that they were sent down to the earth to play their role as vicegerents of God. They were promised Divine guidance, and assured that those who followed that guidance would be successful.

Islam does not contribute to any theory of the "fall of man'. There was no fall at all. Man was purposefully created to be God's vicegerent on earth to fulfill God's Will. It, therefore, actually represents 'rise of man' to new challenges, not his fall.

According to the Islamic teachings, Eve did not lead Adam to sin and disobedience. Satan caused both to disobey God, and both of them were responsible. Both repented, and were forgiven. They came down to earth without the stigma of the original sin.

Islam teaches that the human nature is pure and man has been created in the best of all forms. Man and woman are made from the same substance, and everyone is born in a state of purity and innocence. Success or failure depends upon one's own beliefs and behavior, and no one is responsible for the actions of others.

Man is given a choice to do good or bad, and will be held responsible for his actions. Freedom can be misused, and this has great dangers for man in his life on earth, as Satan is always trying to mislead him. Divine Guidance is provided for the success of mankind on earth, but man has not been provided complete protection against error, which would negate freedom of choice. He may commit errors, but his redemption lies in his realization of those errors, seeking repentance, and turning back to the right path.

TO BE PATIENT IN ADVERSITY AND HARDSHIP

Suffering or misfortune is not necessarily a punishment from God for something we have done. Islam teaches that through physical and other sufferings, God may remit minor sins of the believers and facilitate our spiritual growth. What is important to Muslims is how they bear the tests, seeking God's help through prayer and patient perseverance.

In adversity, a Muslim is required to seek a solution, but if it is not immediately forthcoming, he is expected to bear it with patience and not hold God responsible for the difficulty or misfortune. He will not cease to love God, Who is his only real support. A true Muslim follows the old adage: God may not take away the storm from us, but He may give us peace in the midst of the storm.

TO BE GRACIOUS IN FORGIVENESS—AN ISLAMIC VIRTUE

In Islamic teachings, there is a great emphasis on the act of forgiveness. There are at least 30 verses in the Qur'an that deal with forgiveness. Most of these verses refer to forgiveness by God, one of Whose 99 Attributes is Al-Ghaffar, which means "The One who forgives again and again."

In at least ten of these verses, we are commanded to exercise forgiveness in our dealings with other people. For example, in the following verses we are commanded to forgive others:

"Forgive and overlook, do you not wish that God should forgive you?
For God is Oft-forgiving, Most Merciful."
(Qur'an 24:22)

"Hold on to forgiveness, command what is right,
but turn away from the ignorant."
(Qur'an 7:199)

It is human nature to extract recompense for an unjust injury and we are not forbidden from doing so as long as the recompense is equal in degree. But Islam teaches that there is a better way than 'getting even', and it is to forgive and make peace. This is taught in the following verse of the Qur'an:

"The recompense for an injury is an injury equal thereto (in degree),
but if a person forgives and makes reconciliation,
his reward is due from God,
for God loves not those who do wrong (to others)."
(Qur'an 42:40)

Exercise of patience and forgiveness can be difficult even when one is in a good or pleasant mood, so it can require extraordinary self-control and courage to forgive someone when you are in a fit of anger. Whosoever can do so, will find a special reward with God according to the following verse of the Qur'an:

"Whatever is given to you [here] is for the enjoyment in this life,
but that which is with God is better and more lasting.
It is for those who believe and put their trust in their Lord;
those who avoid the greater sins and indecencies
and who forgive even when they are angry."
(Qur'an 42: 36–37)

God commands those of us who are well off to forgive and overlook (the faults of) those who are less fortunate than we are. So, He commands:

"Be gracious in forgiveness."
(Qur'an 15:85)

That by exercising forgiveness for others one can earn the pleasure of God is also obvious from a historical incident that occurred during the life of Prophet Muhammad. In the early days of Islam, their fellow citizens of Mecca subjected Prophet Muhammad and the small group of Muslims to untold brutality and abuse. The people of Mecca boycotted Prophet Muhammad and his followers. They forced them to leave the city because they believed in One True God.

The Muslims left Mecca with few possessions. Left behind were their homes, businesses, farms, and other properties, which were taken over by the Meccans. Despite this unjust treatment, when a few years later the Muslim armies entered Mecca as conquerors under the leadership of Prophet Muhammad, they forgave their enemies. Prophet Muhammad declared general amnesty for the inhabitants of the city. He instructed Muslim soldiers and their commanders that no one was to be hurt unless the Meccans attacked them.

Upon entering Mecca, a Muslim commander got excited and declared, in the Arab tradition of that time, that it was "the day of revenge." When Prophet Muhammad heard, he summoned the commander and reprimanded him, telling him that it was "the day of forgiveness." He then relieved the commander from his post. This incident shows the importance of forgiveness in Islamic teaching and how Prophet Muhammad put this principle into practice.

THE VIRTUES OF COMPASSION AND MERCY

The virtues of compassion and mercy are greatly emphasized in Islamic teachings. The very first line in the Qur'an starts with invocation of the mercy of God Bismillahi Ar-Rahman, Ar-Raheem. It means in the name of God, Most Compassionate, Most Merciful. Ar-Rahman and Ar-Raheem are Divine Attributes. Ar-Raheem means mercy for everything, and Ar-Rahman means the very source of compassion (and mercy).

Each one of the 114 chapters of the Qur'an, except chapter 9 Al-Taubah, opens with the invocation "In the Name of God, Most Compassionate, Most Merciful." In chapter 27, it is mentioned in the beginning as well as in the text. In the Qur'an this invocation is mentioned 114 times, equal to the number of chapters. According to a saying of Prophet Muhammad: "God has more compassion towards people than a mother has towards her baby."

What if there is seemingly a conflict between the mercy of God versus His justice? In that case, according to the sayings of Prophet Muhammad, "the mercy of God prevails over His anger." The Qur'an also teaches us that God is the best of those who are merciful:

> "(O Muhammad) say: My Lord! Forgive and have mercy,
> for Thou art best of all who show mercy."
> (Qur'an 23:118)

Mercy and compassion as human qualities represent sensitivity to others. It is not only sensitivity to their physical pain and suffering, it is also compassion for their overall suffering including spiritual loss and lack of guidance. Thus, Islam teaches compassion for those also who could not find guidance and are not on the right path. It is God's mercy that directs people towards His way and He sent Prophet Muhammad as a mercy for the entire mankind. This is taught in the following Qur'anic verse:

> "We have sent thee not (O Muhammad)
> except as a mercy for (all) the peoples."
> (Qur'an 21:107)

There is a fundamental relationship between a Muslim's faith (Iman) and his compassion. According to a Hadith of Prophet Muhammad, he said: "You will not be true believers until you are compassionate." In this way, compassion is a standard for judging faith. It should be a universal attitude, not merely a feeling for those who are related.

Compassion to others is also a pre-condition for receiving the mercy of God. According to another Hadith of Prophet

Muhammad, he said: "One who does not show mercy to those on earth, shall not receive mercy of Him Who is in the Heaven (God)."

The Qur'an has described individuals who are entitled to our compassion. These include parents (especially in their old age), children, spouses, neighbors, relatives, orphans, the sick and suffering, the servants and slaves as well as the neighbors, the travelers and people in general. It places particular emphasis on compassion for children. According to a Hadith of Prophet Muhammad, he said: "He who has no compassion for our little ones (children) is not one of us."

As God is Merciful to humans, humans are required to exercise mercy towards their fellow human beings, animals, and other creatures. According to the saying of Prophet Muhammad as narrated in Hadith Bukhari, a woman would suffer in Hellfire because she was cruel to her cat, she had confined the cat and would neither feed her nor let her go out.

On another occasion, Prophet Muhammad demonstrated his compassion for dogs. He was traveling with his army and along the way he saw a female dog with small puppies. He became concerned that these animals may get hurt accidentally because of his armed companions. He posted a guard to protect the puppies and their mother until the army had passed.

Taking a life without a just reason, even of an animal, is prohibited in Islam. According to a Hadith of Prophet Muhammad, he said if someone kills even a bird without a good reason, the bird will cry out on the Day of Judgment saying: " O Lord! This person killed me for no reason. He did not kill me for any useful purpose."

GOD LOVES THOSE WHO ARE JUST

Muslims have been commanded to uphold justice. There are several verses in the Qur'an wherein God Commands the practice of justice in our dealing with people. For example:

"Say (O Muhammad) My Lord has commanded justice."
(Qur'an 7:29)

"And act justly; truly, God loves those who are just."
(Qur'an 49:9)

The Qur'an commands Muslims to practice justice even if it goes against the interests of their dear ones. It says:

"O ye who believe! Stand out firmly for justice, as witnesses to God, even though it be against yourselves, or your parents, or your kin; whether he is rich or poor."
(Qur'an 4:135)

Muslims are commanded in the Qur'an to be just when they judge between mankind:

"Verily! God commands you that you return your trust to those whom they are due, and when ye judge between mankind, judge justly. Verily! how excellent is the teaching which He (God) giveth you. Truly, God is He Who hearth and seeth all things."
(Qur'an 4:58)

Every Friday in the sermon of the congregational prayer, the Muslims are reminded to practice justice, help others, and refrain from bad deeds. The Qur'an states:

"Verily! God enjoins justice and kindness, and giving to kinsfolk, and forbids lewdness and abomination and oppression. He admonishes you in order that you may take heed."
(Qur'an 16:90)

In one of his sayings, as narrated in Hadith Bukhari, Prophet Muhammad commanded the Muslims: "Be forgiving and control yourselves in the face of provocation. Give justice to the person who was unfair and unjust to you; give to someone even though he did not give to you when you were in need, and keep fellowship with the one who did not reciprocate your concern."

EQUALITY IN ISLAM

Islam teaches Muslims about universal brotherhood. It seeks to establish bonds of fraternity and equality among them and obliterates all differences and disputes including those of race, language, gender, color, and nationality. It rescues man from economic exploitation and all forms of racial discrimination.

Islam does not permit discrimination based on race, skin color, language, or national origin. Additionally, there is no caste system in Islam. Islam teaches that in the sight of God, all men are equal. The differences in color of the skin, amount of wealth, or social status do not affect the true stature of man in the sight of God. The Qur'an teaches:

> *"The most honored of you in the sight of God is*
> *the one who is the most righteous."*
> (Qur'an 49:13)

Concepts of chosen and gentile people and expressions such as social casts and second-class citizens are meaningless in a truly Islamic society. The virtue of equality is an article of faith and it is deeply rooted in the structure of Islam. An evidence of the practice of equality among Muslims is that interracial marriages are quite common among Muslims. Huston Smith[22] gives the example of Prophet Abraham as modeling this willingness in marrying Hagar, an Egyptian woman of dark skin, as his second wife.

In addition, companions of Prophet Muhammad represented people from all races and skin colors. They included persons with Arab, Persian, African, and Roman backgrounds. A very distinguished companion of the Prophet, Bilal ibn Ribah, was an African slave. He was appointed to the distinguished office of the first muazzen (caller to prayer) of Islam. Salman Farsi, another companion of the prophet, was a Persian.

Huston Smith[22] explains that under Elijah Muhammad, the Black Muslim movement in America (also called The Nation of Islam) was based on militancy towards the whites; but when Malcolm X traveled to Mecca for pilgrimage in 1964, he was impressed to discover that Muslims did not practice racism, and it had no place in Islam. Smith considers the Islamic teaching of racial equality being a big reason for the rapid advancement of Islam in Africa.

Islam seeks to abolish slavery, and considerable progress has been made in this regard. Islam places great value on securing the freedom of slaves and captives of war by paying ransom on their behalf. It is considered a great act of charity. Once a slave is freed, he/she is to be treated equal to other free people in an Islamic society. This is born out by the fact that the first call to prayer at the Quba mosque near Madina, build by Prophet Muhammad himself, was given by the freed African slave Bilal. The Prophet preferred a freed slave for this honor over the noblest Arabs, even his closest companions. This principle of equality and other similar values were the reason that many converted to Islam. The human equality that Islam taught in the 6th century was promised in the U.S. in 1776, and it was delivered in 1964.

The Islamic acts of formal worship are designed to eliminate any sign of prejudice on the basis of race or class differences. For example, in daily congregational prayers, all Muslims stand shoulder to shoulder regardless of their social status. At the time of pilgrimage in Mecca, all Muslim males have identical dress, each wears two pieces of white cloth as a sign of equality; there is no distinction between the prince and the pauper.

IMPORTANCE OF SEEKING KNOWLEDGE AND EDUCATION IN ISLAM

Islam places great importance on the pursuit of knowledge. Both the Qur'an and the Hadith emphasize that man should seek to increase his knowledge to increase his wisdom, his ability to distinguish between the good and the evil, to recognize his Creator, and to appreciate His blessings.

How the Qur'an was revealed is demonstrative of Islam's emphasis on learning. Indeed, the revelation of the Qur'an started with the word Read. Several verses teach the importance of gaining knowledge and the benefit derived from it. For example, it teaches that knowledge increases wisdom, and those who have knowledge are superior in the sight of God than those who lack it.

The importance of seeking knowledge has also been emphasized in several traditional sayings (Hadith) of Prophet Muhammad. For example, he said: "Whoever pursues the road of knowledge, God will direct him to the road to Paradise," and "The angels spread their wings to receive him in the Paradise who seeks after knowledge." He also said: "Seek after knowledge from the cradle to the grave," and "It is the duty of every Muslim man and woman to seek knowledge." The latter Hadith is particularly significant because it specifically mentions that man and woman are equally expected to seek knowledge. It provides additional evidence that in Islam man and woman have equal fundamental rights.

There are two types of knowledge: spiritual knowledge and material/scientific knowledge. Islam teaches that Muslims should increase their knowledge in religious as well as other subjects such as medicine, engineering, mathematics, biology, physics, chemistry, geography, astronomy, architecture and others. The objective is to keep Muslims in tandem with the rest of the world in its march towards human development and progress.

According to the Muslim historian Ibn Khaldun (1332–1406), the curriculum in the Islamic educational institutions of the middle ages included study of two types of subjects:

1. The traditional or transmitted sciences based on revelation. These included study of the Qur'an, Hadith, Fiqh (Islamic law), theology, and linguistic sciences related to the Qur'an and Hadith.
2. Intellectual sciences based on observation and deduction. These included arithmetic, geometry, astronomy, logic, metaphysics, music, and physical and biological sciences (chemistry, physics, medicine, and agricultural sciences).

The curriculum of the modern education system in the Muslim societies depends on the type of institution. In religious institutions, greater emphasis is on the study of the Qur'an, Hadith, Fiqh, and related subjects. In the other institutions not designed to produce religious scholars, all subjects are taught, including biology, chemistry, physics, math, geometry, algebra, calculus, computer science, languages, history, medicine, law and engineering, and social sciences. Islamic studies are also a part of curriculum in these institutions.

As explained in Chapter 13, Muslims contributed to the development of human civilization, especially in the areas of architecture, mathematics, medicine, science, philosophy, poetry, and religion.

ISLAM TEACHES RESPECT FOR PARENTS
AND THEIR CARE IN OLD AGE

Islam teaches that Muslims must fulfill both their duties to God
and to creation. The main duty to God is to worship and obey
Him as is His right to be worshipped and obeyed, to worship
Him alone, without any partners and without any associates,
to worship him with all humility and with all sincerity, and to
obey all His Commandments as given in the Qur'an. The duties
to creation are to people, animals, and the rest of God's creation.
To people, the duties start with members of one's own family,
including husband and wife, children and parents; then extends
to relatives of both spouses, neighbors, friends, fellow workers,
and people in general.

Of the duties to people, the ones towards parents are the most
important. Kindness and respect must be shown to the parents.
Islam places such a great emphasis on showing kindness to parents that in several places in the Qur'an, God has ordained kind
treatment of the parents in the same injunction wherein He has
ordained worship of One God and abstinence from the greatest
sin of Shirk (associating others in worship of God). For example,
it says:

*"And serve God (alone), and ascribe nothing as partners unto Him,
and show kindness to parents."*
(Qur'an 4:36)

*"And Thy Lord hath decreed that ye worship none but Him,
and that ye be kind to thy parents,
whether one or both of them attain old age in thy life.
Say not to them a word of contempt, nor offend them,
but address them in terms of honor.*

And, out of kindness lower to them the wing of humility, and say:
"My Lord! bestow upon them Thy Mercy
as they did take care of me when I was little."
(Qur'an 17: 23–24)

Islam forbids the believers from mistreating their parents, being disrespectful to them, using foul language with them, attacking their dignity or honor, humiliating them, or treating them harshly in any way. The Qur'an commands that the children must be polite and respectful with their parents.

The only time a child is allowed to disobey the parent is if the parent tries to force the child to commit Shirk (associating others with God in worship). Even in this situation, the child has to remain polite to the parent and not be disrespectful.

There are several sayings ascribed to Prophet Muhammad in which he has advised Muslims to be kind and respectful to their parents. For example, in one Hadith (Ibn Majah collection) he is reported to have said: "You will either earn heaven or hellfire, depending upon how you treated your parents."

According to a Hadith narrated by Al-Mughirah, Prophet Muhammad said: " Verily! God forbids you from disobeying your mothers." In a Hadith narrated by Abdullah ibn Amr (at-Tirmizi collection), Prophet Muhammad also said: "Pleasure of God lies in the pleasure of the father, and the wrath of God lies in the wrath of the father."

According to a Hadith narrated in the Abu Dawood collection, a man came to Prophet Muhammad and said that his parents had died, and asked if there was any way he could express his kindness to his dead parents. The Prophet told him that he should make supplication to God for the forgiveness of his parents, honor their commitments after them, and maintain good relations with their friends and relatives.

In Islamic cultures, it is considered a great honor to be able to serve and take care of one's parents. Islam teaches Muslims to accord respectful treatment to teachers, scholars, religious authorities, and elderly people in general.

It can be seen from this chapter how Islam has systematized laws of morality and the Qur'an and Hadith teach the Muslims detailed procedures and methodology for implementing laws of morality in very day life.

15

FAMILY—THE CORNERSTONE OF SOCIETY IN ISLAM

WE LIVE IN an age where the family, as a basic institution of society, is being undermined by powerful and destructive forces. It is rapidly weakening in almost all societies. In Western society, it is disintegrating. This is borne from an explosion of sex outside marriage, an exponential rise in divorce and desertion rates, broken homes, abortions and illegitimate births, same sex marriages, juvenile delinquency, addiction to drugs and alcohol, and by the plight of the elderly.

Islam's position on the family unit is largely formed by the concept of man's role as vicegerent of God. Muslim society is a faith-based society. Activities of life are not compartmentalized as religious and secular. The Islamic code of law, the Shariah, guides life in its entirety. Every activity of a Muslim, whether related to business, education, prayer, politics, sexual relationship, or a civic activity, is religious if it is taken with God-consciousness and according to the values and principles revealed by Him; and it is irreligious if it is in opposition to it.

All differences in language, national origin, race, tribe, geography, and skin color are subordinate to relationship emanating from faith. Anybody who believes in Islam becomes a part of this nation or Ummah. This system of human organization is capable of embracing all of humankind.[55]

In this system, relationships in all social institutions, from the family to the state, are defined by faith-based value system. In Islam, the family is a divinely inspired and ordained institution and faith constitutes the bedrock for the institution of the family. The family institution came into existence with the creation of man. The creation of man and woman and the marriage relationship permeated with tranquility, love, and mercy have been described in the Qur'an as "signs of God."

The family institution plays an important part in Muslim society. It is a basic unit of society, organized in such a way that it operates as its own small-scale society. In Islam, the family institution is so important that a considerable portion of all legal injunctions in the Qur'an relate to the family and its proper regulation.

The purpose of family is to preserve and continue human race, protect morals, provide psycho-emotional stability through sharing of love and kindness, provide social and economic security, create a congenial climate for spiritual and emotional growth of all members of the family, and to promote love, compassion, and emotional stability in the society.

Islam's family system is more a product of law than of custom. It brings the rights of the husband, wife, children, and relatives into a healthy equilibrium. These rights are clearly defined in the Qur'an. In an ideal Islamic family, the family bonds are strengthened by relationship based on love, respect, honor, sincerity, generosity, compassion, and other good virtues. Because the Islamic family system is based on a detailed set of rules about inheritance, orphan rights, and interpersonal relationships, it is better designed to stand up to contemporary pressures than the Western family life, which is held together largely through social conventions and childhood conditioning.[56]

In Islamic teaching, the importance of serving one's parents is a duty second only to the worship of God Almighty, and it is their right to expect it. Muslims are forbidden to show impatience or irritation towards parents as they become difficult due to old age.

In the Islamic world, one rarely finds homes for the elderly, although it is common to find shelters for orphans, widows, and women who may be victims of domestic violence. Children and grandchildren consider the task of caring for the elderly an honor. It is a blessing from God and an opportunity for the spiritual growth of a Muslim to have the honor to take care of his or her parents and grandparents in old age.

As is the case with many aspects of their lives, Muslims strive to emulate the example of Prophet Muhammad in his capacity as a husband and father, as he demonstrated a great amount of love and mercy to his wives, children, and grandchildren.

Islam forbids all forms of sexual relationships outside marriage. The institutions of marriage and the family have been commanded as the 'tradition of the Prophets.' Prophet Muhammad said: "Marriage is a part of my tradition. Whoever runs away from my path is not from amongst us."

Yet marriage in Islam is not simply a sexual relationship, it is a religious and social institution. One objective of marriage is a psychological, emotional, and spiritual companionship between husband and wife. This spiritual relationship sustains and generates love, kindness, mercy, compassion, mutual confidence, self-sacrifice, sense of sharing, and solace. In marriage companionship, each partner seeks ever-increasing emotional fulfillment.

With children in the family, the value of feeling of fellowship, of love and compassion, of sacrifice for others, of tolerance and kindness, are translated into reality and imparted in character. It is the family that provides the most congenial environment for the development of and fulfillment of human personality.

The preservation of the family life is essential for the welfare and prosperity of nations. Muslims possess a stable system of domestic relationships, such as the West is trying to do without, and that is where the strength of the Muslims lies. A stable family offers peace and security, which are essential for the spiritual growth of its members. Muslim families are not limited to traditionally nuclear family, but are extended to include father, mother, sons, daughters, brothers, sisters, grandfather, and grandmother. Such extended family ensures harmony and stability, and reduces incidents of problems such as divorce, extramarital affairs, broken homes, child abuse, domestic violence, and abuse of the elderly.

16

THE STATUS OF WOMAN IN ISLAM

ONE OF THE most misunderstood Western ideas about Islam is the status of women in their society. As taught by the Qur'an, the status of women has little resemblance with the Western stereotype. The latter is a mixture of Islamic traditions corrupted with the local customs. Islam does not teach oppression of women. Any Muslim man who oppresses a woman is doing so out of ignorance and not following the teachings of Islam. Among the countless teachings of Prophet Muhammad, which protected the rights and dignity of women is his saying: *"The best of my followers is he who is fairest in his treatment of his wife."*

Some religions, especially Christianity and Judaism, have historically relegated woman to the lowest level. As a reaction to this teaching, the West has been trying to minimize the difference between the sexes. Islam, on the other hand, gives due recognition to differences between sexes and outlines complementary spheres of activities for the two.

Muslims do not agree with the teachings of the Bible that woman is wicked (Ecclesiasticus 25: 19) or with the teachings of some of the Christian theologians that woman is evil. Islam teaches that woman is as much of the noblest of creation as man is. Indeed, in Islam the role of vicegerency was bestowed upon man and woman equally, each with different roles. Men and women are equal partners in the trial of life on earth. Each will reap the reward in the hereafter for his/her actions in this life. Neither is the shadow of the other. The Qur'an describes the model for men and women in several passages.

According to Islam, it is inevitable for the progress and prosperity of mankind that men and women perform their own respective functions as ordained by nature itself, according to their respective faculties and aptitudes. In the Islamic view, a man or a woman is supreme in his or her own respective sphere.

Women's status in Islam should be discussed in historical perspective. As Professor Huston Smith[22] has pointed out, if one looks at the status of Arabian women before and after the coming of Prophet Muhammad, one can clearly see that Islam has not degraded the status of women, as charged by the West. On the contrary, Islam elevated women and gave them a status which they had never before enjoyed anywhere else in the world.

Before Prophet Muhammad, women were inherited in the Arab culture, as chattels against their will to be disposed off as the father or the husband pleased. Marriage was a loose concept and women were married off against their consent. Sexual perversion was common in the society.

Islam sanctified marriage, making it the sole lawful locus of sexual act and the corner stone of the family. It also made the family the foundation of the society. The consent of both spouses is an explicit condition for a valid marriage under Islamic Law.

In pre-Islamic era, the birth of a daughter in the Arab culture was considered a calamity and they were often buried alive. Islam forbade that practice. Daughters had no inheritance rights, and Islam gave them those rights. Islam gave the women the right to hold property in their name during the seventh century, whereas married women in the United States did not win that right until the twentieth century.[1]

The social status of women in the Western civilization advanced partly because of industrialization and democracy, and not because of religious reforms. For similar reasons, it would be unfair to blame Islam for the social position of Muslim women that is perceived in the West. Once the Muslim majority countries become industrialized and modernized, the status of Muslim women would also be influenced.

Muslims would strive to advance without importing some of the social problems found in the fast-degrading Western society. These include dating, cohabitation, pre-marital sex, and changing of sexual partners until a perfect match is found. Even when such sexual rendezvous culminates in marital bond, it does not last long. The resulting high rate of divorce and a sharp increase in the number of children living with one parent, number of persons living alone, and number of broken families are indications of this social problem.

Muslim societies would have none of this. In a truly Muslim society, a woman cannot be touched until a man comes along who would plan to marry her, treat her like a lady, protect her rights, take the responsibility of a family, and make sure his children can claim legitimacy. It is for these reasons that the divorce rates are low in Islamic countries, and family bonds are very strong and stable.

ISLAM TEACHES THE TREATMENT OF WOMAN WITH LOVE AND RESPECT

The Qur'an teaches that God created man and woman to be a source of love and tranquility for each other:

"And among His signs is this,
that He created for you mates from among yourselves,
that ye may dwell in tranquility with them,
and He has put love and mercy between your (hearts);
verily in that are signs for those who reflect."
(Qur'an 30:21)

Because of woman's status as a mother, wife, and daughter, Islam teaches treatment of women with utmost love and respect. Qur'an places the reverence to woman (the womb that bore you) next to reverence to God:

"O mankind! Be careful of your duty to your Lord,
Who created you from a single soul
and from it created its mate
and from them twain hath spread abroad
a multitude of men and women.
Be careful of your duty towards God
in Whom ye claim (rights) of one another,
and towards the wombs (that bore you).
Lo! God ever watches over you."
(Qur'an 4:1)

Prophet Muhammad was the greatest redeemer of oppressed women and indeed the strongest protector of their rights. According to a saying of Prophet Muhammad: *"Paradise lies under the feet of the mother."*

Additionally, in his farewell address on the occasion of his last pilgrimage, Prophet Muhammad declared: *"O my people, you have certain rights over your wives and so have they over you . . . They are God's trust in your hands. So treat them with utmost kindness."*

Islam grants women numerous rights in the home and in

the society. Among them are the right to work and earn money, to financial support, to earn an education, to inheritance, to a dowry, to keep their maiden name, to worship in a mosque, to being treated with respect and kindness, to vote, and the right to compete for an electoral office.

In England, a woman was not considered a legal entity until 1882. She could neither stand in a court of law on her own nor own property in her own name. On the other hand, Islam gave several basic rights to women as early as in the seventh century when, in Europe, women were condemned as evil and many were burnt alive as witches until as late as the eighteenth century.

WOMEN HAVE THE RIGHT TO INHERIT IN ISLAM

Before the advent of Islam, women did not inherit at all. For the first time in history, the Qur'an created female heirs. It was promulgated at a time when such laws were unheard of in any other part of the world. Its greatest beneficiaries have been women.

Referring to the rights of women in Islam, Professor Ramakrishna Rao[19]states: "Islam came as defender of the weaker sex and entitled women to share in the inheritance of their parent's property. It gave women, centuries ago, the right of owning property. Yet it was only 12 centuries later, in 1881, that England, supposed to be the cradle of democracy, adopted this institution of Islam and an Act was passed, called "The Married Woman's Act." But centuries earlier, the Prophet of Islam had proclaimed: "Women are the twain halves of men. The rights of women are sacred."

According to Islamic law, on the death of a parent, a son inherits double the share of a daughter. The main reason for this is that the son has the financial responsibility for the care of his family and his parents, which the daughter does not. Another reason is that the daughter on marriage may also get the share in her husband's assets as dowry. A woman is absolute master of all that she holds and possesses.

No Muslim woman can be forced to marry without her consent. In some Muslim societies, marriages are arranged by a woman's relatives. Arranged marriages are allowed in Islam, but not required. The woman's agreement to the marriage is required; or as Huston Smith[1] has put it: "not even a sultan may marry without his bride's express approval." Forced marriages, wherever they are performed, are local cultural practices, not religious practices mandated by Islam.

In Islamic culture, the objective of marriage is not only to perpetuate human life, but also to provide emotional support and spiritual harmony to the family. It is not just a union of two individuals; it is union of two extended families. Both families familiarize with each other, and chances of any misunderstanding or conflict are reduced. Islam also teaches that a Muslim should respect and love his in-laws just like his own parents.

The Qur'an (30:21) teaches that a man and wife are expected to find love and compassion in each other, treat each other with respect and consideration, and provide each other comfort and protection just as a garment provides the body comfort and protection (Qur'an 2:187).

Divorce is not forbidden but neither is it encouraged. It is allowed, but only as a last resort. Prophet Muhammad said: "*Of all the permitted things, the one I detest the most is divorce.*" Islamic law gives the wife the right to separate from her husband if he ill-treats her. A husband is not allowed to rule over the wife like a dictator.

If the differences between the husband and the wife become

irreconcilable, the wife is allowed to secure a fair and just divorce from her husband, and she can do this in three ways:

- by incorporating such a right in the marriage contract;
- on ground that husband has stopped loving her or started ill-treating her; and
- the husband has failed to maintain her.

The divorce process requires a husband and wife to pass through three periods of arbiters from each family to try reconciliation. The divorce process advances only when attempts for reconciliation fail. Both husband and wife have an equal right to initiate such process.

SUPREMACY OF MAN OR WOMAN

In view of Islamic teachings, one cannot generalize that a man has supremacy over a woman or vice versa. The supremacy can be judged on the basis of the role each gender plays. In most cases a woman has rights equal to a man. For example, Prophet Muhammad received the oath of commitment (al-bai'ah) from both men and women. Additionally, during the time of Prophet Muhammad, Muslim women went out to do shopping, to get water, to tend and nurse the wounded in battlefield and to go to the mosque for prayer along with men. There was no segregation in public places.

It would be fair to say that man has supremacy in some areas and the woman has supremacy in others. The Qur'an grants supremacy of the husband in family affairs, because he is responsible for maintenance of his wife, for treating her fairly with kindness, love and justice. If he fails in this task, the wife has the right to ask for divorce. If he fulfills his responsibilities, the wife has to give not only her love and care, but her loyalty to

ensure the harmony which is essential to keep the family institution intact, as it supports the pillars of civilization. Except in
family affairs, there is no specific injunction in the Qur'an to con-
clude that woman has to be subordinate to man.

The woman as a mother has supremacy over a man as a
father. Muslim scholars also consider women morally superior
to men, and to be instinctively more pious than men. She is more
protective of her honor and the integrity of her family, and is less
likely to succumb to temptations than man.[57] There are certain
areas where women is regarded as equal or superior to men.

Women are allowed to maintain a degree of independence
within the sphere of marriage. It is demonstrated by the fact
that, while Western women take the surname of their husband
after marriage, the wife usually retains her maiden name in
Islamic culture.

Islam does not prevent women from participation in public
affairs. There is no warrant in the Qur'an or sayings of Prophet
Muhammad to indicate that women cannot rise to high posi-
tions, spiritually as well as materially. There are many examples
from the early history of Islam and the time of Prophet Muhammad that indicate Muslim women actively participating in public affairs.

Women have risen to high political offices in several Muslim
societies. For example, in Turkey, Pakistan, Bangladesh, and
Indonesia, all of which are Muslim countries, women have been
elected as heads of government. In the largest Islamic country Indonesia, Megawati Sukarnoputri was first elected as the
Vice President (1999–2001) and then the President of Indonesia
(2001–2004). Whereas, not a single woman has been elected as
the President or even the Vice President in the history of the
United States.

The late Benazir Bhutto was elected Prime Minister of Pakistan twice. Women in Muslim countries have also risen to high

posts in academia, courts of law, and as cabinet ministers. Dr. Fahmida Mirza, the Speaker of Pakistan's National Assembly (Parliament); Ms. Hina Rabbani Khar, the Foreign Minister; and Dr. Firdaus Awan, Information Minister of Pakistan, are all women.

Islam also allows women to join armed forces in Muslim countries. Many women took an active part in the battles that Prophet Muhammad fought in defense of Islam. For example, Islamic history mentions a woman named Umm Atiyyah who took part in seven battles led by Prophet Muhammad. She would cook food for the Muslim soldiers, supply them medicines and dress up their wounds.[57] Other women nursed the injured and carried food and water for them in the battlefield, included Prophet Muhammad's wife Aisha and his daughter Fatima.

In early days of Islam, Muslim women participated in discussion of the Shura (the consultative council), and appointed to high administrative posts. For example, Caliph Omar Ibn Al-Khattab had appointed a woman, Shifa bint Abdullah, to one of the key posts in his administration as the controller of the market in the city of Medina. A Muslim woman can also achieve high spiritual level. Rabi'a al-Adawiyya, a female Muslim Sufi saint, is known to have achieved spiritually sublime heights.

DO MUSLIM WOMEN HAVE TO WEAR A VEIL IN PUBLIC?

During 2004 when a Louisiana legislator proposed a bill that would ban the wearing of low-riding pants that reveal underwear or the cleft of the buttocks, the state chapter of ACLU immediately condemned the measure as a violation of 'freedom of expression' and called the measure stupid.[58]

With images of a provocatively dressed young generation in the West, the concept of "modesty" is often seen as a strange relic of another age. In the popular TV shows, modest dress seems to be limited to the likes of Caroline Ingalls and her daughters in the reruns of the TV show 'Little House on the Prairie.'

Modesty is defined as propriety in dress or behavior, simplicity, moderation, and freedom from vanity and boastfulness. Yet, the meaning of the word modesty is not well known in today's culture. Modest dress is not practiced any more. It was not long ago that immigrants came to the USA wearing long dresses with women covering their hair, and men would not go shirtless in public.

Islam teaches Muslims to practice modesty. The Qur'an teaches the Muslim men and women to "lower their gaze and guard their modesty in order to preserve their purity"(Qur'an 24:30). Prophet Muhammad once said: "Every religion has its defining character and the defining character of Islam is modesty (internal and external)."

In dress, the parts of the body that must be covered differ for Muslim men and women. The Muslim man must be covered from navel to the knee, and the Muslim woman must be covered from the neck down to the ankles and wrists.

When in public, Muslim women are required to cover their hair and wear an over-garment, or clothing that does not caricature their bodily form, which means to conceal, rather than reveal and project, their bodily figure. The face does not need to be covered. Different terms are used for the description of head and face coverings. The term hijab has been used for a variety of coverings. In this book, the term hijab will mean a scarf that is used to cover the head, leaving the face uncovered. The term veil is used for a covering on the head as well as the face.

The use of hijab by women to cover their heads in public is not unique to Muslims. Other faith traditions practice it or contain references to it in their religious texts. In Genesis 24:62–65, we find that on seeing Isaac, Rebekah "took a veil and covered herself." Similarly, in almost all pictures and paintings, Mary, the mother of Jesus, is depicted as wearing a head cover or hijab. All Catholic nuns wear hijab on their heads, as did the late Mother Theresa.

Orthodox Jewish women wear hijab to cover their heads in public, and many women of Hindu and Sikh religions in India wear hijab, locally called *dopatta*. The public use of hijab by women is not limited to any given faith tradition.

However, when Muslim women wear the scarf, it takes on political connotations. Some women in the West wear heads-carves for fashion, but when Muslim women wear the same scarf or a hijab, they are promptly labeled as victims of oppression and inequality or dubbed as extremists. The hijab or scarf protects a Muslim woman's modesty; it cannot be equated to a Christian woman wearing a cross, as the French have done.

The French have gone to the extreme of passing a law in 2004 against the use of hijab or scarves in their public schools, and later passing a law that outlawed face-covering veils. Some French Muslim women consider it an attack on their individual liberty, freedom of religion, and freedom of conscience. Ironically, instead of helping some women integrate, the law may force women to be cloistered in their homes to avoid exposing their faces in public.

Similarly, in parts of Germany, Belgium, and the Netherlands, public school teachers are forbidden to wear Muslim heads-carves, although Catholic attire for nuns and priests is allowed, making for a clear discrimination against Muslim women. They are forced to choose between their modesty and education. The ban violates the ideal of liberty, equality, and fraternity.

Many Muslim women choose to wear hijab to identify themselves as Muslims following the teachings of Islam. Some do it to express their disapproval of Western society's promotion of women as objects of sexual exploitation, and to express their disgust at the Western woman's public display of her most intimate anatomy for the amusement of men.

Although some Muslim women use a veil to cover their faces, it is not widely used. The Qur'an does not say that an ordinary Muslim woman has to cover her face. During the time of Prophet Muhammad, Muslim women were active in public life, including the battlefield and tending the wounded. It would be hard to imagine that they had their faces covered with a veil. They would be tumbling all over the battlefield. However, they most certainly wore hijab to cover their heads.

In some parts of the world, including the rural areas of Afghanistan, India, Pakistan, and the Persian Gulf states, women use a head-to-toe covering called Burqa when in public. This practice is not sanctioned by the Qur'an or in the sayings of Prophet Muhammad. It is a socio-cultural practice, and it should not be exclusively associated with Islam.

It is interesting to observe that during the time when India and Pakistan were British colonies, Muslims had a lower education level, and most Muslim women wore Burqas. After their freedom from the British rule, Pakistani women became more educated, and the use of Burqa reduced to a minimum. In Afghanistan, which remains underdeveloped and under the occupation of the U.S. and NATO forces, the use of Burqa is still quite common. The use of Burqa seems to be directly related to the education level of women, and not to their religion.

ISLAM ALLOWS POLYGAMY BUT VIRTUALLY ENJOINS MONOGAMY

The term polygamy is one of the first labels used by those non-Muslims who wish to stereotype Muslims. Study of history shows us that even before the Qur'an was revealed, man could marry any number of wives. Christianity and Judaism allowed the practice. We know well from the Bible that David and Solomon had multiple wives, and Jacob had two sisters for his wives at the same time. So why single out Islam for allowing polygamy?

In fact Islam introduced certain restrictions that apply to those who practice polygamy. Thus, although the Qur'an gives permission that a man can have up to four wives simultaneously, it also states that the husband has to treat all his wives equitably and justly:

> *"If you cannot deal equitably and justly with (more than one wife),*
> *then you should marry only one."*
> (Qur'an 4:3)

In another verse on this subject the Qur'an states:

> *"You shall never be able to do justice among your wives,*
> *no matter how much you desire."*
> (Qur'an 4:129)

As Huston Smith[1] has pointed out, the Qur'an virtually enjoins monogamy because it is almost impossible to practice equality and justice with all wives, especially in distribution of love and affection. A polygamous husband would also be required to provide for a separate living quarter for each wife, which would be a limiting factor in itself. As a result, multiple wives are seldom found in truly Muslim societies. As a security precaution, a woman can also insert a condition in her marriage contract barring the husband from polygamy.

Nevertheless, Islam does grant permission of polygamy to man. Under certain circumstances, polygamy may be morally preferable to its alternatives. One example of such a situation would be if, early in marriage, the wife contracts paralysis or a disease that would prevent her from sexual union. Another example would be if, as a result of war, the male population is reduced, leaving more women than men in the population. Under these and similar situations, monogamy may foster prostitution and illicit sexual relations in which man will not have any responsibility for his sexual partners and for any children resulting from such immoral relationships.

Such a situation would offer a choice between polygamy and depriving a large proportion of women of their right to motherhood and having a family. Obviously, polygamy may be a better choice under these circumstances.

Therefore, although polygamy among the Muslims is not common, the permission granted to a Muslim man to simultaneously have more than one wife under certain circumstances, provided he can treat them with equality, would bring more benefit to the society than harm.

It can be seen from this chapter that Islam does not teach oppression of woman at all. On the contrary, it.has granted woman rights which she did not enjoy in the pre-Islamic era. The Qur'an and Hadith give the woman the right to agree to her marriage, right to divorce, right to inherit and own property, right to work, right to education, right to vote, hold a public office, and many other rights.

17

TERRORISM—NOT TAUGHT OR CONDONED BY ISLAM

THE USE OF the term terrorism can be highly subjective. It depends on who is defining it. In present day terminology, terrorism is understood to involve premeditated, politically motivated acts of violence committed by individuals, sub-national groups, or clandestine agents to frighten and intimidate noncombatant target victims and/or undermine confidence in an authority. Some people include in it violence committed by a government to intimidate a populace. The conventionally used term 'terrorism' must be distinguished from a national liberation movement.

Although the stereotypical profile of the present day terrorist projects a Muslim or Arab extremist bent on carrying out some perverted act of revenge against a Western society, there are many others who fit the definition of terrorist. An editorial in the Sunday May 20, 2007 issue of the Trenton Times newspaper of Trenton, New Jersey describes some of America's own 'homegrown' terrorists and cautions that terrorists can take a variety of forms.

Timothy McVeigh, for example, was as much a terrorist as Osama Bin Laden. Although they came from completely different backgrounds, and had different beliefs, one was a Christian and the other a Muslim, each was responsible for the death of many innocent people. The editorial also mentions Eric Rudolph, known for bombing at the 1996 Olympics in Atlanta and attacks on abortion clinics that resulted in the death of three people and injury of at least 150 others.

Similarly, Theodore Kaczynski, the Unabomber, carried out his own terrorism against what he considered the evils of modern technology. He killed three persons and injured many with his mail bombing from the late 1970s to the early 1990s.

More recently, a 32-year-old Christian terrorist, Anders Behring Breivik, went on a killing spree and slaughtered 77 innocent people in Oslo and on the Island of Utoya in Norway. As expected, initial reports from the media immediately focused on the possibility of 'Islamic militants.' Even soon after the incident, when it was found out that the terrorist was a home grown fundamentalist Christian, the Muslims were not completed absolved, because the so called "terrorism specialists" claimed that the other (meaning non-Islamic) terrorists were 'learning from al-Qaeda and mimicking its tactics.'

The discourse on terrorism would be incomplete without the mention of the Zionist, Jewish terrorists, who in 1946–47 waged an intense and bloody campaign of terrorism against the Palestinians, the British, and even some Jews who opposed them. Two major Jewish terrorist organizations in pre-independence Palestine were the Irgun and the Stern gang. These organizations were led by some very prominent Israeli leaders.

Irgun was a dominant Jewish terrorist organization. Its most spectacular feat was the July 22, 1946 blowing up of the King David hotel in Jerusalem, killing 91 people including Arabs, British, and Jews. In the May/June issue of The Washington Reporter on Middle East affairs, Donald Neff [59] describes terrorist attacks in Palestine during 1947 that resulted in the deaths of 374 Arabs and British. Most of the attacks were carried out by Irgun and the Stern Gang. These acts of terrorism were not limited to shooting and conventional bombing, but included poisoning the water supply of the non-Jewish part of Jerusalem with botulism and other bacteria; letter bombs were also introduced to the Middle East by Jewish terrorists.

Terrorism is neither a new thing, nor is it limited to particular individuals or groups. Some governments use terrorism as a tool to intimidate their own citizens and other people over whom they may have military control or superiority.

During the 1920's and 1930's, the term "terrorism" was more associated with the repressive practices employed by dictatorial states than with non-state groups. Such practices included beatings, unlawful detentions, torture, death squads, and other forms of intimidation. Such practices were employed against their own citizens by Nazis in Germany, fascists in Italy, and totalitarian regimes in the USSR.

Similarly, During the 1940s and 1950s, nationalist organizations fought the powers in Asia, Africa, and the Middle East to get rid of the colonial rule. The violence used by these anti-colonial organizations was labeled as terrorism.[60]

Repressive methods of intimidating their own citizens have also been used by military dictatorships during the 1970s. Such state-sanctioned acts of violence are generally termed terror and their practice by governments continues even today.

The present day organizations most active in carrying out acts of terrorism and suicide bombings (al-Qaida and Taliban) are geographically of Middle Eastern and South Asian association. However, the first modern terrorists were European and American anarchists at the end of the nineteenth century, and it was from Europe that Muslims learned the techniques of terrorism.

Some of the earliest terrorists—the Palestinian airplane hijackers of the 1970's—were not Muslims; in fact, some were Marxist

atheists, some of Christian origin. Tamil Tigers, a Hindu sepa-
ratist group in Sri Lanka had the largest tally of suicide bombing
techniques at one time; some of the most famous suicide bombers were the Japanese kamikaze pilots.

Depending on the political view of a given act, it may be
described as an act of terrorism under some circumstances, and
called an act of heroism under different circumstances. When
the Mujahedeen (Muslim freedom fighters in Afghanistan)
were blowing up Soviet soldiers and civilian 'advisors' during the 1980s, they were termed heroes in the West and some
(such as Maulvi Yunis Khalis) were invited to the White House
to meet U.S. President Ronald Regan. However, when the same
people were later blowing up American soldiers and civilians
in Afghanistan, no American saw them as heroes; they were
labeled 'terrorists.'

University of Chicago Professor Robert Pape and James Feldman have written a book on suicide terrorism: *"Cutting the Fuse:
The Explosion of Global Suicide Terrorism and How to Stop It."*[61]

After analyzing 2200 suicide attacks that occurred between
1980 and 2009 in Israel, Chechnya, Sri Lanka, Iraq, Afghanistan,
and Pakistan, they discovered new evidence that, contrary to
popular and dangerously mistaken belief, religion alone moti-
vates only a tiny minority of these attacks. Instead, the root
cause of most of the attacks is the foreign military occupation,
which triggers secular as well as religious people alike to carry
out suicide bombings.

They have investigated the real causes of suicide terrorism
and have demonstrated that the U.S. military strategy serves
only to breed a new generation of terrorists.

Tom Kean, Co-Chair of the 9/11 Commission, has stated that
this analysis is correct, and has called for a total reexamination
of U.S. military strategy. Lee Hamilton, Co-Chair of the 9/11
Commission, has recommended this book to both scholars and

policy makers who have an interest in the U.S. national security policy.

Terrorism, unjustified violence, and killing innocent people are forbidden in Islam, as terrorism involves the indiscriminate use of force, and innocent people are likely to get hurt. Instead of creating fear, Islam is meant to bring peace to a society, whether its people are Muslims or non-Muslims. There is no verse in the Qur'an that teaches or condones terrorism.

Islam does not teach that Muslims can kill or harm civilians as a result of resentment, even if the resentment is based on legitimate grievance. It is mandatory in Islam that grievances are addressed by implementation of rules of justice.

In the Qur'an Muslims are commanded to uphold justice:

"O you who believe! Be steadfast witness in justice for God;
and let not hatred of any people cause you to deal with them unjustly.
Be always just. That is near to righteousness.
And observe your duty to God.
Surely, God is aware of whatever you do."
(Qur'an 5:8)

Even in a just war or military jihad, where Muslims are allowed to fight to defend Islam or to fight tyranny, oppression, and injustice in a society, they are not allowed to harm innocent or unarmed civilians, especially women, children, the sick, and the elderly. Hurting innocent people in a conflict goes against the teachings of Islam.

The extreme actions of individuals or groups who claim to be Muslim may be the result of their ignorance or uncontrolled anger. Those who commit acts of terrorism in the name of Islam are simply not following the teachings of Islam. These people are following their own views and political agendas.

This brings us to the question many people ask: What have

the Muslims done to fight terrorism? Muslims have said and done a lot against terrorism, but Western mainstream media has paid little attention. It is a well-known fact that Muslims are as much victims of terrorism as any other people, and they are in the forefront of the war against terrorism. In addition, they have taken a lot more casualties than any other people. [62, 63]

Muslim scholars, religious leaders, and organizations around the world have issued Fatwas (religious rulings) containing Islam's absolute condemnation of terrorism, religious extremism, suicide bombings, and similar violent acts against innocent civilians. Fatwas have been issued in Australia, Egypt, Pakistan, Saudi Arabia, Spain, UK, and USA.

One such Fatwa was issued on July 28, 2005 by the Islamic religious juristic body in North America, called the Fiqh Council of North America (FCNA). This body represents Muslims of the United States and Canada. In their Fatwa, the FCNA has declared all acts of terrorism, extremism, suicide bombings and other methods of targeting innocent civilians and their properties forbidden (*haram*) and those who commit such acts have been declared criminals, not "martyrs."[64]

The Fatwa also declares that it is forbidden (haram) for a Muslim to cooperate with any individual or group that is involved in any act of terrorism or prohibited violence. Further, it mandates Muslims to cooperate with the law enforcement authorities to protect the lives of civilians against all acts of extremism and terrorism. This Fatwa against terrorism is described in detail in the January-February 2010 issue of The Message International magazine of the Islamic Circle of North America (ICNA).

All major American Muslim organizations have endorsed this ruling. The most prominent organizations include Islamic Society of North America (ISNA), Islamic Circle of North America (ICNA), Muslim Public Affairs Council (MPAC), Muslim American Society (MAS), the Council on American-Islamic

Relations (CAIR), Muslim Student Association of the US and Canada (MSA), Canadian Council on American-Islamic Relations, American Federation of Muslims of Indian Origin, American Muslim Alliance (AMA), Council of Shia Muslim Scholars of North America, and Islamic Networks Group & Affiliates.

On March 2nd, 2010, an influential Muslim scholar from Pakistan, Dr. Tahir ul-Qadri, issued a Fatwa against terrorism and suicide bombing. His 600-page Fatwa dismantles al-Qaeda's violent ideology. The scholar describes al-Qaeda as an "old evil with a new name" that has not been sufficiently challenged. The scholar's movement is growing in the UK and has attracted the interest of the policy makers and security chiefs. In his Fatwa, delivered in London, Dr. Qadri said that Islam forbids suicide bombings and the massacre of innocent citizens. Although many scholars have made similar religious edicts in the past, Dr. Qadri's Fatwa goes much further by omitting "ifs and buts" added by other scholars.

Irrespective of the legitimacy of grievances related to persecution or oppression, terrorism is not the solution. Rather, it is the epitome of injustice because it targets innocent people. Innocent civilians should not have to pay for the crimes of others in settlings political or military conflicts. Muslims are prohibited in the Qur'an from taking an innocent life (5:32, 17:33). It is considered as one of the gravest sins in Islam. Moreover, the Qur'an clearly commands that Muslims act with justice and impartiality, even in dealing with an enemy (4:135, 5:8).

Condemning terrorism is only one side of the coin. It would be naive to talk about terrorism without discussing the causes that drive terrorists to such extremes. Terrorism may not be curtailed without addressing its causes. Terrorists must have some grievance or feeling of injustice that forces them to take these extreme actions. Graham Fuller, writes in August 24th, 1998 issue of Los Angeles Times that it is dangerous to separate terrorism from

politics, yet the U.S. media continue to talk about war on terrorism without mentioning the issues and reasons behind it. Similarly, Charley Reese writes in August 24, 1998 issue of Orlando
Sentinel that terrorism is a political issue, and a response to a
faulty U.S. foreign policy.[65]

Fuller and Reese identify some of the reasons behind terrorism against the United States. They include faulty U.S. foreign
policy in the Middle East, based on one-sided support of Israel
against the Palestinians; U.S. support for almost any ruler or
regime in the Islamic world, even if they are in power against the
wishes of their people, as long as they protect the U.S. interests
(oil and Israel); U.S. invasion of and military presence against
the wishes of the people in several Muslim countries; U.S. economic sanctions against Muslim countries; and U.S. support of
countries or regimes where Muslim minorities are fighting for
their freedom and/or fundamental human rights, such as Palestine, Kashmir, Chechnya, and Xinjiang Uygur Autonomous
Region of China.

Obviously, some groups feel that even though they may not
be strong enough to take on the U.S. and its allies by conventional military means, they can cause enough hurt to force the
U.S. and its allies to review their policies in the Middle East and
towards the Muslims in a more just manner. In his book The War
on Islam, Enver Masud quotes Sir Peter Ustinow who once said:
"Terrorism is the war of the poor, and war is the terrorism of the
rich." Although the United Nations has no official definition of
terrorism, its Member States have demanded that it is important
to distinguish between terrorism and wars of liberation.[66]

FANATICISM AND EXTREMISM

Fanaticism is another phenomenon incompatible with Islamic
teachings of live and let live in peace and harmony. The tradition

of Islam is meant to be simple, easily applied, realistic, and practical. Islam is built more on glad tidings than on warnings. It is a religion of moderation and balanced conduct, and does not teach indulgence in the extreme of anything, whether it is related to life in this world or in the Hereafter.

Extremism and fanaticism are not condoned in Islam, especially if an extreme action hurts innocent people. Prophet Muhammad actually spoke out very firmly against extremism and fanaticism.

It is important to recognize, however, that extremism and fanaticism are problems that are common to followers of all religions, so it would be unfair to blame only Muslims for these problems. Fanatical Muslims are no more representative of the true Islamic teaching than Eric Rudolph, who blew up abortion clinics and workers therein, Timothy McVeigh or David Koresh were of Christianity.

Advice to non-Muslims is to not draw conclusions about Islam from the actions of a few violent individuals who do not represent Muslims at large. Similarly, they should also be aware that there are people in our societies who are suffering from Islamophobia (fear and hate of Islam) because of their ignorance about the true teachings of Islam. They demonize the entire global community of Muslims for the actions of a few, and hinder efforts to provide a moderate voice and promote mutual understanding and peace.

18

ISLAMIC FUNDAMENTALISM

MANY WITHIN WESTERN media and political circles do not know what Islamic fundamentalism is. They confuse fundamentalism with radicalism, religious extremism, and terrorism, thereby misleading non-Muslims. A Muslim fundamentalist, according to the literal meaning of the word, is someone who tries to live his/her life according to the fundamental teachings of God as described in the Qur'an, and according to the traditions of Prophet Muhammad. The term Islamic fundamentalist can be applied to someone who wants to reintroduce an Islamic system based on its fundamental teachings. Those who are in favor of introducing modern reforms that are based on Islamic teachings can also be included in this category.

In America, liberals describe conservative Christians by the term 'fundamentalism'. Fundamentalists are people who believe that all statements made in the Bible are literally true. They stand against critical study of the Bible, scientific theories of evolution, and openness towards non-Christians. Thus 'fundamentalism' has acquired a meaning of fanaticism and obscurantism. Islam knows no such phenomena, because the status of the Qur'an has never been in question. On the contrary, Islam has always stressed the use of reason and logic.

What is erroneously labeled as Islamic fundamentalism is actually a different movement. A movement that can best be described as Islamic traditionalism is pervading the whole Muslim World. Traditionalists claim that Muslim leadership has blindly imitated the West, westernizing itself without significant improvement to the status of their people.

Traditionalism is not the only political movement in Muslim countries. The leadership in Muslim lands has tried socialism, capitalism, secularism, nationalism, and democracy. According to these traditionalists, western law, institutions, education system, and way of living, have all been tried and have failed. Naturally, these traditionalists look to the Qur'an for guidance. They look to the great men of Islam of the early periods for moralizing exemplification of their values.

Among Muslims, there is a desire to see Islam find its proper place in shaping the spiritual, moral, ethical, social, economic, and political life of their people. There is a sense of distrust and frustration within the post-colonial regimes, whether military, monarchic, or dictatorial, and even, at least in some cases, democratic who are presently ruling the Muslim world. Many feel that most of these regimes support feudalism, act as puppets of the Western powers, and have failed their own people and their aspirations. They have kept the masses uneducated and backward, and that serves their interest and that of their Western masters. Masses fear them but they do not respect or love them. They have seen that simple westernization or secularization is not the answer. This should help explain the underlying reason for the current unrest in the Muslim World.

Many Muslims do not question the value of Western achievements in the fields of science, technology, education, health, or communication. However, according to the traditionalists, some of the decadent manifestations of westernization such as alcoholism, drug abuse, pornography, sexual perversion, spiritual bankruptcy, disintegration of the family system, financial corruption, and excessive hunger for materialism are unacceptable to them. American pop culture appears to be a lot like paganism, a cult that worships money, sex, and power. For them, Islam is an oasis of old-fashioned family values. Therefore, it is natural for Muslim traditionalist to exercise caution in their approach to Western values.

Over the last two centuries, most Muslim countries were colonized. The colonial powers had little interest, if any, in learning about the religion, culture, and way of living of their subjects. When they departed, they left the Muslim lands economically poor, educationally backward, and culturally bankrupt. There is still an arrogant tendency in some quarters of the West, especially the Western Europe, to look upon the Muslim world as backward and uncivilized.

Like all others, Muslims want to be masters of their own lands and natural resources, and designers of their own destinies according to their cherished principles and values. They seek independence of their lands from all direct or indirect control, occupation, and manipulation by foreign powers.

The Islam and the Judeo-Christian worlds do not have to be locked in conflict; they believe in the same fundamental values of love for God and love of the neighbor. The true followers of Islam give the highest possible importance to the values of life and liberty, justice and equity, universal equality, and home and family integrity. They are both opposed to tyranny and exploitation. It was for these values that Muslims around the world laid down their lives in the struggle for independence and liberation from colonialism. In this regard, the Muslim and American experiences are similar.

Those who know about Islam, Judaism, and Christianity know that there are more similarities than differences between them. Rapprochement and critique on the basis of what Muslims,

Jews, and Christians hold in common can only serve the interests of followers of three faith traditions. The areas in which their traditions are identical or similar are significant. Therefore, the result can only be beneficial to all involved. Christians, Jews, and Muslims have lived together harmoniously in the past. To learn about this one only needs to study the history of Muslim Spain.

19

THE REAL MEANING AND ROLE OF *JIHAD* IN ISLAM

THE TERM JIHAD is misunderstood by many Westerners as well by as some Muslims. The anti-Islamic elements of Western media regularly use this term in an effort to vilify Islam and Muslims. Western commentators, right wing politicians, Islamophobes, and some of the non-Muslim religious leaders use it as a rallying cry to spread fear and hatred against Islam in the minds of largely uninformed general population.

The Arabic word *Jihad* comes from the root JHD which means to "strive and struggle." In Islamic context, it means to struggle in the way of God. It refers to struggle in different contexts.

According to a famous Islamic scholar Ibn al-Qayyim al-Jawjiyya, there are no less than 14 forms of Jihad. Only one of these involves military combat, the other 13 represent various types of struggle of a person within himself and within the society. [67]

In the first context, it refers to inward Jihad, or the struggle against evil inclinations within oneself and putting God's Will into daily practice (Qura'an 22:77–78; 29:5–7). In his book *Illuminations—Compiled Lectures on Shariah and Tasawwuf*, Shaykh Muhammad Hisham Kabbani[67] explains that waging Jihad against one's self is necessary in order to purify himself from bad desires, morals, and manners that lead to the displeasure of God and His Prophet.

Trying to purify one's soul by prayer, fasting, and acts of charity towards God's creatures is considered Jihad Akbar, meaning the greater Jihad. Similarly, a person who supports a family, educates his children by working honestly, and avoids bribery, corruption, and unlawful means of earning money, is participating in the greater Jihad.

On one occasion, when returning from a battle, Prophet Muhammad said to his companions: *"You have come from the lesser Jihad to the greater Jihad."* His companions asked: "What is the greater Jihad?" He answered: *"The battle against one's idle desires."* It implies struggle against the rebellious elements of the soul.

The second context is the social Jihad. In this case a Muslim struggles in defense of truth, justice, goodness, and charity in society (Qur'an 49:15; 61:10–11). Muslims are required to fight against social injustice, tyranny, and evil in society. In Islamic teaching, standing in the presence of a tyrannical ruler and speaking the truth is a form of Jihad.

Jihad can also be accomplished in several other manners. It can be accomplished by donating financial resources to a beneficial cause, or through speaking, writing, diplomacy or any other peaceful means, or by creating awareness through news against injustice, tyranny, and evil in society.

The third context involves military action in the battlefield, which is often referred to in the Qur'an as Qital. Military Jihad is allowed in the Qur'an for legitimate self-defense in resisting and fighting aggression, persecution, or oppression (Qur'an 2:190–193; 22:39–41). Under these circumstances, it is justified as a last resort to prevent a greater wrong. Military Jihad is undertaken by a Muslim nation when it is under attack, to defend its freedom and liberty, and to fight a potential invading or occupying force. All Muslims able to fight have to answer the call to join the national army. In this sense, it is similar to the draft in the U.S. armed forces.

Huston Smith[1] has compared Islam's military Jihad with the 'Just War' concept in Christian canon law, including the notion in both Christianity and Islam that the martyrs will go to the heaven. He states that in both cases the war must be for defensive purpose and to right a wrong. Islam, like Christianity, considers those who die in such wars to be martyrs, and promises them Paradise.

The Qur'an teaches forgiveness and return for evil with that which is better under the right circumstances, but this does not mean tolerating evil and wrong doing. For wanton wrong doing, Qur'an allows befitting punishment. Similarly, Muslims are required to resist injustice, oppression, tyranny, and anarchy. Defense of collective life against such evils would call for all forms of resistance, including armed resistance, and that would be Jihad.

If attacked, Muslims are allowed to defend themselves, but they are not to initiate a fight. In this regard the Qur'an states:

(Permission is granted to) Fight in the way of God
against those who fight against you, but do not start the hostilities.
God loveth not the aggressors"
(Qur'an 2:190)

This verse was revealed to grant permission for the first time to the tiny Muslim community to defend themselves and their faith in One God against the relentless hostility of the idol worshippers of Arabia. Prophet Muhammad had to choose between fighting to defend himself, his community, and his faith or to see his faith and community of Muslims wiped out.

When a Muslim state is threatened, invaded, or forcefully

occupied by a non-Muslim army, it is the Muslims' duty to defend its land and people at all cost. Only a legitimate and representative authority can declare military Jihad, and the decision to declare military Jihad is always taken seriously. Muslims are required to rise up, defend Islam, end the occupation of their land, end all kind of injustice, tyranny, oppression, and anarchy, and restore freedom and justice.

Importantly, the rule of military Jihad requires that once the enemy surrenders or leaves, all hostility is to cease. There should be no reprisals, all prisoners should be treated humanely, and if possible, returned to their families. During the time of Prophet Muhammad one of the ways a prisoner of war could gain his freedom was to teach and educate ten Muslims. This also shows how important learning and education is considered in Islam.

Prophet Muhammad humanized the battlefield and established traditions regarding decent conduct of war. These included honoring agreements; prohibition of torture, rape, or injury to prisoners; and prohibition of disfiguration of the dead. The women, children, elderly, and the religious leaders or clergy not engaged in the war were not to be hurt. Similarly, crops, plantations, orchards, and sacred objects, including houses of worship, were to be spared.

Islam laid down these rules for humane treatment of prisoners fourteen centuries before the Geneva Convention. This is the reason why the Muslim world was so shocked to learn about the inhuman and disgraceful treatment of some of the Iraqi, Afghan, and other Muslim prisoners in Abu Gharaib, Guantanamo Bay and Afghanistan prisons by the occupying American and NATO forces. These revelations have created enormous anger, hatred, and contempt for the West, and have very badly damaged the image of the United States in the Muslim world.

Muslims regard human life as a gift from God that must be returned to Him or be laid down for a just cause. This belief is not much different from what Jesus taught, when he said: *"Greater love hath no man than this, that a man lay down his life for his friends"* (John 15:13), or if need be, for God. A Muslim who gives up his or her life for God in a righteous cause is considered a martyr or Shaheed and is promised a great reward in the hereafter. Islam, however, does not allow any person to kill others because of differences based on race, religion, culture, or language.

To have differences among people is a sign of vitality, dynamism, and healthy competition. Therefore, Islam is resolutely against killing of innocent people. The Qur'an, in this relation states:

"If anyone slays a human being,
unless it be for murder or for spreading corruption on earth,
it shall be as if he had slain all mankind;
whereas, if anyone saves a life,
it shall be as if he had saved the lives of all mankind.
(Qur'an 5:32)

The Qur'an teaches the Muslims peaceful co-existence with others in kindness and justice. It recognizes plurality in human societies, including religious plurality, as a part of God's plan in creation. This is the reason it commands respectful dialog, not forced conversion.

In conclusion, Jihad means to struggle and make the best effort to put in practice the fundamental teachings of Islam: to love and worship God, love His creatures, practice justice in society, strive to spiritually purify oneself by prayer, fasting and doing charitable works, and to fight oppression and injustice in society.

20

THE MOSAIC OF SECTS
IN ISLAM

LIKE CHRISTIANITY AND Judaism, there is diversity and pluralism within the faith of Islam. Diversity has been praised as an essential component of a healthy human communal experience, and is considered desirable and indicative of a faith's overall health. As far sectarianism in Islam is concerned, the news media reporting on the Iraq war have familiarized Non-Muslims with the terms Sunnis and Shi'as. Non-Muslims, especially those in the west, are curious to know about Sunnis and Shi'as.

All Muslims share the same essential belief system, and they all follow the same Qur'an and Sunnah as sources of their teachings. However, there are some differences of opinion among the global Muslim community (Ummah) with respect to the interpretation of the teachings of Islam and its history. The majority of Muslims in the world are Sunnis, comprising 85% of all Muslims. The remaining 15% of Muslims belong to the Shi'a sect. The split between the Sunnis and the Shi'a traces its origin to the earliest days of Islam and is based on historical disagreements about who should have succeeded Prophet Muhammad.

The Sunnis believed that Prophet Muhammad died without

establishing a system for selection of a successor. After the death of Prophet Muhammad in 632 AD, his closest companion and father-in-law Abu Bakr was selected by the leadership of Medina to become the first Caliph (successor). He was accepted by majority of the Muslims as their leader.

A minority of Muslims believed that succession should be hereditary. Since Prophet Muhammad had no surviving sons, they believed his closest relative, his cousin and son-in-law Ali Ibn Abi Talib should have succeeded Prophet Muhammad as the leader (called Imam) of the Muslims.

Ali was passed over three times before he finally became the fourth (rightly guided) Caliph in the year 656 CE. Even after he became the Caliph, some people supported him, while others opposed him, based on the political differences of the time. Those who supported Ali became known as the Shi'aan-e-Ali (the party of Ali) or, for short, the Shi'a.

For the Shi'a, only a descendent of Prophet Muhammad has the right to rule. There is no need to elect the leader, because birthright is enough legitimacy to rule. For Sunni Muslims, any righteous Muslim can be elected as the Caliph (the leader of the Muslims) and he does not have to be a descendent of the Prophet. All of the writing in this book is from the Sunni point of view.

From its inception, the Shi'a community has been led by a leader called Imam. The succession of Imams traces its lineage back to Ali. At some stage, the Imam was forced to go into hiding in order to protect himself. The Shi'a are divided into sects on the question of which Imam had to go into hiding. However, all Shi'a people believe that the hidden Imam will return near the end of the world to usher in an age of peace and prosperity for the Muslim Ummah.

The Sunnis are also subdivided into other groups based mostly on the interpretation of Islamic law, the Sharia. There are four major Sunni schools of interpretation of Islamic law: Hanafi, Hun'bali, Maliki, and Shafi'i. Some Muslims, such as Ahl-e-Hadith, do not follow any of these schools. Within these groups, there are sub-groups who are either liberal or conservative in their interpretation of Islamic law and theology.

For example, the present day Salafis, Wahhabis (mostly in Saudi Arabia), and Deobandis (such as the Taliban in Afghanistan) are ultraconservative and puritanical in their interpretation of the Sharia. They denounce many popular beliefs and practices, such as visitation and veneration of Auwliaullah (Muslim saints) and graves (shrines) of saints. This puts them at odds with Shi'as as well as those Sunnis who follow the Sufi tradition, which teaches reverence for saints and respect for shrines.

The differences between the Sunnis and the Shi'a are based on political differences rooted in old history. The differences of opinion within the Muslim community (Ummah) indicate diversity. But it should be understood that all Muslims, regardless of their affiliation, hold similar beliefs and engage in the same basic practices.

While there were no sects in the Muslim community during the time of Prophet Muhammad, he tolerated some difference of opinion among his companions, but he did not approve of outright division among Muslims. According to a saying of Prophet Muhammad, the difference of opinion among his followers is a mercy (of God) for people.

Regardless of their identification with any sect or school of Islamic jurisprudence, all Muslims believe in the same One True God (called Allah in Arabic), follow the same Qur'an, and declare their faith through the same creed (Shahadah). They all believe in Prophet Muhammad as the last Messenger of God, pray five times a day facing towards Mecca, pay poor-due (Zakat), fast during the month of Ramadan, and undertake pilgrimage to Mecca, in Saudi Arabia.

21

SUFI TRADITION—
THE INNER MYSTICAL
DIMENSION OF ISLAM

IDEALLY, THE APPARENT and observable conduct of a Muslim and the fulfillment of his religious duties should comply with the Sharia or Islamic law. For example, when a person performs his mandatory act of worship or Salat, Sharia judges him on the basis of apparent requirement, such as making ablution, facing towards the Ka'ba, and performing Salat at the right time. However, the spirit of the conduct, which is in the heart and therefore not easily observable, is also very important.

The aspect of Islamic practices concerned with the spirit of conduct is known as Tasawwuf. Tasawwuf judges the quality of Salat by the degree of sincerity, concentration, and devotion one has in the performance of the Salat, and the effect Salat has on the morals and manners of the person.

Mawdudi[68] has given a beautiful analogy which shows the relationship between Sharia and Tasawwuf. He said that the performance of Salat with correct procedure, but without the spirit is like a handsome man who is defective in character. On the other hand, the performance of Salat with all sincerity, but with defects in its execution is like a man who is noble in character but deformed in appearance.

Tasawwuf is also known by other commonly used names, such as mysticism, Islamic mysticism, and Sufism. It is understood to be the inner mystical dimension of Islam. It is an expression of the esoteric form of the religion of Islam. The philosophy of the Sufi tradition is best summed up in the words of the great Sufi saint of India, Khuwaja Mueenuddin Chishti in his following discourse quoted in *The Book of Sufi Healing* by Shaykh Hakim Moinuddin Chishti:[69]

"Love all and hate none.
Mere talk of peace will avail you naught.
And mere talk of God and religion will not take you far.
Bring out all of the latent powers of your being
and reveal the full magnificence of your immortal self.
Be surcharged with peace and joy, scatter them
wherever you are.
And wherever you go, be a blazing fire of truth.
Be a beauteous blossom of love, and be a soothing
balm of peace.
With your spiritual light dispel the darkness of ignorance.
Dissolve the clouds of discord and war,
and spread goodwill, peace, and harmony among the people.
Never seek any help, charity, or favors
from anyone except God.
Never go to the courts of kings,
but never refuse to bless and help the needy, the poor,
the widow, and the orphan, if they come to your door.
This is your mission: to serve the people.
Carry it out dutifully and courageously."

According to Sufis, their tradition goes back to the life of Prophet Muhammad himself. They call him the exemplar of God-oriented lifestyle and claim that they are simply continuing that tradition. This lifestyle is based on purification of the inner self (Tazkiyyat an-nafs) through the worship and remembrance (Zikr) of God; selfless love for others; frugality in worldly possessions; self denial; development of good character traits such as patience, contentment, thankfulness to God, and reliance on Him alone; and getting rid of bad character traits such as anger, greed, vanity, miserliness, hatred, selfishness, lust, and problems related to ego.

A Sufi is defined as the one who seeks most direct way to God through purification. The objective of Sufism is reparation of the heart and turning it away from everything except God.[70] This can be achieved by renunciation of the materialistic pleasures of the lower self (the ego), removal of the reprehensible traits from one's character, such as anger, arrogance, love of the world, malice, jealousy, vanity, stinginess, avarice, ostentation, heedlessness, and replacing them with virtuous and praiseworthy traits, such as love, tolerance, peace, justice, compassion, humility, generosity, and truthfulness.

Dhun Nun Misri has defined a Sufi as one whose speech accords with his behavior.[71] In the words of the great Sufi saint Hasan Al-Basri, a true Sufi is one whose face shows modesty, heart is purified, tongue is wet with the praise of God, hands are generous in giving, whose promise is binding, and whose advice cures afflictions.

In his book, *Deliverance from Errors*, Al-Ghazali[72] describes the purification of the heart completely from what is other than God most high as the first condition towards attaining the purity that is required in the Sufi tradition. Sinking the heart completely in the remembrance (Zikr) of God is also required.

Practicing Sufi tradition shows the way to the realization of inner peace, true happiness and success. Such an individual attains heightened consciousness, perceives God continuously, and his every act is in compliance with God's command. The ultimate objective of a Sufi is to struggle and achieve such spiritual perfection.

There are three levels of faith: Islam, Iman, and Ihsan. Islam involves actions and behavior based on Shariah, and Iman involves the underlying belief. Ihasn means to worship God as if you see Him, and if you do not see Him, then to know that He sees you. Ihsan is the highest level of faith and it comes with certainty and perfection of character. Tasawwuf and Tazkiyyat an-nafs facilitate the achievement of this level of faith.

According to a saying of Prophet Muhammad (Hadith Qudsi), God has said the following about the person who attains a level of such spiritual perfection: "My servant draws near to Me through voluntary worship until I love him. And when I love him, I will be the ears through which he hears, the eyes with which he sees, I will be the tongue with which he speaks, I will be the hand with which he grasps, and I will be the foot with which he walks."

Training in Tasawwuf is facilitated under the guidance of a spiritual mentor/ teacher or Shaykh (also known as Murshud). The other activities that help the seeker on the path of Tasawwuf include practice of the ritual of remembrance of God (Zikrullah or Zikr) alone or in group, contemplation on God and His creation (Tafakkur), night vigil (Qiyam-al-layl), self-purification through abstinence from materialism and its corrupting traits, and occasional seclusion for worship.

The Shaykh must be someone who has deep knowledge of the religion, including the Sharia and Tasawwuf. He must have authorization from a Master/ Grand Shaykh in the Tariqa (chain in the Sufi order), who himself is usually a link in the chain going all the way back to Prophet Muhammad. The objective of the Shaykh is to purify the heart of the student (the Mureed) through transmission of knowledge.

After finding a teacher/Shaykh, a disciple typically lives with him, serves him for years, and learns from him before he can achieve purification of the heart and a high spiritual level. These days, it is not always possible; many students live elsewhere and visit their Shaykh as frequently as they can. Shaykh Hisham Kabbani[73] has described in his book *Classical Islam and The Naqshbandi Sufi Tradition*, that Muhammad Bahauddin Shah Naqshband, the founder of the Naqshbandi Sufi order, served his first teacher, Shaykh Muhammad Baba As-Samasi, for 20 years until the teacher died. Then he served several other teachers. The training under the teachers was extremely difficult and demanding.

What is taught by a Shaykh in order to cleanse the heart of his students can be assessed from the teachings of Shaykh Muhammad Nazim Adil al-Haqqani, the head of the world's largest Naqshbandi Haqqani Sufi spiritual order, in his transcribed lectures in the volume 1 of a book series called *Liberating the Soul*.[74] Shaykh Nazim lives in Lefke, Cyprus, where thousands of people from all over the world visit to learn wisdom from him. More information about the Naqshbandi Haqqani Sufi order is available on the following website: www.Sufilive.com

According to a Hadith narrated by Ibn Umar, Prophet Muhammad said: "When you pass by the gardens of Paradise, avail yourselves of them." The Companions asked: "What are the gardens of Paradise, O Messenger of Allah?" He replied: "The groups of people performing Zikr. There are roaming Angels of God who go about looking for the groups of people performing Zikr, and when they find them they surround them closely." This hadith of Prophet Muhammad indicates great blessings for those who perform Zikr.

Muslim scholars have mentioned many benefits of Zikr.

For example, Ibn al-Qayyim has said that Zikr makes a barrier between the Hellfire and the person performing the Zikr, and even if he is on his way to Hellfire for some bad deeds, his Zikr of God will stand as a barrier in that path and the Angels will ask for God's forgiveness for that person.

The Shaykh or his representative usually leads Zikr. He chants out the liturgy and the group (of Mureeds) follows him, like a choir. The participants wash themselves before the ceremony and may also use costumes, such as turbans and robes. Some Sufi orders also use musical instruments, such as a duff, in the Zikr ceremony. Zikr may also be performed in the form of meditation, and even as dance, such as in the case of the Whirling Derveshes.

Zikr means to remember, mention, or celebrate praises of God. The practice of Zikr in a Sufi tradition involves glorification of God by repetitively reciting verses of the Qur'an or Attributes of God. One has to permeate his thoughts and acts with the presence of God. Prophet Muhammad had taught his companions to chant certain verses of the Qur'an. He also said that the best Zikr is to recite: La ilaha illallah, which means "there is no one worthy of worship except God."

The Qur'an states that the hearts become calm and contented with the remembrance (Zikr) of God, and through Zikr, one can also express his/her gratitude to God for all the blessings (Qur'an 13:28 and 2:152). The Sufis consider Zikr as the food for the soul, and the Shaykh has the expertise of feeding the spiritual food to the followers. He is like a spiritual nutritionist, and knows what kind of Zikr should be 'prescribed' for the followers (Mureeds).

Imam Feisal Abdul Rauf,[75] in his book What's Right with Islam, gives a beautiful analogy of zikr as a music and the Mureed as a player in the orchestra. The Shaykh is analogous to the maestro, who leads and guides the orchestra.

According to Imam Rauf, different parts of the body may be

involved in the performance of the Zikr. For example, Zikr of the mind involves intellectual contemplation. Zikr of the tongue is repeating the divine attributes or verses of the Qur'an. Similarly, Zikr of the heart is increasing the love of God and Prophet Muhammad; removal of the diseases of the heart, such as anger, ego, jealousy, lust, greed; maintenance of proper behavior and etiquette towards God, Prophet Muhammad, and mankind. All aspects of Zikr function in harmony.

Compliance with Islamic laws (Sharia) is a necessary condition for following a genuine Sufi path. Contrary to what some people may believe, real Sufis strictly conform to and practice the teachings of the Islamic laws (Sharia) and their teaching is also in adherence to the laws of Sharia. There is no authentic Sufi tradition without following the laws of Sharia; one cannot follow Sharia without applying the principles of Sufism, the core value of which is sincerity in turning to God.

Shaykh Hisham Kabbani[67] has mentioned a reference to Imam Ahmad Bin Hanbal in which he advised his son to find the company of the (true) Sufis, because they were like a fountain of knowledge, they practiced the Zikr of God, and they had the most spiritual power. Similarly, Al-Ghazali[76] has stated that he has learned with certainty that the Sufis walk on the road of God, their life is the best life, their method the soundest method, and their character the purest character.

In his book Reliance of the Traveller, Nuh Ha Mim Keller-[77]quotes the famous Muslim jurist Imam Malik who said: "He who practices Sufi tradition without learning the laws of Sharia corrupts his faith, and he who learns about Sharia without practicing (the principles of) Sufism, corrupts himself. Only he who combines the two proves true."

It can be concluded that a Muslim strives to achieve the pleasure of God and a more fulfilled life by externally following the laws of Sharia and internally practice of Tasawwuf in daily life.

Since the Middle Ages, Sufi tradition has been institution-
alized into several devotional Orders or Tariqas, each headed
by a founder. All Orders, Shi'a as well Sunni, trace their origin
to Prophet Muhammad, through his cousin Ali, or his father-
in-law and friend Abu Bakr. The major Sufi orders are Chishti,
Qadiri, Naqshbandi, and Suhrawardi. There are also several
other orders.

Sufism is quite popular in some parts of the world, especially in Afghanistan, Pakistan, Iran, Iraq, Morocco, Senegal,
Turkey, and Indonesia. It has made some important contributions to the faith of Islam. For example, poetry of the Sufi-saint
poet Jalal-ud-Deen Rumi is very popular in the United States.
In North America, his anthologies of poetry sell more than any
other poet. His poetry has provided insights on the relationship
between man and God.

Rabi'a al-Adawiyya, an early female Sufi, has expressed the
sincerity of her belief in the following poem:

O Allah! If I worship You for fear of Hell,
then let me burn in it;
and if I worship You in the hope that I go to Paradise,
then exclude me from it;
but if I worship You for Your own sake,
then do not withhold from me Your everlasting beauty."

Sufi orders played an important role in the political life of
Muslims and in the spread of Islam. Al-Ghazali[72] stated that the
spread of Sufism has been a definitive factor in the spread of
Islam and in the creation of integrally Islamic cultures, especially in Africa and Asia.

It is important to note that although the Sufi tradition of Islam
follows and teaches the inner peaceful and loving mystical
dimension of Islam, it does not teach passiveness in the face of

aggression and injustice. Several Sufi leaders have participated in and led armed resistance against the colonial and imperial powers of their times, and have fought against them in Africa, South Asia, and Caucasus.

For example, Qadiri Sheikh Emir Abd el-Kader al-Jazairi led the Algerians in war of liberation against the French occupiers of Algeria. Similarly, Shaykh Amadou Bamba and Hajj Umar Tall fought against the colonial powers in sub-Saharan Africa, and Sheikh Mansur Ushurma and Naqshbandi Sheikh Imam Shamil Daghestani led the fight in the war of liberation against Russians in Caucasus in the 19th century.

As Sufism was the main organizing body of many traditional cultures in Muslim lands targeted by the colonial powers, it is not surprising that the imperial powers chose to attack Sufi masters as a way of undermining the native resistance movements.

Al-Ghazali, in his greatest treaties, *The Revival of Religious Sciences* (Al-Ihya Al-Ulum Addeen), has argued that Sufism originated from the Qur'an and was, therefore, compatible with the mainstream Islamic teachings. He reasoned that it did not contradict Islamic Law (Sharia), and it was necessary to its complete fulfillment.

For the true Sufis, the Qur'an and Hadith are the only textbooks from which they derive their knowledge; they put this knowledge into practice to attain a high spiritual level, which enables them to resist temptations of the materialistic world and submit to the Will of God. Anyone who deviates from the teachings of the Qur'an, the teachings of Prophet Muhammad, and the laws of Sharia, cannot be considered a Sufi, regardless of what he may claim to be.

Mawdudi has observed that many people who claim to be Sufis pollute Islamic mysticism with absurdities that could not be justified in the teachings of the Qur'an and Sunnah.68 Such spurious Sufis have proclaimed themselves immune to the requirements of the Sharia, setting themselves free from Salat, fasting, Zakat and Hajj. By doing so, they have deviated from the Divine commands and their claims of the love of God and His Messenger are false.

The above description has been entirely about the traditional Muslim Sufi Orders, which are considered by traditional Islamic scholars as integral discipline within the faith of Islam, and are never distinct from it. However, there are other groups who are labeled non-traditional Sufis, who may not comply with the laws of Islamic Sharia in their practice. In addition, some non-Islamic groups use the Sufi title. However, any group that does not follow Islamic Sharia are not categorized Sufi by conventional Islamic scholars.

In conclusion, Muslims and non-Muslims alike need to take extra care in determining who is a genuine Sufi and who is not. Scholars of Islam teach us that whoever does not follow Islamic law (Shariah) in his practices, cannot be a true Sufi, regardless of what he calls himself.

22

MUSLIMS ARE NOT ANTI-WEST

IT IS IMPORTANT for a non-Muslim reader to remember the diversity within Islam. Not all Muslims think and act alike, and approaches to Islam among Muslims range from ultraconservative and fundamentalist to progressive and reformist. There is also a range of opinions with respect to the question of how Muslims should relate to non-Muslims, especially the Western world. This is similar to the range of attitudes people in the West have towards Muslims. Some Westerners are very friendly towards Muslims, while some can't wait to inflict harm on them.

Islam teaches that God has created diverse peoples and cultures for a purpose, which indicates that He intended the world to remain pluralistic in religion. It is incorrect to believe that all Muslims hate the Westerners for what they believe in.

In the past, contact between Muslims and non-Muslims has varied, depending on the socio-political environment at that time. In Spain, as well as during the Abbasid rule during the Middle Ages (from the 8th century to the 13th century), Muslims lived and worked with Jews and Christians in peace and harmony; all three communities benefited from the experience.[2]

At other times, Muslims and non-Muslims have found themselves disagreeing in an antagonistic, sometimes hostile, ways.

Between the eleventh and thirteenth centuries, Christian crusaders invaded Muslim lands several times with the intention to "liberate" the Holy Land from the Muslims, whom they called infidels. Crusades lasted for 200 years, and this period in Muslim-Christian relations resulted in mutual distrust and hatred.

Commenting on the first Crusade by Europe's Christendom against Islam, Jonathan Lyons[49] writes that the first call for a Crusade came from Pope Urban II on November 27, 1095. Around that time, the Christians of Europe were divided and fighting amongst themselves. The Crusade was designed by the church to unite them against a perceived enemy, of whom they knew nothing but that the church had labeled them infidels and barbarians. Crusaders were promised eternal reward and remission of sins. The church was also competing with Europe's secular rulers for power, and the Pope saw the crusade as a way to restore the authority of the church in the Christian world.

The warriors were an army of uneducated Christians who could not tell time or even date their holy days on a calendar. They had no understanding of mathematics, science, or the technology of the time, such as papermaking, use of lenses and mirrors, or any idea about contemporary scientific instruments, such as the astrolabe of the Muslims. They estimated the time of day from the position of the sun, and at night from burning candles of a certain diameter. These fanatics marched under the sign of the cross towards the lands of the infidels. They committed great savagery and brutality against the Muslims in the captured territories.

The crusade also provided an excuse for fanatical Christians to kill Jews, whom the Christians had labeled "enemies of Christ" and had accused them of scheming with the far-off Muslims. At Worms in 1096, five thousand Jews, who had sought the protection of the local Catholic leaders, were massacred. Another thousand were killed in Mainz during anti-Jewish rioting, and more were massacred in Prague and at the border of Hungary. Jewish leaders organized mass suicides rather than let their families fall into the hands of the attacking crusaders and face forced conversion.[49]

In the years shortly before the First Crusade, one Muslim traveler found Jerusalem to be an intellectual melting pot teeming with experts of the three monotheistic faiths, where scholars of Islamic law gathered to debate in the al-Aqsa mosque. All of that was put to an end by the crusaders. The city's scholarly class was killed wholesale, along with much of the rest of the citizens.

Describing the carnage in the city of Jerusalem resulting from the First Crusade, Jonathan Lyons quotes chronicler Raymond of Aguilers who stated that piles of heads, hands, and feet were to be seen in the streets, and one could only find his way by walking over the bodies of men and horses.

The extreme violence of the First Crusade reflected Christian propaganda at a time when the West knew very little about Islam and its teachings; the church ideologues successfully painted a highly damaging portrait of the Muslims in order to sow the seeds of the holy war. Lyons states that the less the Christians knew about the Muslims, the more they hated them.[49] The same hate also led to the idea of Reconquesta in Spain. Living in peace with the Muslims was not considered a good option. It should come as no surprise that the Muslims are discomforted when they hear the word 'Crusade.'

The period of colonialism in the Muslim world also fermented similar antagonism. After the crusades, taking advantage of the much weakened and disunited Muslims, the European powers—notably England, France, Italy and the Netherlands—invaded Muslim lands and colonized them for extended period of time.

Colonization of the Muslim lands by the Europeans did such a great harm that they have still not fully recovered from it.

Because the primary interest of the colonial powers was to sub-jugate the colonized lands and use the manpower and resources of the colonies to benefit their own industries back home, they made no effort to understand the religions or cultures of their subjects, and never tried to educate them. As a result, the colo-nies remained underdeveloped and the inhabitants remained largely uneducated and backward.

Muslims remained under the yoke of colonialism well into the twentieth century, and in most colonies, people had to wage wars of national liberation to free themselves from shackles of foreign domination and exploitation. When the colonial pow-ers were finally forced out, they left behind impoverished and uneducated people, and a number of unsettled political disputes. Some of these disputes have caused a lot of division among their former subjects and have led to wars. These events have cre-ated a painful memory in the minds of the Muslim people, and remains as one of the main reasons for the mistrust that some Muslims have for Western powers.

While some Westerners are quick to blame Islam for low developmental levels in Muslim countries, they fail to real-ize that underdevelopment is due to economic factors, limited resources, and a lack of education—not because of Islam. It should be noted that there are many non-Muslim countries in the world that are underdeveloped. Muslims contribution to human civilization has been and continues to be significant (see Chapter 13). It would be wrong to associate underdevelopment with the faith of Islam.

Islam is quite compatible with modernization; the use of modern technology is as prevalent in Muslim countries as it is in any non-Muslim country. All Muslims, whether religious or non-religious, conservative or progressive, take advantage of airplanes, automobiles, cell phones, computers, fax machines, internet, TV, and satellite dishes. As described in Chapter 13, some Muslim inventions provided the basic ideas for present day technology.

Although many Muslims feel no hesitation in becoming modernized, they wish to maintain their Islamic faith, identity, and values. There is no conflict between Islam and modernity. The history of Islam during its golden age has clearly demonstrated that both faith and reason, and religion and science can co-exist. A Muslim can become modern without the danger of losing his faith or Islamic values.

Muslims greatly admire the modern concepts that are commonly associated with Western culture, such as democracy, freedom of religion, freedom of expression, civil liberties, human rights, system of justice, and achievements in the areas of science and technology. These values are not new to Muslims, as Islam teaches similar values. Muslims identify with them and feel at home associating and working with those who subscribe to these values, whether they are Muslims or non-Muslims.

One proof of this is that every year, thousands of students from Muslim countries travel to Europe and the USA for education, returning home to share western knowledge and values with their compatriots. At the same time, significant numbers of them prefer to stay in Europe and USA to become citizens.

Presently, there are sizeable populations of Muslims in Europe and the USA, and they actively contribute to their economic and social development as architects, economists, lawyers, scientists, engineers, doctors, journalists, social scientists, sportsmen, and legislators.

Reportedly, there are 3,540 Muslims on active duty in the United States Armed Forces.[78] However, it is suspected that the actual number is much larger than this because some Muslims avoid identifying their faith for fear of discrimination. Several Muslim soldiers have been deployed in Iraq and Afghanistan, and many of them have been killed. Two hundred and twelve have been awarded Combat Action Ribbons. More than half these troops are African-American Muslims, who were born and raised in the U.S.

American Muslims are credited with their contribution to the overall development of American society and the strengthening of American institutions. Speaking at the 46th Convention of the Islamic Society of North America (ISNA), the largest Muslim organization in North America, Valerie Jarrett, a Senior Advisor to President Obama, paid tribute to the diligent work of Muslim Americans on behalf of the country, and commended ISNA for addressing critical national issues.

Secretary of State Hillary Rodham Clinton, in a statement made on April 12, 2011 at the annual U.S.-Islamic World Forum in Washington, D.C. acknowledged the contribution of American Muslims. She said: "I am proud that this year we are recognizing the contributions of the millions of American Muslims who do so much to make this country strong. As President Obama said in Cairo, "Islam has always been a part of America's history," and every day American Muslims are helping write our story."

Muslim populations are also exerting their influence in national elections in the United States and Europe. According to a Washington Times report of November 14, 2006 by Eric Pfeiffer, Muslim voters played a key role in turning over the control of the Senate to Democrats during the 2006 Congressional elections. The Muslim political leadership identified states with close races and heavy Muslim populations, and influenced the election outcomes by well-organized campaigns.

During this election, Muslims also celebrated the victory of the first Muslim Congressman, Democrat Keith Ellison, from the 5th Congressional District in Minnesota. Interestingly, Congressman Ellison received the backing of the National Jewish Democratic Council, even though his opponent, Republican Alan Fine, was Jewish.

The encounter between the Western World and Islam is not a clash of two separate and antithetical civilizations. As Professor Esposito[3] said in his book *What Everyone Needs to Know About Islam*, Jews, Christians, and Muslims are children of Abraham, and part of a Judeo-Christian-Islamic tradition. They need to cooperate with, and not confront, one another. Our common future demands a new, more inclusive sense of pluralism and tolerance based upon justice, fairness, mutual understanding, and respect.

Yet, many Muslims believe that some of the policies of the USA and other Western countries towards them are unfair and unjust. They wish to see such policies become more balanced. Some of reasons for the Muslim anger towards the West, especially the United States, is because of the following reasons:

1. Almost all Muslims are unhappy at the United States' unbalanced, one-sided foreign policy in the Middle East, in respect to its blind support of Israel, and leaders in the West are aware of this. For example, General David Petraeus, hero of Iraq and America's commander in the Middle East, told a Senate committee that the unresolved conflict in Palestine was fomenting anti-Americanism in the region.[79]

    Oppression and unjust treatment of the Palestinians and occupation of their land by the Israelis are a major reasons for Muslim terrorism. The United States needs to be seen as real and honest broker in the Israel-Palestinian conflict. Once the Palestinians are granted their just rights, terrorism may disappear altogether.

2. US invasion and occupation of Iraq and Afghanistan, the presence of the U.S and other Western troops in these countries and in the Arabian Peninsula; the drone and helicopter gunship attacks in Pakistan, and off and on

threat of invasion of Pakistani territiry by the American and NATO forces from Afghanistan are also fueling anti-American sentiment among Muslims in that part of the world.

Thousands of U.S. soldiers march through these impoverished lands, bringing fear and the threat of death, all in the name of peace, often in the name of Christ. There seem to be no reduction in bloodshed too soon.

Pakistan, which is allied with the United States in war against terrorism, claims to have suffered deaths of 35,000 civilians, 6532 soldiers, and 3629 police and paramilitary personnel so far in the war on terrorism. They also claim to have arrested hundreds of operatives of al-Qaeda and other terrorist organizations. Despite so many casualties of Pakistani civilians and men in uniform, the Americans seem to be dissatisfied with the performance of the Pakistani government, as they always keep asking them to 'do more.' This has led to widespread anger against the United States in the Pakistani public.

President Obama announced during November 2010 that the Afghanistan war will continue at least through 2014. This means there are plans to continue this counterproductive occupation. Terrorism, against which the war is claimed to be fought, will likely increase because there are reports that show that the occupation of Muslim lands, and not religious fervor, is the main cause of a sharp increase in terrorism attacks.[66]

3. Frequent imposition of economic sanctions against several Muslim countries is another cause of distrust between USA and the Muslim world.

4. Muslims minorities in Russia, China, India, and Israel are also not happy with the U.S. for its lack of support for their liberation from these countries. There is a need to

differentiate between terrorism and national liberation movements.

5. The questionable US attitude with respect to the system of governments in the Muslim world. The U.S. administrations talk a lot about democratization in the Muslim world, but in practice, they appear to support the corrupt, dictatorial, and tyrannical governments, which serve the interest of the West rather than of their own populations. Arab masses are fighting and dying for liberation from their ruthless and tyrannical rulers in a number of Arab countries, but the USA and European powers are not helping them in any substantial way.

6. Governments elected by popular votes in some Muslim lands have been opposed by the Western countries because elections were won by parties that had contested them on the basis of their Islamic character.

7. Muslims are also unhappy at America's use of international financial institutions such as the IMF and the World Bank that use financial aid and loans as leverage to pressure governments in Muslim countries to adopt policies favorable to the West.[80]

Muslims want to see the U.S. and Europe adopt policies based on fairness and humanitarian values when dealing with Muslims, and not the policies of occupation, colonialism, and imperialism. The U.S. needs to have an even-handed approach to the Israel-Palestine conflict, and to be seen as an honest broker. For decades, the U.S. has traditionally been seen as tremendously one-sided in this dispute, and this is the core issue that needs to be resolved. People in Muslim countries are fed up with such discriminatory policies and wish to be treated with respect, equality, and dignity.

This mistrust of Western Europe, and America, is more a

product of resentment against the foreign policy of the Western nations than any feeling of ill-will directed towards Europeans or Americans themselves. So when some Americans ask: "Why do they hate us," they are assuming that the majority of the people in the Muslim world hate America. This is simply not true. What they fail to see is that those who have disagreements with the U.S. foreign policy do not necessarily hate America or Americans.

While the overwhelming majority of Muslims prefer to deal with the West on the principle of mutual respect, there is a small minority of extremists who do not hesitate to use violence and confrontation to make a point, stemming more from political motives than religious fervor.

Virtually all Muslims denounce such violent actions as not representing Islam, yet this seems to be ignored by the Western media, who seem to pay no attention to these denunciations. On the contrary, it is a popular complaint in the West to ask, "why aren't the Muslims speaking out against terrorism?" The fact is that they are speaking out, rather, they are crying out, but nobody in the West seems to be taking notice. All the Western media have to do is to give fair coverage when Muslim people and their leaders denounce terrorism. For example, one of the major American TV networks could invite or interview the great Muslim scholar Dr. Tahir al-Qadri to explain his Fatwa (religious edict) against terrorism. Dr. Tahir al-Qadri lives in Canada and may be readily available for this.

It can be summarized from this chapter that Islam is a religion of peace and tranquility and it does not teach or condone terrorism, and violence. Those who undertake acts of terrorism and indiscriminate violence are not following the teachings of Islam. They are following their own political agendas.

23

ISLAM TEACHES REASON AND DIALOGUE, NOT VIOLENCE

THE WORD ISLAM means self-surrender and submission to the Will of God. Anyone who submits to the Will of God and lives his life as God commands, is a follower of Islam and is a Muslim. The name Islam is derived from a root word 'silm' which means 'peace,' and 'surrender'. Its full connotation is the peace that comes when one willingly surrenders himself to the Will of One God. This meaning is also reflected in the Islamic greeting of 'Assalam-o-alaikum,' meaning "peace be upon you."

Islam is meant to be a religion of peace, mercy, and forgiveness. In the Qur'an, God's compassion and mercy are cited 192 times as against 17 references to His wrath and displeasure. Most Muslims are a peace loving 'silent majority,' who are moderate in their outlook and have nothing to do with the grave events that have come to be associated with their faith.

Yet in the West, and particularly the United States, the underlying assumption is that the majority of Muslims are not moderate. Some in the West even talk about moderating the religion itself, assuming that there is something in the religion that promotes violence and extremism.

This kind of talk is the result of lack of proper understanding of the teachings of Islam in the West, especially in the media. The Western media seem to pick up isolated incidents committed by a tiny minority of extremists, who do not represent the 1.5 billion Muslims of the world. The news is magnified, sensationalized, and promoted as representing Islam. As a result, overwhelming majorities of peaceful, innocent Muslims are unjustly victimized. They are always on the defensive, and apologetic for something they have nothing to do with.

As Huston Smith has said in his book *Islam — A Concise Introduction,* the popular Western image of Islam as a religion of violence is utterly untrue.[1] Muslims do not hate non-Muslims, be they Christians, Jews, Hindus, Buddhists, followers of any other religion or have no religion. Islam does not teach or condone injustice and violence, and it does not allow killing of any innocent person regardless of his or her religion. The life of all human beings is sacrosanct, according to the teachings of the Qur'an and guidance of Prophet Muhammad. The following Qur'anic verses indicate value of life in Islam:

"Take not life, which God has made sacred,
except by way of justice (and law);
thus He commands you, in order that ye may learn wisdom."
(Qur'an 6:151)

"Whoever kills a person, except as a punishment for murder
or mischief in the land, it shall be as if he had killed all of mankind,
and whoso will save the life of one person,
it shall be as if he had saved the life of all mankind."
(Qur'an 5:32)

> *"Nor take life which God has made sacred, except for just cause.*
> *And if anyone is slain wrongfully,*
> *We have given his heir authority (to demand compensation or forgive)*
> *but let him not exceed bounds in the matter of taking life,*
> *for he is helped (by the law)."*
>
> (Qur'an 17:33)

Some passages in the Qur'an are quoted by critics out of context in an attempt to prove that they teach violence. For example: *"kill them wherever you find them."* (Qur'an 2:191 and 4:89)

To be fair, one should always read these verses in their textual and historical context. The full text says:

> *"Fight in the cause of God against those who wage war against you,*
> *but do not transgress limits, for God loves not transgressors.*
> *And kill them wherever they confront you in combat,*
> *and drive them out of the places from which they have driven you,*
> *(though killing is bad) oppression is worse than killing . . .*
> *and fight them until there is no more oppression*
> *and there prevails faith in God;*
> *but if they cease, let there be no hostility except*
> *against the wrong doers."*
>
> (Qur'an 2:190–193)

These passages were revealed in Medina, where Prophet Muhammad and a small group of his companions had been forced to migrate from Mecca after 13 years of suffering and persecution at the hand of the idol worshipers. Prophet Muhammad and his followers were struggling to protect Islam from being wiped out in its initial stages.

Even after the migration, the Meccans continued attacking the Prophet and his followers. In these verses, Muslims were given permission for the first time to fight back and defend their religion, their lives, their families, and their properties. Even in these passages, one can see how much restraint and care is emphasized.

It is very important that religious texts are studied in their proper context. When they are not read in their proper textual and historical contexts they become distorted, and give a completely different meaning. This problem is not limited to the Qur'an—many Bible verses would seem violent if removed from their textual context.

Many violent Jewish and Christian groups use these texts for their own goals. Crusaders had used them against Muslims and Jews, Nazis used them against Jews, Serbians used them against Bosnian Muslims, and Zionists are using them against Palestinians.[81]

Following are some of the examples of such verses from the Bible:

*"When the Lord Thy God shall bring thee into the land
whither thou goest to possess it,
and hath cast out many nations before thee . . .
and when the Lord thy God shall deliver them before thee;
thou shalt smite them, and utterly destroy them;
thou shalt make no covenant with them,
nor shew mercy unto them . . .
But thus shall you deal with them;
ye shall destroy their altars, and break down their images,
and cut down their groves,
and burn their graven images with fire."*
(Deuteronomy 7:1–5)

*"And when the Lord thy God hath delivered it into thy hands,
thou shalt smite every male thereof with the edge of the sword.
But the woman, and the little ones and the cattle,*

and all that is in the city, even all the spoil thereof,
shalt thou take unto thyself,
and thou shalt eat the spoilt of thine enemies,
which the Lord thy God hath given thee . . .
thou shalt save alive nothing that breatheth."
(Deuteronomy 20: 13–16).

"Now therefore kill every male among the little ones,
and kill every woman that hath known man by lying with him.
But all the women children,that have not known a man
by lying with him,
keep alive for yourselves."
(Numbers 31:17–18).

Obviously, if these verses are read out of context, the Bible would appear to be teaching hate, vengeance, and extreme kind of violence, almost genocide. Even the New Testament seems to teach violence. For example, Jesus is telling the people:

"But those mine enemies, which would not
that I should reign over them,
bring hither, and slay them before me."
(Luke 19:27)

There are many other passages in the Bible that, if read out of context, seem to teach intolerance for and killing of people whose religious views are different from those of Jews and Christians and who may worship entities other than God (Exodus 22:20). Such people are to be killed by stoning them to death (Deutronomy 17: 2-7), even if they are friends or family (Deutronomy 13:6-10), and even if an entire city has to be killed including humans and their cattle (Deutronomy 13:12-16). Jesus also seems to be teaching violence against the inhabitants of a city who refuse to receive his followers. They are to be punished in a manner more savage than that of Sodom and Gomorrah (Mark 6:11).

Quoting passages out of context from any holy book can have grave consequences. For example, insurgents of the Lord's Resistance Army (LRA), a Christian extremist group in Uganda, have terrorized, mutilated, and killed innocent people in the name of God, quoting passages from the Bible. They have justified cutting off peoples' hands, feet, ears, noses, and lips and gouged out their eyes while quoting passages such as Ezekiel 23:25-34, Matthew 5:29-30, Matthew 18:8–9, and Mark 9:43–47.

Some in Western media pick up isolated incidents of violence that are committed by a tiny minority of extremist Muslims, magnifying them in an effort to demonize the entire faith of Islam. Fortunately, there are some fair-minded people in Western media who reject such misleading distortions of Islam. For example, Tom Regan, in an article published in the May 31, 2005 issue of Christian Science Monitor, has debunked allegation that Muslims are disrespected in the West because they become violent when their religion is insulted.

Of course it would be untrue to say that no Muslim becomes violent when his/her religion is insulted. But it would be unfair to say that most of them are violent or to claim that Muslims are the only people who become violent. In his article, Tom Regan pointed out the decades long Christian violence in Northern Ireland, the murder of hundreds of Palestinian refugees by Christian militias in the Lebanese refugee camps of Sabra and Shatila in 1982, and the murder of 20,000 Bosnian Muslims by Serbian Christians in 1995. To this list, he added murder in America of abortion providers and the people who work for them, and approval of this violence by Christian preachers.

He also points out that there is no shortage of violent Jewish extremists, and gives the example of religious leaders in Israel who threatened violence and riots against Israeli Prime Minister Ariel Sharon and his supporters, if he went ahead with his disengagement plan. Those religious leaders believed they had 'God-given right' to the Gaza (and the West Bank), and that by defending the settlements through force and threats, they were carrying out God's will.

Regarding Buddhism, Regan reminds us that most people in North America see Buddhism personified in the presence of Dalai Lama. In the Buddhist countries, such as Sri Lanka and Thailand, violence against minorities is a serious problem. In Sri Lanka, for example, thousands of people have been killed in clashes between the Hindu Tamil Tigers and the Buddhist government. In Thailand, Buddhists have attacked Catholic churches, and violence against religious minorities is a big problem.

Regan states that there are countless examples of religious violence of the kind ascribed to the Muslims being committed by non-Muslim religious groups (and individuals). There is no shortage of religious extremists in the West who only want to spread hate for other religions. The most recent example is that of Terry Jones, pastor of The Dove World Outreach Center, a little known church in Gainsville, Florida.

Terry Jones sparked a firestorm by inviting Christians to join him in burning of the Qur'an to commemorate the anniversary of 9/11. Although later he cancelled his plan under pressure, his announcement infuriated Muslims all over the world, with widespread street demonstrations, increasing danger to the American troops in Afghanistan and elsewhere and turning into a disaster for the US foreign policy. A copy of the Qur'an was, nevertheless, burned at The Dove World Outreach Center on March 9, 2011. As a reaction to this senseless gesture of hate widespread protests took place in the Muslim world in which eleven people died in Afghanistan, including seven foreign workers of the UN staff.

This kind of act of extreme hate gives support to the argument presented by Nicholas Kristof in the OP-ED section of the New York Times on August 21, 2010 that historically, some of the most shocking brutality has been committed in the name of the Bible, not the Qur'an. He describes that the crusaders massacred so many men, women, and children in Jerusalem that a Christian chronicler, Fulcher of Chartres, described ankle-deep blood in an area from this massacre. He also mentions burning of Jews alive by the crusaders, while singing, "Christ, we Adore Thee."

As Huston Smith[1] describes in his book *Islam—A Concise Introduction*, that Muslims, just like the adherents of any other faith, have struggled and taken up arms to protect their faith when necessary. Professor Smith quotes Norman Daniel who states in his book, *Islam and the West—The Making of an Image*, that Islam has resorted to violence no more than Christianity. His example is that Spain and Anatolia changed hands at the same time. Many Jews and Muslims in Spain were killed, expelled, or forced to convert to Christianity; Muslims committed no such atrocities against Christians when they conquered Constantinople—a city that was and still is the capital of Orthodox Christianity.

It is also important to remember that not every case of violence in Muslim countries is related to Islam. Giving an example, in his August 21, 2010 OP-ED column in New York Times Nicholas Kristof describes the case of a young woman in Pakistan whose brother wanted to kill her for honor. It turned out that they were Christian people, not Muslims. This indicates that honor killing, which is usually blamed on Islam, is a cultural problem, not religious.

In view of what has been described above, one can say that while it is right to decry violence in the name of religion, it would be wrong to associate this problem with one particular religion. This kind of association would serve to prevent us from stopping all religious violence, and keep us from exploring the messages of hope, justice, love of God, and love of fellow man that all religions contain at their cores.

In some cases, Islam has been used to mitigate or outright eliminate violence. For example, Israelis initially supported the rise of Hammas in Gaza. Their theory was that if Gazans became more religious, they would spend more time praying in the mosques rather than fighting in the streets for their rights.[66]

Islam forbids violence, especially against people of other faiths. Muslims are taught to treat adherents of other religions with kindness and justice, as long as they do not mistreat them because of their faith. The Qur'an teaches:

"God forbids you not,
with regard to those who fight you not for (your) faith
nor drive you out of your homes,
from dealing kindly and justly with them,
for God loveth those who are just."
(Qur'an 60:8)

Historically, there have been ups and downs in the relations among the Muslims, Jews, and Christians, and they seem to still continue now, albeit at a reduced level. It is hoped, however, that as the world keeps shrinking into a global village, there will be more understanding among these three Abrahamic faith traditions of the world, and Muslims, Christians, and Jews will reach out to one another in peace and mutual understanding.

In September 2006, Pope Benedict XVI delivered a speech at the University of Regensberg in Germany, in which he quoted a 14th century Byzantine emperor, Emperor Manuel II Paleologus. He said: "Show me just what Mohammed brought that was new, and there you will find things only evil and inhuman, such as his command to spread by the sword the faith he preached." Muslims considered the Pope's quotation of the Byzantine emperor inappropriate and offensive. As expected, reference to the statement by the Pope triggered widespread demonstration in the Islamic world.

According to Catholic World News[82], the Pope told a Sunday audience that he was deeply sorry about the reactions in some countries after his speech. According to The Catholic World News, the Pope did not intend to insult Muslims or show disrespect for Islam. Instead, he hoped to capture the attention of the Muslim world, to challenge their leadership to a dialog based on reason, and to stimulate a discussion of faith and reason—a discussion that is both necessary and possible.

The Pope's challenge to the Islamic world had been heard, as the world's most influential Islamic leaders have responded to his call. They declared that Islam is a religion of reason, and that they were ready for inter-religious dialogue based on reason.

According to BBC News[83] of October 12, 2007, 138 Muslim leaders wrote a letter to Pope Benedict XVI and more than thirty other leaders of the world's Orthodox Christians and Anglicans. The letter is entitled "*A Common Word Between Us and You,*" and it urges greater understanding between the followers of Islam and Christianity. The letter pointed out that world peace depended on improved relations between Muslims and Christians.

The letter shows similarity of passages from the Qur'an and the Bible, and points out that Muslims and Christians worship the same God and that both Islam and Christianity emphasize the importance of total love and devotion to God and love of the fellow humans. The letter stated in part the following:

"As Muslims, we say to Christians that
we are not against them and that Islam
is not against them—so long as they do not wage war

against Muslims on account of their religion,
oppress them and drive them out of their homes.

If Muslims and Christians are not at peace, the world cannot be at peace. With the terrible weaponry of the modern world; with Muslims and Christians intertwined everywhere as never before, no side can unilaterally win a conflict between more than half of the world's inhabitants. Thus our common future is at stake. The very survival of the world itself is perhaps at stake.

So let our differences not cause hatred and strife between us. Let us vie with each other only in righteousness and good works. Let us respect each other, be fair and kind to one another and live in sincere peace, harmony and mutual goodwill." (www. acommonword.com)

Muslim scholars and leaders consider this document to be a landmark, as it has been signed by representatives of all Muslim scholars from a wide range of theological schools across Sunni, Shia, Salafi and Sufi traditions, as well as prominent Muslim political leaders and intellectuals.

The letter has also been signed by the Grand Muftis of Azerbaijan, Bosnia and Hercegovina, Croatia, Dubai, Egypt, Kosovo, Russia and Syria; the Secretary General of the Organization of Islamic Conference (OIC); Muslim intellectuals and representatives of several Muslim organizations in Europe and USA; and present and past senators, and ministers of several Muslim countries. Both Washington Post[84] and Newsweek[85] have reported that several Christian leaders have welcomed this initiative.

Rowan Williams,[84] Archbishop of Canterbury and spiritual leader to the world's 17 million Anglicans has said that "the letter provides an opportunity for Muslims and Christians to explore together their distinctive understandings. The call to respect, peace and goodwill should now be taken up at all levels and in all countries."

NEWSWEEK has reported that the early responses indicate that Christian leaders were welcoming the "Common word" with open arms. In Britain, the Bishop of London told NEWS-WEEK that the letter would "invite" young people to view the world as "a place where dialog is possible, instead of a place full of threats." [85] Similarly, Rod Parsley, senior pastor of the World Harvest Church in Ohio, said: "My prayer is that this letter begins a dialog that results in Muslims and Christians uniting around the love we have for each other as God's children."

This effort demonstrates what mainstream Muslims and Christians can achieve by working together. For Muslims, they can reclaim the true message of Islam, which forever remains a message of love, peace, and mercy. Through this letter, the Muslim leaders have taken a historic step to assure Christian leaders that they envision a world where leaders of all faiths are working side by side to foster harmony and mutual understanding.

Interfaith dialog and cooperation are not new to the Muslims. Muslims were very active in interfaith work throughout their history. John Kaltner,[2] Hugh Salzberg,[44] and Mark Graham,[48] describe that during the Golden Age of Islam Muslim, Christian, and Jewish scientists and scholars worked together to advance and preserve knowledge.

Christian scholars such as Yahya bin Masawaih and Hunayn ibn Ishaq worked together with their fellow Muslim scholars in the House of Wisdom, a center of excellence for scholarship sponsored by the Abbasid Caliphs Hartun Ar-Rashid and Al-Mamoon in Baghdad. Jerald Dirks[47] states, Muslim Spain (Andalusia) was a monument to interfaith dialog. Jewish, Christian, and Muslim religious scholars of that era were active in fostering mutual religious understanding and cooperation and inter-religious scholarship.

Dirks also describes that under the leadership of Bishop Raymond of Seville, Muslim scholars, Jewish rabbis, and Christian

monks sat together around a table studying old manuscripts.
Jews and Christians were appointed to high government posts
in Muslim Spain. Caliph Abd Al-Rahman III appointed a Jewish
rabbi as his foreign minister, the physician and scholar Hasai
ibn Shaprut.

AMIR ABDEL KADER—A MUSLIM LEADER WHO SAVED THE LIVES OF CHRISTIANS

Muslim effort in interfaith dialog and cooperation is not limited
to Baghdad or Muslim Spain; there are many examples of Muslims known for interfaith dialog with non-Muslims. One person
who won great admiration for his interfaith dialogue effort was
Amir Abd el-Kader, an Algerian freedom fighter and scholar of
the Qur'an who lived during the first half of the 19th century.
In a story written about him, Louis Werner[86] states that Abd
el-Kader became famous both as a freedom fighter against the
French and as an advocate for religious tolerance.

He led the Algerians in a resistance against the French occupation of their country. Although his military struggle was not
successful in removing the French from Algeria, he won fame
and respect in the West for his great effort to build bridges
between Muslims and Christians. He focused more on common-
alities between the two religions, and less on differences.

He was admired for his work on peace and good treatment
of the French prisoners of war, and was praised for feeding the
French prisoners better food than his own troops. For such acts
of chivalry and generosity, he won many friends among the
westerners, including church leaders who similarly worked to
bridge gaps between East and West. For example, Archbishop
of Algiers, Monseigneur Henri Teissier, praised Abd el-Kader as
a seeker of peace even in the presence of violent confrontation.

Abd el-Kader's resistance struggle could not match a merciless French campaign of warfare, and in 1847, he decided to lay down arms. As a part of the deal, the French accepted his condition of asylum in another Arab country, but the French broke their part of the deal and imprisoned him. He stayed in prison for 5 years, and after his release, he travelled to Syria, which was under Ottoman rule.

While in Syria, Abd el-Kader continued to play the peacemaker role amongst the Muslims, Christians, and Druze. In 1860 during religious riots in Damascus when the lives of 12,000 Syrian Maronite Catholics were in danger, he sent his own armed men to escort the Christians to his own guarded quarters, and saved their lives. He did this despite opposition of the Ottoman governor.

This act of compassion for the Christians was greatly admired by President Abraham Lincoln, who wrote him a letter of thanks. The farmers of Iowa were so impressed by this story that they named a town (Elkader, Iowa) after him. Today, he is remembered as an example of a Muslim who respected other religions.

MUSLIMS SAVED THE LIVES OF MANY JEWS

There are many examples where Muslims saved the lives of Jews at the risk of their own lives, especially during the Holocaust of World War II. One of these stories is told by Dr. Robert Satloff, who conducted eight years of research, discovering many examples of Muslim Arabs saving the lives of Jews. The story has been told in the form of a film called Among the Righteous—a 2011 McNeil/Lehrer Production. Its website is www.amongtherighteous.com.

The story shows Arabs saving the lives of Jews during World War II in Tunisia, Algeria, and Morocco, which were at that time under Nazi, Vichy France, and Fascist rule. The most prominent Arabs who saved Jews were Khaled Abdul Wahab, Si Ali Sakkat, and Hamza Abdul Jalil.

Khalid Abdul Wahab, also referred to as "Arab Oskar Schindler," lived on a farm in Mahdia, Tunisia at the time German troops invaded Tunisia. He was 31 years old when the Germans occupied Tunisia in 1942. He shrewdly cultivated relations with German officers in order to gain their confidence and learn about their plans to persecute Jews. He learnt that a German officer had his eye on Odette Boukhris, a beautiful Jewish woman whom he planned to rape.

Khalid spent the night secretly transporting Odette, her husband, other members of their family, and several other Jews in his van to his farm, hiding them in a stable. They stayed there under his protection for four months. One night, a drunk German soldier happened to come by and threatened to kill the Jewish women, but Khaled showed up in time to save them. One of the women later said, "It was like the coming of Messiah."

Other examples of Muslims who saved the lives of Jews from the Nazis during World War II include Tunisians Hamza Abdul Jalil and Si Ali Sakkat. Hamza Abdul Jalil was the owner of a Turkish bath house (Hammam), who gave shelter to his Jewish neighbor Joseph Naccache. His son later reported to have said his father acted out of common humanity, and there is good in everyone. Si Ali Sakkat gave shelter to 60 Jews, who had managed to escape from a Nazi labor camp in the Zaghouan valley. Looking for shelter, they came upon Ali Sakkat's farm compound and asked for protection. Ali ordered his farmhands to give them food and shelter.

In Algeria, anti-Jewish measures of the French were met by opposition from Muslim religious authorities. The Imam of Algiers issued a religious edict (fatwa) forbidding Muslims from serving as custodians of properties confiscated by the Nazis from the Jews. All Algerian Muslims accepted the edict, showing their solidarity with their Jewish compatriots.

The Vichy regime, in trying to please the Germans, attempted to drive a wedge between the Algerian Muslims and Jews. They tried to gain Muslim support by offering them goods seized from Jews, but the Muslims chose to take a pro-Jewish stance. Despite the economic difficulties of that time, the Muslims, to their great credit, refused to take advantage of the Jewish sufferings for personal gain.

Those who helped Jews included Muslim monarchs and mullas alike. Among those who were committed to justice were two Muslim religious scholars, Shaykh Abdelhamid Ben Badis and Shaykh Taieb el Okabi. Shaykh Ben Badis, who was a reformer, founded in 1931 the unifying Algerian League of Muslims and Jews. He was a great supporter of the Jews, and opposed the anti-Semitic acts of the Vichy in Algeria.

Shaykh Okabi had very good relations with Algerian Jews, and he issued a formal prohibition on Muslims from attacking Jews or benefitting from their sufferings. He also issued instructions to the Muslims to help the Jews and protect their properties.

Although the Germans occupied Algeria, Morocco, and Tunisia, the rulers of these countries—the French and Italians—were sympathetic to the Jews and did everything they could to defy anti-Jewish laws imposed upon them. It is said about the Tunisian king Moncef Bey that he treated Jews no different from the Muslim Tunisians. He extended protection to his Jewish citizens in as much as he could. He hid Jews from Nazis and helped many others avoid arrest and deportation.

Similarly, the late King Muhammad V of Morocco was known to treat Jewish people in his kingdom the same way he treated the Muslim citizens. He was very unhappy with Vichy's anti-Jewish laws, and did everything possible to resist their implementation. He defied the Vichy French authorities by telling them that in Morocco there were no Jews or Muslims, only Moroccans. When the French told Moroccans that they would provide them 200,000 yellow Stars of David for Moroccan Jews to wear, the king told them to add twenty more. When asked why twenty more, he replied that is how many individuals were in his royal family. The Moroccan Jews saw him as a hero, and he is celebrated as a savior in Moroccan Jewish lore.

Arabs were not the only Muslims who saved Jews from the Nazi Holocaust. Albanian Muslims, Turks, Bosnian Muslims, and other European Muslims saved thousands of Jews. One untold story is on display at a Jewish temple in St. Louis, Missouri. This photographic exhibit features portraits of Albanian Muslims in a documentary called 'Besa' produced by JWM productions. Its official website is http://www.missingpages.co.uk. The website features stories of Jews who were saved from Nazi Holocaust by Albanian Muslims.

Another fascinating story of Muslims saving Jews from Nazis is told by Karen Gray Ruelle and Deborah Durland DeSaix in their book *The Grand Mosque of Paris: A Story of How Muslims Rescued Jews During the Holocaust* (Published by Holiday House, Inc., 2010). According to this story, rector of the Grand Mosque in Paris, Si Keddour Benghabrit and other Muslims gave refuge to Jews and worked in the resistance to help them escape Nazi persecution during World War II. The grand mosque had been built in honor of the 100,000 Muslim soldiers who died fighting for France in the First World War.

Si Benghabrit was French Algerian and deeply loyal to France. He was appointed as a Muslim Chaplin in the French army, and took care of the needs of the Muslim soldiers. After the First World War, the French Parliament acknowledged his loyalty by authorizing the building of the Grand Mosque in

Paris. Benghebrit was appointed its rector. During World War II, the mosque became a sanctuary for Jews escaping persecution.

Benghabrit saved the Jews by issuing them fake certificates identifying them as Muslims. Although the majority of those who found refuge there were Jews, others also found safety there, including fighters or escapees from German prison camps and Allied pilots whose planes had been shot down.

During the Nazi occupation of Paris, Jews were not safe, and few Parisians were willing to risk their own lives to help them. Many Jews found a hiding place in the Grand Mosque of Paris. The Mosque was not just a place of worship, but also a community center, and it was an ideal temporary place for escaped prisoners of war and Jews of all ages, including children.

Similarly, Bosnian Muslims formed a resistance force against the Nazis, saving many Jews. Some Muslims defied Nazi warnings that threatened the death penalty for those who harbored Jews. Muslims were sent to concentration camps for rescuing Jews. One example is of the Hardaga family who were honored as "Righteous Among Nations"; a tree was planted in their memory at Yad Vashem. There were also Muslims who saved the cultural heritage of the Jews. A Medieval Jewish manuscript, an old Haggadah, was saved by a Bosnian Muslim.

A Turkish diplomat, Salahattin Ulkumen, saved many Jews on the island of Rhodes during a German occupation. Turkish Muslims saved thousands of European Jews by arranging boats to ferry them to safety in Turkey, allowing Jews to cross through the Greek-Turkish border even if they had no papers.

Fundamentally, Muslims value life and liberty no less than Jews and Christians do, they believe in peaceful coexistence with non-Muslims, and they practice humanitarian values similar to those of Jews and Christians. In the present day atmosphere of Islamophobia, Muslims are making an effort to educate non-Muslims, especially in America, about Islam and Muslims.

Presently, Muslims all over the United States are actively engaged in interfaith dialogues with Jews and Christians. Ironically, this is happening in the backdrop of a sharp increase in derision, misinformation, and outright bigotry directed by some ultra right wing, Islamophobic groups, and bloggers against Muslim Americans. However, Muslims have also found support in several political leaders and leaders of many Christian and Jewish groups who have defended Muslims and declared their support for them.

MUSLIMS HAVE USED NON-VIOLENT RESISTANCE

A favorite weapon of the opponents of Islam is associating Islam with violence. It seems like even justifiable resistance would be viewed as violence. Some people have asked if there is nonviolent resistance in the Muslim culture—there is. Not all Muslim resistance has been violent. There has been non-violent resistance to persecution, occupation of their lands, and other forms of injustice committed against them. Everyone seems to have heard leaders of non-violent resistance such as Mohandas Gandhi, Martin Luthar King, and Nelson Mandela, but not too many people seem to know Abdul Ghaffar Khan or, as he is also known, Badshah Khan.

Abdul Ghaffar Khan was born in British India (present day Pakistan) in 1890. He spent 80 years of his life fighting for peace and justice through nonviolence means, and he did this because of his Muslim faith.

In the November 24, 2010 issue of National Catholic Reporter, John Dear describes that Ghaffar Khan displayed an Islamic perspective that the non-Muslim world seldom sees, evidence that nonviolent resistance is within the scope of Islam.

Ghaffar Khan was a Pathan political, as well as religious

leader, who led thousands of people to oppose British rule in India. Although Pathans are known to be warrior people, Ghaffar Khan was a soldier of nonviolence. He claimed that he learned nonviolence from the Qur'an and Prophet Muhammad.

He had 100,000 followers, who conducted a campaign through peaceful rallying, speeches, strikes, sit-ins, and other nonviolent methods of resistance campaigns to demonstrate their opposition to the British rule. In one such demonstration in 1930, 250 of his followers were surrounded by the British soldiers and gunned down. The British arrested, imprisoned, and tortured many of Ghaffar Khan's followers, and burned their homes.

John Dear refers to a book *"Nonviolent Soldier of Islam: Badshah Khan: A Man to Match His Mountains"* (Nilgiri Press, 1984, 1999) by Eknath Easwaran. Easwaran wrote "if Badshah Khan could raise a nonviolent army out of a people so steeped in violence as the Pathans, there is no country on earth where it cannot be done." He also recommended that Badshah Khan's legacy of nonviolent resistance needed to be built upon, taught, and practiced.

Badshah Khan was a friend of Gandhi, who commended his use of active nonviolence to achieve social change. His nonviolent opposition to the British, and later to the dictatorship in Pakistan, earned him 30 years of imprisonment, mostly in hard labor and solitary confinement.

When he died in 1988, he was 98 years old and under house arrest. When Badshah Khan explained the fundamental laws of nonviolence in the Qur'an to Gandhi, Gandhi was stunned. Khan demonstrated that nonviolence was in perfect harmony with the teachings of Islam. He said nonviolence was not a new concept for him; Prophet Muhammad had followed it 1400 years ago.

In his book, Easwaran explained that when Ghaffar Khan compared nonviolence to the "weapon of the Prophet," he meant exercise of the concept of Sabr, as taught in the Qur'an.

The concept of Sabr is often translated as "patience" or "endurance" and is counseled repeatedly in the Surahs (Chapters) of the Qur'an revealed in Mecca during the earlier days of Islam.

Prophet Muhammad and his followers endured ridicule and harsh persecution at the hands of idol worshipers of Mecca, but held on to their faith in One God, without retaliating and without retreating, and in perfect submission to the Will of God (Islam). Sabr is all this and more. Easwaran adds to its meaning more virtues, which include tenacity in a righteous way, cheerful resignation in misfortune, forgiveness, self-control, renunciation, and refraining from revenge. He also quotes a statement from Umar Ibn al-Khattab, the second Caliph of Islam, who said: "We have found the best of our life in Sabr."

24

MUSLIM REACTION TO CARTOONS OF PROPHET MUHAMMAD

ISLAM FORBIDS THE depiction of God or His prophets in the form of images, drawings, statues, idols, cartoons, movies, or any other form. For this reason, there are no images of God or Prophet Muhammad in Muslim places of worship or homes. Muslims fear that such representations may lead to worship of these symbols, which would distract them from the worship of God.

This is also the reason why movies about Jesus Christ, such as "The Last Temptation of Christ" and "The Passion of Christ" were banned in many Muslim countries. Muslims believe that depiction of Jesus in these movies is an insult to a person whom Muslims love and revere as a Prophet of God.

The publication of the infamous 12 cartoons depicting Prophet Muhammad in the September 30, 2005 issue of the Danish Newspaper Jyllands-Posten caused an outrage among Muslims worldwide for similar reasons. The cartoons showed Prophet Muhammad in very insulting postures. In one cartoon he was shown with a bomb shaped turban that had a burning fuse, in another he was declaring that paradise had run out of virgins for suicide bombers, and in yet another he was shown with a sword and two veiled women.

Not only Muslims found the images insulting to the person of someone beloved and revered, the derogatory nature of the images were perceived as an attack on Islam and Muslims. It indicated the arrogance of Western society, its lack of respect for other cultures and religions, and dire need for its education about Islam. For the Muslims in the West, incidents of this type make them feel threatened, disempowered, and marginalized.

Gwladys Fouche wrote in a February 6th, 2006 issue of The Guardian that in the past editors of Jyllands-Posten had rejected the idea of publishing cartoons of Jesus in their newspaper on the ground that they could be offensive to readers and that they could provoke an outcry. In view of this, the decision of the editors to run Prophet Muhammad's cartoons clearly shows a double standard, and the newspaper owes an apology to the Muslims.

The violent reaction to the cartoons can be attributed not only to Muslims, but also to the Western media, which played a role in initiating and then wickedly fueling the perpetuation of the violence. Indeed, Muslims are constantly subjected to western media's bigotry and stereotyping.

Bigotry seems to become more acceptable when it accompanies stereotypes, helping the subjugation and oppression of a minority. This recalls the historical example of the Western media stereotyping the Native Americans as savages, thereby enabling the Europeans to carry out atrocities against them.

Jews in pre-WWII Germany were also subjected to media prejudice due to their religion. The so-called 'free' press in Nazi Germany enabled the propagation of hatred against Jews, and ultimately helped create a hateful environment in which six million innocent Jews were killed. Nazis began by burning books, which led to burning people.

In an article in the Dawn newspaper, Hyder[87] points out that among those found guilty in the Nuremburg Trial was Julius Streicher, a newspaper publisher and a journalist who was found guilty of crimes against humanity. Streicher certainly knew the power of the press in influencing public opinion; he used arguments of free speech to accomplish his evil goals.

Today, the anti-Semitism that has plagued many Western minds over the course of history no longer aims at Jews, but now at Arabs, Muslims and all things Islamic. Spiteful stereotyping of religious Muslims has replaced the past stereotyping of the other 'less civilized' peoples.

The suspicion that Muslims face in the West gives the feeling of being threatened and pushed against a wall. They have the feeling of drowning in the abounding stereotypes. It makes them wonder if this is the way to live and what contribution can they make to society under their prevailing circumstances. They are concerned about their family's future in the West. Protesting is one way for them to express their insecurity and regain self-respect.

In her article in The Guardian, Sarah Joseph[88] explains that there is a good reason for this fear and insecurity. She explains that the countries who have republished the cartoons of Prophet Muhammad—Spain, France, Italy and Germany—have a nasty history of fascism. The Holocaust did not occur overnight. It took time to brew and to establish a people as subhuman, and the media and the cartoons played their part. In its new role, fascism now seems to be using the Freedom of speech as a weapon.

The editor who commissioned the cartoons of Prophet Muhammad said that the cartoons were carried to test how integrated and compatible the religion of Islam was with a modern secular society. It was also said that the cartoons were designed to "test the growing tendency for self-censorship when handling Islamic subject matter." Whatever the objective, it is clear that it has done more to reveal the prejudices of Europe and increase the insecurities of its Muslim minorities. Europe has a history of turning on its minorities and expressing contempt for other cultures.

In an article in The Guardian titled "Europe's contempt for other cultures can't be sustained," Martin Jacqeus[89] wrote that even if we believe free speech is a fundamental value, it does not give us the right to say whatever we like to say in any context, regardless of consequences or effect. Respect for others in this increasingly interdependent world is also important.

As Martin Jacques points out, Jyllands-Posten decision to publish the cartoons in France, Germany, Italy and to reprint them elsewhere, was a deliberate, calculated insult to the beliefs of Muslims. It was not only done in the tradition of free speech, but in the tradition of European contempt for other cultures and religions.

For 200 years, Europe colonized most of the world and never needed to take the sensitivies, beliefs and cultures of their colonies into consideration. The colonial powers imposed their rulers, religion, language, educational system, racial hierarchy, customs, and value system on their colonies. They still display an attitude of racial bigotry, superiority, and disdain towards the people they once colonized and their religions, cultures, and value systems. Occasionally, this attitude appears in the form of 'free speech.'

Dr. Ingrid Mattson[90], a professor at Hartford Seminary, said Muslims are not just upset because the Danish cartoons disregard their religious beliefs; these are racist depictions, and they are along the lines of anti-Semitic depictions once seen in Europe. They are deliberately offensive and aimed at a minority which is already feeling marginalized. Muslims love the Prophet Muhammad, and an attack on him is perceived as an attack on Islam.

Susilo Bambang Yudhoyono[91], the President of Indonesia (the largest Muslim country), wrote that reprinting the cartoons to make a point about free speech is a senseless act of gambling and a disservice to democracy. It sends a conflicting message to the Muslim community: that in a democracy, it is permissible to offend Islam.

Commenting on the republishing of one of the twelve cartoons of Prophet Muhammad, U.N. Secretary General Ban Ki-moon stated that free speech should respect religious sensitivities, and the freedom of expression should be exercised responsibly and in a way that respects all religious beliefs. In 2006, when the cartoons were published in Jyllands-Posten, the U.N Secretary General Kofi Annan, said that the freedom of the press should always be exercised in a way that fully respects the religious beliefs and tenets of all religions (Reuters in Yahoo News, February 20, 2008).

According to January 30, 2006 report of Agence France Presse, former President Bill Clinton called these cartoons "totally outrageous against Islam" and warned of rising anti-Islamic feelings. He also wondered if anti-Islamic prejudice was going to replace anti-Semitic prejudice.

This message damages efforts to prove that democracy and Islam can co-exist. The average practicing Muslim needs to be convinced that the democracy he or she is embracing—and is expected to defend—also protects and respects Islam's sacred symbols. Otherwise, democracy will not be of much interest to him or her.

Many western commentators have defended the publication of the cartoons by arguing against any limit on the freedom of expression. However, they exercise a double standard. For example, when the British historian David Irving was sentenced by an Austrian court to three years in jail for publicly questioning the extent of the holocaust, the western journalists and intellectuals did not defend his freedom of expression, and chose to remain silent.

By preferring to criticize the Muslims for protesting against the cartoons but choosing to remain silent on the David Irving case, the western journalists and intellectuals' claim on the issue of freedom of expression appears hypocritical.

Muslims lack the resources to respond to the incessant media attacks on their religion, but they do have the right to freedom of expression, so their street demonstrations against the publication of the offensive cartoons may be justified and necessary. Violence, however, is neither justified nor necessary. Peaceful demonstrations are common in the West, and they are effective; even in the USA and Europe, however, not all demonstrations are peaceful—some turn violent and result in arrests.

25

MUSLIMS HAVE LOUDLY CONDEMNED THE TRAGEDY OF SEPTEMBER 11

MANY MUSLIMS AND Muslim organizations condemned the terrorist attacks of September 11, 2001 in New York, Washington, D.C. and elsewhere. For those who complain that the Muslims did not condemn the terrorist attacks of 9/11, or did not condemn them loudly enough, it is important to realize that there is no central authority in the Muslim world who could represent all 1.5 billion Muslims in condemning the terrorist attacks of 9/11. The condemnations did take place, and it came from individual Muslims, Muslim groups, organizations in North America and Europe, as well as leaders in Muslim countries. Several Muslim organizations in the United States have condemned terrorism in the strongest possible terms.

Muslims went beyond just condemning the attacks. They also took and continue to take active steps to combat extremism and the exploitation of religion for violent political purposes. They have expressed their opposition to terrorism and extremism by speaking out publicly against them in radio and TV talk shows, during sermons in mosques, in interfaith dialogue meetings and seminars, on websites, in newspaper ads, and by rallying against terrorism.

All over the United States, Islamic groups took out ads in major newspapers condemning terrorism and expressing their sympathy for the victims of attacks. The Council on American Islamic Relations (CAIR), the most prominent national Islamic civil rights and advocacy group, issued the following statements on the events of September 11:

"We at the Council on American Islamic Relations (CAIR), along with the entire American Muslim community are deeply saddened by the massive loss of life resulting from the tragic events of September 11. American Muslims utterly condemn the vicious and cowardly acts of terrorism against innocent civilians. We join all Americans in calling for the swift apprehension and punishment of the perpetrators. No political cause could ever be assisted by such immoral acts."

"All members of the Muslim community are asked to offer whatever help they can to the victims and their families. Muslim medical professionals should go to the scenes of the attacks to offer aid and comfort to the victims."

CAIR also launched a 'Not in the name of Islam' petition drive and urged Muslims to sign online petition against terrorism. The petition on the web site (www.cair-net.org) was designed to disassociate the faith of Islam from any violent acts that may have been committed by any Muslims. It allowed Muslims to help correct misperceptions of Islam.

The "Not in the Name of Islam" petition stated:

"We, the undersigned, wish to state clearly that those who commit acts of terror and murder in the name of Islam are not only destroying innocent lives, but are also devastating the image of the faith they claim to represent. No injustice done to Muslims can ever justify the massacre of innocent people and no act of terror will ever serve the cause of Islam. We repudiate and disassociate ourselves from any Muslim group or individual who commits such brutal and un-Islamic acts. Islam must not be held hostage by the criminal actions of a tiny minority acting outside both the boundaries of their faith and the teachings of the Prophet Muhammad."

CAIR's petition was launched following the videotaped beheading of an American civilian in Iraq that shocked television viewers worldwide. It was hoped that the petition drive would finally demonstrate that Muslims in America and throughout the Islamic world reject any violence committed in the name of Islam. The petition denounced hatred in the name of Islam. It was signed by 690,000 individuals.

CAIR also coordinated a group of North American Muslim scholars to issue a fatwa reiterating Islam's repudiation of religious extremism and violence against innocent people—including suicide bombings.

The St. Louis, MO branch of CAIR took out an ad in the September 16, 2001 issue of the Washington Post, that in part read:

"American Muslims, who unequivocally condemned terrorist attacks on our nation, call on you to alert fellow citizens to the fact that now is a time for all of us to stand together in the face of this heinous crime."

A letter was sent to President Bush from several Muslim organizations, condemning terrorist attacks in the United States. The letter was signed by the leaders of the American Muslim Alliance, the American Muslim Council, the Council on American-Islamic Relations, the Muslim Public Affairs Council, the Muslim American Society, the Islamic Society of North America, the Islamic Circle of North America, and the Muslim Alliance in North America. Together, these groups represent most of the seven million Muslims in the United States.

Political leaders of several Muslim countries have also condemned the acts of terrorism perpetrated on 9/11. According
to Agence France Presse news dated 9/9/06, former Iranian
President Mohammad Khatami, when speaking in Arlington,
VA, condemned the September 11, 2001 terrorist attacks on the
United States, saying that those who carried them out would
never go to heaven. "We, Muslims, should condemn this atroc-
ity even more strongly," Mr. Khatami told the Council on American-Islamic Relations.[92]

26

HOW ARE ISLAM AND AMERICA RELATED?[93]

"We hold these truths to be self-evident, that all men are created equal, that they are endowed by their Creator with certain un-alienable rights, that among these are life, liberty and the pursuit of happiness." [Declaration of Independence]

These ideals are a part of the Islamic faith also. Islam teaches that all humans are created equal and are blessed by their Creator with certain rights—the right to life, the right to pursue eternal happiness, and the right to liberty. Liberty, as Muslims see it, is not just defined as freedom of religion, assembly, and speech but, more importantly, freedom from subservience to any creation of the Creator. It is the freedom to serve the Creator, God Almighty, alone.

While many so-called Muslim nations are not, Islam is democratic in spirit. It advocates self-governance, and the right to self-determination. The Qur'an enjoins Muslims to rule themselves through consultation and consensus. Muslims believe that each person is responsible for his or her own deeds, and that all stand equal before God. This independent spirit, coupled with an egalitarian worldview, are both uniquely American.

Prophet Muhammad established the first known constitution in the world in the 7th century, known as The Covenant of Medina. It has been hailed as one of the greatest political documents in the history of mankind, and was designed to give a political structure to the city of Medina, to which Muslims had immigrated from Mecca. It was a pact of friendship, alliance, and cooperation among both the native and immigrant Muslims, and the Arabs and Jewish tribes. It guaranteed peace, social justice, religious freedom, and political unity to all inhabitants, men and women, of Medina.

The American ideals of independence, liberty, democracy, equality, and especially monotheism " . . . one nation under God," are all found within Islam's Covenant of Medina. Also, there is a very relevant verse of the Qur'an, which says: "Verily, this nation of yours is one nation and I am your Lord, so worship Me (alone)."(Qur'an 21:92).

For most Americans, the Qur'an seems like a foreign book full of strange invocations, yet it will not remain as foreign once it is realized that some of the Founders of the United States read the Qur'an and kept their own copies of this book.

The Qur'an affirms many of the earlier traditions of Christianity and Judaism because it is a revelation from the same one source, God Almighty. It brings good news to those who believe in God and do righteous deeds, and brings warning to the disbelievers and evildoers.

One marvels at the wisdom of America's founding fathers. When it came to religion, they had a vision to build a country of many different faiths, not just Christianity. They put all religions on an equal footing by saying no one religion would be the official religion of America. They did this to avoid any kind of religious violence. In order to implement their vision they also read the Qur'an and studied Islam with a calm intelligence.[94] Therefore, as Ted Widmer states in Boston Globe of September 12, 2010, that the Qur'an is not alien to American history—but inside it.

John Adams, the second president of United States, owned a copy of the Qur'an which is now found in the personal collection of John Adams, located in the Boston Public Library, and is known as Adams 281.1.

Reports of the Qur'an in American libraries go back to 1683, when an early settler of Germantown, Pennsylvania, brought a German translation of the Qur'an to United States. The first English translation of the Qur'an published in the United States was printed in Springfield, Massachusetts in 1806. Ted Widmer states that there was a long tradition of New Englanders reading in the Qur'an.[94]

Cotton Mather (1663–1728), a New England Puritan minister and prolific author, was familiar with the knowledge of Arabs, Turks, and other Muslims, and was known for quoting Qur'an in his writings. When he learnt that the Ottoman Turks in Constantinople and Smyrna had successfully controlled smallpox by inoculating patients against it, he led a public campaign to do the same in Boston. The campaign was successful and many lives were saved. (Ironically, some people were opposed to it and vilified Mather for using inoculation, calling it 'work of the devil.')

The 1780 Massachusetts Constitution, which John Adams helped to write, was designed to ensure the most ample liberty of conscience for "Deists, Mahometans (Muslims), Jews, and Christians." It was used as a model for the United States Constitution, which was written in 1787 but not ratified until 1789. New England is known to be most hospitable to immigrants, including Muslims, to the United States.

The Founding Fathers carefully considered the ethnic make

up of the new country they were creating, and took into consideration the probability that one day there would be Muslim Americans among other ethnic groups, and how their rights would be protected. Richard Henry Lee insisted that the right to practice religion was protected for Mahometans (Muslims), Gentoo (Hindus) as well as Christians. George Washington praised the Muslims and suggested that he would welcome them if they came to United States in search of work. Benjamin Franklin argued that Muslims ought to have the freedom to preach to Christians if the Christians insisted on the right to preach to them. [94]

Thomas Jefferson was known to be one of the Americans who was most knowledgeable about Islam, possessing his own copy of the Qur'an. He bought this 1764 English translation while studying law at the College of William and Mary in Virginia. In 2008 the first Muslim ever elected to United States Congress, Keith Ellison, a Democrat from Minnesota, asked for Jefferson's Qur'an to put his hand on for taking oath of his office.

John Adams and Thomas Jefferson cultivated very good relations with the Islamic countries of their time, especially Morocco, as Moroccans considered the Americans fellow Ahl al-Kitab or the People of the Book, with both groups eschewing idol worship. Consequently, favorable treaties were signed with Morocco.

It is also reported that about 20% of the African American slaves came from Islamic background, keeping their knowledge of the Qur'an alive by reciting its verses from memory. Some were known to have brought copies of the Qur'an with them. Ted Widmer reports that in the war of 1812, African Muslim slaves fought and helped to defend America from a British attack.[94] To those who question the loyalty of Muslims to the United States, this should serve as a proof that the Muslim Americans can be just as loyal as any other people.

After one year into his Presidency, George Washington wrote

about the children of the Stock of Abraham (who include Muslims, Christians, and Jews). "May the children of the Stock of Abraham, who dwell in this land, continue to merit and enjoy the good will of the other inhabitants; while everyone shall sit in safety under his own vine and fig tree, and there shall be none to make him afraid." Washington closed with an invocation: "May the father of all mercies scatter light and not darkness in our paths, and make us all in our several vocations useful here, and in his own due time and way everlastingly happy."

In Who Speaks for Islam, a research report by the Gallup World Poll, John Esposito and Dalia Mogahed reported that Muslims around the world want the same things that Americans want, and they share the same values.[66] They reject terrorism and violence.

MUSLIMS IN AMERICA—A HISTORICAL PERSPECTIVE

Jerald F. Dirks, in his book Muslims in American History: A Forgotten Legacy[47] gives an account of the history and establishment of Muslims in America. He shows that some Muslims were here long before Christopher Columbus discovered America.

Islam is typically seen as an alien religion that has little, if anything, in common with the average American or the American history. Americans of the 1950s and 1960s generation may associate Islam with the Black Muslim movement of that era, and younger Americans may associate it with the September 11, 2001 tragedy. In both cases, the perceptions are negative.

In reality and in contrast to these perceptions, historians have traced the history of Islam in America back several centuries. Even though most of this history has been forgotten, modern day scholars have been able to find the presence of Islam in old American history through the study of archeological inscriptions and linguistic analysis carved into stones.

Jerald Dirks describes a number of pre-Columbian voyages by Muslim sailors, traders, and adventurers from Andalusia (contemporary Spain and Portugal), the Ottoman Empire, and other parts of the Mediterranean, as well as from different parts of Africa towards the West. The first documented voyage of Muslims from Andalusia to the Americas took place during the late ninth century, six hundred years before Christopher Columbus discovered Americas in 1492. That travel to Americas during 889 by Khashkhash ibn Saeed ibn Awad, a resident of Cordoba, Spain was recorded by the famous Muslim geographer and historian Ali Al-Masudi (871-957) in his book.[47]

Many of the Spanish explorers who undertook voyages to the Americas during the pre-Columbian period were Muslim traders and colonizers. They were of Arab and Berber descent, and brought Islam to Americas. Similarly, some of the sailors who travelled with Christopher Columbus to Americas were also Muslims, and they knew the use of the astrolabe.

In their writings on their voyages to Americas, Christopher Columbus and his son Ferdinand gave evidence about the pre-Columbian presence of Muslims in America. They reported having seen Indian women dressed in long veils and Indian men wearing breechcloths of the same design and material as the shawls worn by the Muslim women of Granada, Andalusia (Spain).

Al-Idrisi, a 12th century Muslim geographer, physician, and advisor to King Roger II of Sicily, also described a voyage by North African Muslims who sailed west from Portugal. Presumably, they arrived at a Caribbean Island and were taken prisoners by native Indians. Dirks also mentions that there is some evidence from inscriptions that the Mandinka people, who were Muslims from Mali, West Africa, sailed to Brazil, and from there west and north to Peru, Mexico, and the present day United States. [47]

AFRICAN MUSLIMS BROUGHT TO AMERICA AS SLAVES

It was not just Muslim sailors, traders, explorers, and adventurers who brought Islam to America. In a substantial way, Islam came to America with the millions of African slaves who were shipped to America from Africa starting in the 16th century and continuing through the early part of the 19th century. Between 15 and 20 million slaves were brought to the New World, and 20-30% of them were Muslims.[95] This means three to six million African Muslims were enslaved in Americas. Only 15-20% of the Muslim slaves were women.[47]

In contrast to the illiterate and uneducated stereotype of savages, the African slaves, especially the Muslim slaves who were brought to Americas, were mostly educated. During the 16th through the 18th centuries, education was quite common in West Africa. West African slaves were mostly educated, whereas the vast majority of Europeans and Americans were not.[47] Jonathan Curiel suggests that Muslim slaves were more literate because they were trained in recitation (and reading) of the Qur'an.[95]

Among the Muslim slaves who were brought to America were lawyers, teachers, doctors, professors, Muslim religious leaders, and other professionals. Several museums in the American South contain Arabic manuscripts written by these African Muslims. Some manuscripts contain material from the Qur'an and material related to Islamic law (Shariah).

Jonathan Curiel wrote a story on the life of Omar ibn Said, a Muslim scholar and a teacher in West Africa who was captured and brought to America as a slave. He was more educated than many of the slave masters he encountered in Carolinas.[95] He was a great believer of co-existence between Muslims and Christians; despite being enslaved by Christians, he had good things to say about them. One of the Arabic manuscripts written by Omar ibn Said was displayed at the Civic Center in Atlanta.

In this manuscript, he advocated interfaith dialogue between Muslims and Christians.

Sadly, once in America, the slaves were subjected to all kind of hardship, degradations, and humiliations. Horrors were inflicted upon them. In some Southern States, there was no law to protect the slaves against physical abuse and deprivation. Some owners literally worked their slaves to death. Slaves had no right to own property, and if a slave owned anything, it automatically became the property of the owner.

In several States, freeing slaves or teaching them to read and write was unlawful. They were usually ruthlessly persecuted for their Muslim faith, and forbidden to teach their religion to their children.[47]

In some Southern States, slaves were forbidden to marry, and even if in some cases they were allowed, they could marry only people of their own race. To make things worse for the slaves who married and had families, their owners would destroy their families by selling off a spouse or a child—more or less like selling an animal.

Muslim slaves in America suffered greater hardship than their non-Muslim counterparts. They found it impossible to practice their Islam. They could not perform the mandatory acts of Islamic worship, meaning the five daily prayers (Salat), fasting during the month of Ramadan, paying Zakat (poor due), and going to Mecca for pilgrimage. They also did not have access to copies of the Qur'an.

It was also difficult for them to follow dietary restrictions mandated by their religion. For example, the meat they were given to eat was usually pork, because it was the cheapest meat. Because it was almost impossible to keep their faith, many Muslim slaves did not get married or have children.

Jonathan Curiel states that many Muslim slaves in the Southern United States were under powerful pressure to convert to

Christianity. Some of them, including Omar ibn Said, attended church and read the Bible—in Arabic. But there are indications that in some cases the conversion was superficial and the slaves kept their Islamic faith in secret, like Moriscos of Spain (see Chapter 12). Curiel quotes examples of some of the slaves who renounced their conversion to Christianity after winning their freedom.[95]

In conclusion, it appears that most of the Muslims who came to Americas during the 16th through 19th centuries lost their Islamic identity due to difficulty in practicing their religion, disproportional men to women ratio, not marrying at all or intermarrying with non-Muslims, forced conversion to Christianity, and other reasons. As a result, by the late 1700s and early 1800s, they were mostly Christianized.

MUSLIM IMMIGRANTS IN THE UNITED STATES

Many Muslims have immigrated to America for higher education, better life, or economic opportunities. Many have come here to avoid life of hardship in their countries of origin, and some have come to escape religious or political persecution.

Muslims have been immigrating to America as free men and women for centuries, and participated in the revolutionary war as well as in the conquest of the American Wild West.[47] Initially, their numbers were small, but after the civil war, large numbers of Muslims started to immigrate to America.

The first wave of Muslim immigrants came to the USA from the Arab provinces of the Ottoman Empire during the late 19th century. These Muslims were primarily from Syria, Lebanon, and Jordan. Later, during the 20th century, Muslim immigrants came from the Middle East, Indian subcontinent, and elsewhere. Muslims immigrating to America led to the establishment of mosques and a variety of Muslim institutions, and also sparked an interest in African Americans to discover their Muslim roots. However, some of the resulting institutions, although claiming to be Islamic, such as the Nation of Islam, had little in common with genuine faith Islam. (Chapter 27).

The Muslim population of America has been increasing rapidly through conversion and immigration, and Islam had become the fastest growing and second largest religion in America.[47] Presently, there are between six and eight million Muslims in America. While the greatest number of converts to Islam in America come from the African American background, others including European Americans, Latino Americans, and American Indians are also converting to Islam in substantial numbers.

MUSLIMS AMERICANS ARE PATRIOTIC

Some people in America view Muslim Americans as disloyal to their country. Eliyahu Stern, a Professor of religious studies at Yale University, has written an article in the September 3, 2011 issue of The New York Times; it is titled: "Don't Fear Islamic Law in America." In his article Professor Stern quotes a Gallop poll which found that only 56 percent of Protestants think that Muslims are loyal Americans.

Accusations of disloyalty of a minority to their country is not a new thing, nor is it limited to Muslim Americans. European Jews were also accused of disloyalty to their countries. Leaders of 19th century Europe argued that Jewish laws called into question the ability of the Jews to be civil servants, made it difficult for them to identify with their fellow citizens (of other faiths), and made them hostile to all other peoples.

Jews were considered at best an unassimilable minority, at worst a fifth column, and Jewish law was considered a competing legal system. Christianity, on the other hand was seen as a faith that harmoniously coexisted with the secular law of the country.

The suspicion and mistrust of Muslim Americans is driven by the notion that Muslim Americans are similar to certain extremist Muslim groups of the Middle East. The truth is that there is no similarity between the two groups; they are two completely different groups. Professor Stern quotes a Pew Research Center poll which found that Muslim Americans exhibit the highest level of integration among major American religious groups, and they express greater degree of tolerance towards people of other faiths than do Protestants, Catholics or Jews.

There are many facts which show that Muslim Americans are patriotic. They are serving the nation in all walks of life. They include doctors, nurses, firefighters, paramedics, policemen, lawyers, teachers, bankers, business executives, elected representatives, and other professions. They work hard to make this country a great country. Thousands of Muslim Americans are serving in the armed forces of United States, and some have made the ultimate sacrifice for their country. They include army specialist Kareem Khan, who gave his life in Iraq, and now rests with his fellow heroes at Arlington.

President Barak Obama hosted an Iftar Dinner on August 10, 2011 at the White House, and in his speech he reminded the American people that Islam has always been a part of our American family and Muslim Americans have long contributed to the strength and character of our country in all walks of life. He pointed out that the Americans who lost their lives to the attacks of 9/11 included many patriotic Muslim Americans. They included Muslim workers in the twin towers, Americans by birth and Americans by choice, who used to come together for prayers and meals at Iftar. One married couple was looking forward to the birth of their first child.

They included first responders; a former police cadet who rushed to the scene to help, and then was killed when the towers collapsed on him; a nurse, who helped many; a naval officer at pentagon, who rushed into the flames and pulled the injured to safety; and others. The President of the United States honored these Muslim Americans as "American Heroes."

The President reminded the American people that since the day of 9/11 Muslim Americans have helped us in protecting our communities as police officers and fire fighters; worked in federal government, keeping our homeland secure; guided our intelligence and counter-terrorism efforts, and upheld civil rights and civil liberties of all Americans. So they have helped in keeping all Americans safe.

These and other facts reject the accusation made by some people that Muslim Americans are somehow less patriotic than the rest of the Americans.

America's strength has been in its ability to transform itself—economically, culturally and religiously, In the 20th century Judeo-Christian ethic was promoted, and common elements of the Jewish, Catholic, and Protestant traditions were accentuated. Now, there is a pressing need for promoting Abrahamic ethic that includes Islam into the religious tapestry of American life.

27

ISLAM IS DIFFERENT FROM THE NATION OF ISLAM

ISLAM AND THE so-called Nation of Islam are two completely different religions. Islam is a religion that was revealed to Prophet Muhammad of Arabia in the seventh century. It is a religion of 1.5 billion people from all races and cultures of the world and enjoins the worship of One True God, who is free from anthropomorphic characteristics.

The Nation of Islam is a movement initiated by its founders as a reaction to the discriminatory policies of the white Americans against the African Americans. The movement was designed to elevate the social level of the minorities in America. They continued to suffer from subhuman treatment despite the end of slavery in America with the Emancipation proclamation and passage of the 13th Amendment to the Constitution in 1865.

African Americans continued to suffer restrictions on their rights to a proper education, employment, and other rights enjoyed by white Americans. They suffered humiliation in the form of segregation, second-class status, and discrimination in almost all aspects of life. Many were lynched, burned alive, shot, and killed during the last part of the 19th and early part of the 20th centuries. During the 15 year period from 1900 to 1914, 1,100 African Americans were lynched. As a reaction to this racial hatred and bigotry against African Americans, the movement of the Nation of Islam was launched in Detroit in 1930.[47]

The doctrine of the movement is based upon racial mythology, with some elements from the teachings of Islam and some elements against the teachings of Islam incorporated into it. The movement started with an individual by the name of Wallace D. Fard. He started teaching the African Americans about the glorious history of black Africans, and that the religion of their ancestors and of all dark-skinned people in the world was Islam. He quoted references from the Bible, the literature of the Jehovah Witnesses, and the Qur'an, and established the first house of worship or Temple. He also taught that white man was responsible for the sufferings of the black Africans.

Fard described himself as 'the Supreme Ruler of the universe,' and some of his followers considered him as divine. In 1934, Fard disappeared and Elijah Muhammad assumed control as the Minister of Islam in his place. He was born Elijah Poole in Georgia, the son of a Baptist minister. He met Fard in 1930, and Fard changed his name to Elijah Muhammad. He assumed the title of prophet and messenger of Allah. At this point, Fard was recognized as Allah or as an incarnation of Allah.[47]

Under the leadership of Elijah Muhammad, the Nation of Islam became popular. By 1962, membership may have reached a million people, with the number of Temples exceeding 69. Its success was largely due to the work of Malcolm X, who was a great orator.

Malcolm X joined Nation of Islam in 1952, and was an enthusiastic follower of Elijah Muhammad. In 1963, he was suspended for making statements following the death of John F. Kennedy. In 1964, he left the Nation of Islam, embraced orthodox Islam, changed his name to Malik El-Shabazz, and formed his own Islamic organization called the Muslim Mosque, Inc.

He also began to talk against the racial mythology of the Nation of Islam; the followers of the Nation of Islam became his enemies. That same year he went to Mecca for Hajj, and was assassinated soon after his return. In 1964, 22-year-old Cassius Clay won the world heavyweight boxing title, announced that he had joined the Nation of Islam, and changed his name to Muhammad Ali.

Elijah Muhammad had built a national movement of "Black Muslims" based on racist ideology. It taught that white people were devils and black people should separate themselves from white society. It taught black supremacy and black separatism, things that completely contradict Islam's teaching of brotherhood and equality of all believers in a community regardless of color, ethnic background, or national origin.

The Nation of Islam did not teach practice of the five mandatory acts of worship called "the Five Pillars" of Islam. In orthodox Islam, one cannot be a Muslim without practicing these five mandatory acts of worship.

The followers of the Nation of Islam adhere to some Islamic principles that are mixed with teachings that are alien to Islam. The Nation of Islam teaches social, personal, economic, and political separation of the races, prohibits interracial socializing and marriage, promotes separate educational facilities for different races, and mandates support for only African American businesses.

This racial exclusivity taught by the Nation of Islam directly contradicts the universal brotherhood taught by the religion of Islam. There is nothing in orthodox Islam that has any similarity with the racial mythology of the Nation of Islam. To understand the difference between Islam and the Nation of Islam, one needs to read the story of Malcolm X in his book *The Autobiography of Malcolm X*.

During his visit to Mecca for pilgrimage, Malcolm X was

impressed to see true brotherhood and equality among Muslims of all races and nations. He returned from the pilgrimage a true Muslim, rather than a Black Muslim, and changed his position on black nationalism to pan-Africanism.

Describing his impression, he stated in *The Autobiography of Malcolm X*: "America needs to understand Islam, because this is the one religion that erases from its society the race problem. Throughout my travels in the Muslim world, I have met, talked to, and even eaten with people who in America would have been considered 'White'—but the 'white' attitude was removed from their minds by the religion of Islam. I have never before seen sincere and true brotherhood practiced by all colors together, irrespective of their color."[96]

The belief system of the Nation of Islam has several fundamental differences with orthodox Islam. The Nation of Islam teaches that all Afro-Asians were divine and that the supreme man among them was Allah.[47] This black person was incarnated in the person of Wallace D. Fard. This sort of belief completely violates Islamic teaching about the nature of God Almighty. The teachings of the Nation of Islam that Elijah Muhammad was a prophet and messenger of Allah also directly contradicts the teachings of orthodox Islam that Prophet Muhammad was the last Messenger of God, and there will be no other Prophet after him.

There are also serious differences in the religious practices of the orthodox Islam and the Nation of Islam. Orthodox Islam requires bowing, kneeling, and prostration in its mandatory daily prayers; the Nation of Islam requires no such movements. Orthodox Islam requires fasting during the lunar month of Ramadan; the Nation of Islam teaches its follower to fast during the solar month of December.

Many of the practices of the Nation of Islam were challenged by Malcolm X and also Elijah Muhammad's son, the late Wallace

ISLAM FOR FELLOW AMERICANS

D. Muhammad, who questioned many of the teachings of the Nation of Islam.

When Wallace D. Muhammad succeeded his father as the leader of the Nation of Islam, he implemented major reforms in doctrines and the organizational structure of his movement, so that they would conform to the teachings of orthodox Sunni Islam.

Wallace D. Muhammad performed pilgrimage to Mecca, and changed his name to Warith Deen Muhammad. He also changed the name of the 'temples of the Nation of Islam' to 'mosques,' and changed the title of 'ministers' to 'Imams.' The majority of the community now observes the "Five Pillars" of Islam in solidarity with the worldwide community of Islam to which they now belong.

Lately, one of the most vocal representatives of the Nation of Islam has been Louis Farrakhan, who rejected the changes implemented by Malcolm X and Warith Deen Muhammad in the doctrines of the Nation of Islam. However, in recent years he has also been moving his position closer to a more orthodox Islamic identity.

28

THE WAVE OF
ISLAMOPHOBIA IN AMERICA

OPPOSITION TO ISLAMIC SHARIAH

An anti-Shariah movement has been spreading in the United States for the last several months, and more than two dozen American states have considered measures to restrict judges from consulting Shariah, several states are considering outlawing aspects of Shariah law, and statutes have been enacted in three states. Some of these efforts would curtail Muslims from settling disputes over dietary laws and marriage through religious procedures, while others would directly affect Muslims who try to live life according to teachings of Islam.

In Tennessee, a state legislator introduced a bill that would make following Shariah a crime, punishable with up to 15 years in prison, and a bill recently passed by the Tennessee General Assembly equates Shariah with a set of rules that promote "the destruction of the national existence of the United States." Similarly, in Oklahoma, voters approved a constitutional amendment that bars courts from considering Shariah. Similar measures have been introduced or passed in several other states.

Anti-Muslim political operatives have been spreading Shariah-phobia for some time, but lately it seems to have acquired new momentum. Several factors have fueled the anti-Shariah movement, including the rise of the Tea Party. The sad part is that most of these people who are introducing or supporting anti-Shariah bills don't know what Shariah is. They have not been able to answer basic questions about Islamic law or why they see it as a threat.

In the July 31, 2011 issue of New York Times, Andrea Elliott wrote an article about the man who is behind the anti-Shariah movement. She identified a little known lawyer, David Yerushalmi, a Hasidic Jew with a history of controversial statements about race, immigration and Islam. He is the founder of the Society of Americans for National Existance.

On the group's Website, he has proposed a law that would make observing Islamic law a felony punishable by 20 years in prison. He has likened Islamic law to sedition. Characterizing a religious law as seditius is not new. In the 19th century Europe, the Jewish religious law was considered 'seditious.'

Despite his lack of formal training in Islamic law, he has promoted himself as an expert on Shariah, and seems to have convinced some people that Shariah is the greatest threat to American freedom since the cold war. Among those who are echoing Mr. Yerushalmi's views are two Republican presidential candidates, a former director of CIA, and other prominent figures.

Although the anti-Shariah movement is directed at a problem more imagined than real, it seems to be sending out message of alarm about Islam, the kind of message that influenced Anders Behring Breivik to carry out his slaughter of 77 innocent civilians in Norway on July 22, 2011.

WHAT IS SHARIAH AND WHY SHOULD ANYBODY
FEAR IT IN AMERICA?

Shariah is Islamic law. It is an Arabic word for "way" or "path."
It is Islam's roadmap for living morally and achieving felicity,
salvation, and the pleasure of God Almighty. Muslims define Islamic law as the law of God. It is not only law, but also includes
procedures through which jurists apply teachings of religious
texts of Islam to ascertain the Will of God. The result of this process is called Fiqh, which is the moral and legal underpinning of
a Muslim's existence.

It is not based on any legislation in the traditional concept of
the legal system. It is based on four sources: two primary and
two secondary. The primary sources are the Qur'an and the
Sunna. Muslims consider the Qur'an as the uncreated Word of
God Almighty. It is not exclusively a legal code or constitution.
Legal rulings constitute only 350 verses—a small part of the
total 6,235 verses. The Sunna are actions and sayings of Prophet
Muhammad, or what he approved. These Sunna are related in
tradition called Hadith.

The secondary sources are Ijma (consensus of legal scholars
and jurists, and sometimes even entire communities of the Muslims) and Qiyas (reasoning by analogy). Juristic preferences,
public interest, and customs may also be used as secondary
sources.

The belief in One God is an essential principle of Shariah, as
all discussions of morality and law proceed from here. Accordingly, Shariah does not divide between the facets in human life.
Religion and morality are not separated from economics or politics. It regulates legal rights and obligations as well as non-legal
matters—moral rights and obligations.

Shariah governs every aspect of a Muslim's life. It applies to
marriage, estate planning, finance, and business transactions. It

also teaches a Muslim how to pray, fast, and give charity, among other acts of worship. It is a complex body of law, but very flexible.

US courts are required to regularly apply foreign law, including Islamic law, to a number of things. These may relate to validity of a marriage, recognition of a foreign divorce, child custody, probating of Islamic will, and payment of damages in a commercial disputes. Shariah is relevant in a U.S. court as a foreign law or as a source of information to understand the claims of parties in a dispute.

For example, Muslim marriage involves a marriage contract, which is signed in front of witnesses at the time of marriage ceremony. Among other requirements, the contract specifies a mutually agreed upon amount called Mehr, which is pledged by the groom to his bride in accordance with Shariah. The contract specifies whether the payment is due immediately or later. An American court would require expert testimony to understand what Mehr and a Muslim marriage contract are, and what the expectations were of the parties involved. Such testimony would be necessary for the court to make an appropriate judgment on disputes involving a Muslim marriage.

Shariah law is used in American courts the same way as Jewish law, canon law, and any other foreign laws are. For example, Shariah law, like Jewish law, most commonly comes up in U.S. courts through divorce and custody proceedings or in commercial litigation. These type of cases usually involve contracts that failed to be resolved in a religious setting.

In the West, there is a misunderstanding about Shariah. When the word Shariah is mentioned, stoning, lashing, and amputations as punishments come to mind. Islamic law includes not only criminal law but also moral and ethical rules and perspectives. These rules guide Muslims through the life.

The Qur'an does not mention stoning for adultery; it prescribes lashing. However, stoning for adultery is required in the Bible (Deutronomy 21:20-21; 22:22; Leviticus 20:10). It is unlikely that U.S. courts will consider such a provision in a foreign law, because our constitutional protection and public policy will not allow it. Foreign law or religious law in American courts will be considered within the limits of American constitution.

In some states, bills are introduced and hearings held seeking ban on Shariah law. Many bills are drawn from a template prepared by an anti-Islam hate group. They are doing this to create a fear that Muslims are trying to impose Shariah law on United States courts, which is far from reality. The United States Constitution prohibits U.S. courts from imposing any religious or civil laws. It says, "Congress shall make no law respecting an establishment of religion." Secondly, by seeking to take action against a religious minority, the proponents of anti-Shariah bills are violating the Constitution. They are singling out only one religious group—Muslims, whose religious rights are protected by the United States Constitution, which is the law of the land.

In its spirit, the Shariah law is based on the principles of justice, mercy, and compassion. It prescribes punishments for actions that cause harm in a society, and they are carried out only after careful evaluation of circumstances.

For example, during the reign of the Muslim ruler Caliph Umar Ibn al-Khattab, a man came to him with a complaint that his servant had stolen his food and needed to be punished (according to Islamic law) for stealing. Umar summoned the servant and asked him why he stole from his master. The servant answered that he was hungry and his master did not give him enough to eat. Umar let the servant go, but reprimanded the master for neglecting his duty to feed his servant.

Punishment under Islamic law is carried out to protect the society from greater harm. Under the right circumstances, the punishment of a criminal may even be reversed if the victim's relatives agree to forgive him in exchange for adequate compensation or blood money. This policy saved Raymond Davis, an American citizen and CIA operative, who killed two Pakistanis on a busy street on January 27, 2011 in Lahore, Pakistan. He was arrested, jailed, and faced sentence under Pakistan's penal law.

The US claim for his diplomatic immunity was not accepted by Pakistan's Foreign Ministry. Finally, after 49 days, the matter was resolved when a local court, using a provision in the Shariah law, set him free in exchange for blood money (Arabic: diyya). The money was paid on behalf of Raymond Davis to the relatives of the individuals he killed. In another example, during the summer of 2010, the US embassy in Islamabad made a similar blood money payment on behalf of a U.S. diplomat who, driving while intoxicated (DWI), killed a Pakistani citizen.

Ordinarily, such a payment would be the end of the issue, and once blood money is accepted the accused is acquitted and the matter is closed. Application of Shariah law does not necessarily mean harsh draconian punishment. One can see in these examples that application of Shariah law may actually help to reduce the pain and suffering in a society.

Even in most Muslim countries, Shariah law is not the primary legal system. For example, in Pakistan, an Islamic republic, the legal system is based on Constitution of Pakistan. It does contain some elements of Shariah, but only those elements that are acceptable from the public policy point of view. For example, no stoning, lashing and amputations are carried out in Pakistan. Criminal cases are heard in civil courts. For adultery, for example, one may be sent to jail, but no one is flogged. There are also Shariah courts in the country, where cases of religious nature are heard, but verdicts of the Shariah courts can be appealed to the Shariah bench of the Supreme Court of Pakistan, which has the authority to overrule the Shariah court decisions.

Unfortunately, there are some anti-Muslim elements in the

United States who are determined to find fault with anything Islamic, and spread hate and fear of Islam and Muslims among uninformed citizens. Introduction of bills to ban courts from considering foreign law, especially Islamic law, is an attempt to spread fear of Islam in this country.

If passed, such bills would result in government-sanctioned discrimination against a minority faith. The bills target all religions, and if passed would violate constitutional rights to create private contracts and will deny people the use of Jewish law, Catholic Law, or any other religious law, while also jeopardizing international business contracts that include forms of arbitration, choice of law clauses, or foreign law clauses. Some states have already rejected this type of legislation as unnecessary, harmful to the business community, and unconstitutional.

In an article published in the September 3, 2011 issue of the New York Times, Professor Eliyahu Stern has said that this crusade against Shariah is wrong; because it undermines American democracy, ignores its successful history of religious tolerance and assimilation, creates a dangerous divide between America and its fastest-growing religious minority, and fosters a hostile environment that will hinder the growth of progressive and tolerant strand of Islam in America.

Professor Stern writes that the claim that Shariah threatens American security is reminiscent of the accusation, in 19th century Europe, that Jewish law was seditious. He gave an example that in 1807, Napoleon convened an assembly of rabbinic authorities to address the question of whether Jewish law prevented Jews from being loyal citizens of the republic. Their conclusion was that it did not.

Presently, there seems to be an effort underway by some to scrutinize the Shariah law and then to make that scrutiny a basis to accuse Muslim Americans of disloyalty.

ISLAMOPHOBIA AND HOSTILITY TO MOSQUE BUILDING

For the past several months, a disturbing rise has been seen in Islamophobia. Islamophobia is defined as the dread or hatred of Islam and to fear or dislike all Muslims. It manifests in expressions of suspicion, hostility, and hateful rhetoric against Islam and Muslims, and in discrimination against them by excluding them from economic, social and public life of the country.

It also appears in discrimination against Muslims trying to legally build or expand their mosques across the United States. Muslims see it as a pattern of intolerance that has existed for the last few years, but has deepened in since 9/11.

Hate speech against Islam and the Muslims has started to appear with greater frequency and more toxicity, and it seems to have become an accepted form of racism against Muslims. What was once politically incorrect has become acceptable. A former American Speaker of the House even equated Islam with Nazism. But he forgot to mention the religious affiliation of the Nazis—they were not Muslims.

A more recent challenge for the American Muslims is in the debate surrounding a Muslim proposal to build a community center called Cordoba House. Imam Feisal Abdul Rauf and his wife Daisy Khan, American Muslims well known for promoting interfaith dialogue, conceived this project. The project proposes to build an Islamic community center at Park 51 near Ground Zero in Manhattan, New York City. The plan has been approved by the city authorities and has been backed by Mayor Michael Bloomberg and several members of the Jewish and Christian communities, especially the clergy. However, it has run into severe resistance.

Right wing politicians, political commentators, hard-line Christian ministers, and some families of the 9/11 victims consider the area at and around Ground Zero to be 'sacred ground' and object that an Islamic cultural center would be an insult to the 2606 people who were killed on 9/11. They have declared their opposition to the proposed project, claiming that it would be a 'memorial to terrorists' and insensitive to the memories of those who died at this site.

The backers of the plan tell a different story. They argue that the dead included many Muslims, and that Muslims respect the sanctity of Ground Zero. They also argue that the site of the proposed center is neither at Ground Zero nor is the proposed building a mosque. The proposed building site, Park 51, is located more than two blocks away from Ground Zero, and is designed to be a 15 story non-sectarian cultural and interfaith spiritual center along with a Muslim prayer area and a monument to all those who lost their lives on 9/11. It is designed to house offices, meeting rooms, a performing arts center, a gymnasium, a swimming pool, and a prayer room.

They also point out that there are strip clubs and liquor stores near Ground Zero, which should be more of a concern to the sanctity of Ground Zero. Their project, which is not just a mosque but a cultural center, is designed to promote interfaith dialogue and goodwill amongst Muslims, Christians, Jews, people of other faiths, as well as non-believers. It is not meant to insult anyone; rather, it is to be built as a protest against the radical terrorists who committed the atrocities of 9/11. Imam Faisal Abdul Rauf said the Cordoba House would help rebuild lower Manhattan and send a message of peace.

Pastor Welton Gaddy, Leader of the Interfaith Alliance, had the following to say about Imam Faisal Abdul Rauf: "A great irony disturbs me. For years, public discourse has called for a great moderate Muslim voice to counter extremism. Now, when such a voice is seeking to be heard in meaningful and helpful ways, it faces severe backlash and strong opposition—indicating a continued fear and ignorance of the Muslim faith, even at its most peaceful."

Michael Bloomberg, Mayor of New York, has supported the project, and said: "I happen to think this is a very appropriate place for somebody who wants to build a mosque, because it tells the world that America, and New York City, which is what I'm responsible for, really believe in what we preach."

Cordoba House is not the only Muslim-initiated project that is victim of opposition. Efforts to construct mosques, such as those in Sheepshead Bay, Staten Island; Murfreesboro, Tennessee; Bridgewater, New Jersey, and elsewhere in United States have also run into resistance. There is no denying that there is an increased anti-Islam and anti-Muslim sentiment (Islamophobia) in the United States; opposition to mosque construction, hate crimes, and discrimination against Muslims are only a few of its manifestations.

The term Islamophobia was officially accepted in January 2001 at the 'Stockholm International Forum on Combating Intolerance,' and recognized as a form of intolerance alongside xenophobia and anti-Semitism.

The intolerance of Islam by Islamophobes is evident from the ridiculous accusations that are heaped on Islam and Muslims. As listed by Bobby Ghosh[97] in Times magazine (August 30, 2010 issue), some of these accusations say Islam is a religion of hate, that Muslims are out to wipe out Christianity, Muslims murder their children, and Christian children have enough problems with drugs, alcohol, and pornography and should not have to worry about Islam too. Of course, all of these are false allegations.

Some who have expressed their opposition to Muslims and their mosques allege that American Muslims do not condemn terrorism. This allegation also holds no merit. In fact, many Muslim leaders and organizations have consistently denounced acts of terrorism in the name of their religion (see Chapter 25). The Western media have not found them newsworthy.

Since Muslims are a minority in America, and tend to be much more diffusely scattered, their places of worship are often the most visible targets. When Muslims decide to build formal mosques, they become more exposed and vulnerable. Over the last few years, several mosque projects have faced bitter opposition.

There is so much fear of building mosques that at the Township Planning Meetings, anti-Islam groups bring Islam haters in large numbers to show opposition to building mosques. Even residents who are ordinarily friendly with Muslims turn their backs on them and show scorn and hostility at the hearings. In some cases, the religious leaders have added to the hatred by making statements that the political objective of Islam is to dominate the world with its teachings.

Hateful reaction from opponents has been shown to Muslims seeking local government approval to build mosques in Tennessee, Wisconsin, California, and other states. In California, the opponents brought dogs and picket signs to the Friday prayer at a mosque.

In reaction to this hate mongering, a national coalition of individuals and organizations from different faith traditions, called Interfaith Coalition on Mosques (ICOM), has come together under the sponsorship of Anti-Defamation League (ADL) to fight for the rights of Muslims when they are violated. Announcing this on the ADL website on March 3, 2011, ICOM also stated that the best way to uphold America's democratic values is to ensure that Muslims have the same religious freedom enjoyed by other Americans.

ICOM also stated that they are extremely concerned about discrimination against mosque building in America. The purpose of their organization is to assist Muslim communities who are denied permission to build mosques in their neighborhoods. They promise to monitor incidents of mosque discrimination throughout the country, and raise their voices if they see prejudice.

Charter Members of ICOM include Ambassador Akbar Ahmed; Dr. Saud Anwar, Rabbi Elliort Cosgrove, Abraham Foxman, Rev. Dr. C. Welton Gaddy, Rabbi Yilz Greenberg, Rev. Dr. Katherine Henderson, Dr. Joel C. Hunter, Bishop Paul Peter Jesep, Msgr. Guy A. Massie, Dr. Eboo Patel, and Father Robert Robbins.

Another manifestation of Islamophobia appeared in March 2011 when Rep. Peter King (R-NY), Chairman, House Sub-Committee on Homeland Security, started hearing on alleged "radicalization in the American Muslim community." This hearing is based on the assumption that most American Muslims are radicalized. It has been widely condemned by members of Congress and interfaith and civil liberties groups.

This atmosphere of increased Islamophobia risks making American Muslims feel increasingly marginalized and insecure. One of the dangers of Islamophobia is that it will discourage Muslims from assimilation into the society at large. Americans need to be just and fair towards minorities, especially Muslims who already feel threatened and excluded.

It is likely that Islamophobia and hostility towards Muslims is a result of ignorance about the faith of Islam and its followers. Islam is a religion of peace and harmony, and there is no need for non-Muslims to have suspicion of Islam and the Muslims or to hate them. Non-Muslims need to participate in Interfaith dialogue programs with Muslims in order to learn about who the Muslims are and what Islam teaches. They will find that Muslims are peaceful people, and may be surprised to find that some of their neighbors including doctors, teachers, and businessmen are Muslims and live as peaceful citizens just like themselves.

Non-Muslims should also visit mosques to see how Muslims worship. They will see that mosques are very simple buildings without any decorations or idols. Muslims worship the One and Only God (in Arabic called Allah). He is the same God that Jews call Yahweh and Christians call Our Father in the Heaven. Muslims do not worship Muhammad, who was a man and the last Messenger of God to mankind. Muslims may explain to them that the worship service is basically glorification and praise of God and asking Him for His guidance to fulfill His Will.

There are several reasons for Islamophobia. One reason is the string of terrorism-related incidents involving American Muslims, like the accused Fort Hood shooter Major Nidal Hasan and the would-be Time Square bomber Faisal Shahzad. These incidents increased negative attitude of American public against Muslims. It should be remembered that several would-be incidents of terrorism were prevented because of Muslim cooperation with law enforcement agencies. A second reason is the rapidly increasing Muslim population in the West, especially in Western Europe.

The third reason for perpetuation of Islamophobia is Western media. In the Encyclopedia of Race and Ethnic Studies, Elizabeth Poole cites articles in the British press from between 1994 and 2004, in which Muslim viewpoints were underrepresented and issues involving Muslims usually depicted in a negative light. Such portrayals included the depiction of Islam and Muslims as a threat to Western security and values. Expressions used in the media such as "Islamic terrorism," "Islamic bomb," and "violent Islam" have resulted in a negative perception of Islam.

The fourth reason is the shadow of suspicion cast over all Muslims in the West, especially those who are travelling. For example, many Muslim travelers are subjected to special screening by security agencies at the airports giving the public an impression that Muslims are inherently threatening.

Another important reason for Islamophobia is the lack of education in the West about Islam and the Muslims. According to August 19–22, 2010 Pew Survey Report, 55% of Americans said they know some or very little about Islam and its practices, and 25% said they know nothing at all about them. Only about 9% knew a great deal about Islam, and only 37% Americans know a Muslim American. Lack of knowledge about Islam and Muslims can certainly be a reason to fear Muslims.

Once people get to know one another they find out that overwhelming majority of Muslims are peace-loving citizens who cherish the same values non-Muslims do. Muslims love God and their neighbor, they value life and liberty no less than Jews, Christians, and other non-Muslim Americans do. Once this is realized, the barriers start to break. It is very important for Muslim and non-Muslim Americans to participate in open-minded interfaith dialogue programs.

The author of this book is active in interfaith dialogue programs, and has come to know from his experience that many Jews and Christians have never met a Muslim. Once they meet them, they learn that Muslims, like other Americans, strive to work hard, raise their families in peace, and make sure their children have good educations and prosperous future.

During the present hard times, Muslims of America have received support from fellow Americans, especially the leaders and clergy of several Jewish groups and Christian denominations, Japanese Americans, and others; they gratefully appreciate this support.

President Barak Obama has said Muslims have the right to practice their religion and build the Islamic Center in Lower Manhattan. However, later he said he was not endorsing the specifics of the (building) plan. Commenting on Mr. Obama's backing off, Dick Cavett[98] said in his article under Opinionator in the August 20, 2010 issue of the New York Times, that "he was dismayed to see Mr. Obama shed a few vertebrae the next day and step back."

Secretary of State Hillary Rodham Clinton, in a statement made on April 12, 2011 at the annual U.S.-Islamic World Forum in Washington, D.C. acknowledged the contribution of American Muslims. She said: "I am proud that this year we are recognizing the contributions of the millions of American Muslims who do so much to make this country strong. As President Obama said in Cairo. 'Islam has always been a part of America's history,' and every day American Muslims are helping write our story."

New York Mayor Michael Bloomberg was in strong defense of building a community center and mosque near Ground Zero (at Park 51). He delivered an impassioned speech on Tuesday, August 24, 2010 at the dinner in observance of Iftar, the breaking of the daily fast during Ramadan. He said that not allowing a proposed mosque to be built near ground Zero would be "compromising our commitment to fighting terror with freedom, and we would undercut the values and principles that so many heroes died protecting." He also said that the compromise to find another location for the mosque won't end the debate (Christian Salazar,[99] Associated Press, Yahoo News, Aug 25, 2010).

Several members of Jewish and Christian clergy have expressed their solidarity with American Muslims. Only a few examples can be cited here. Rev. David A. Davis of Nassau Presbyterian Church, Rabbi Adam Feldman of Jewish Center of Princeton, and Rev. Jana Parkis-Brash of Princeton United Methodist Church wrote a letter to the editor of The Princeton Packet, Princeton, New Jersey (September 3, 2010 issue) in which they said that as elected leaders of the clergy association, they wanted to express their support of their Muslim neighbors.

They states that they believe in religious freedom and equality for all under the law in our nation and give thanks for the

Muslim tradition that falls in the lineage of Abraham. They sought to send a clear message of welcome and inclusion that counters the hateful and divisive actions and beliefs of some who have been given way too much attention in the media. They pledged to stand in solidarity with the Muslim community and to actively counter any disrespect, discrimination or vandalism of worship space, business, schools, or homes.

Leaders of the Franciscans of Holy Name Province have also raised their voices against this tide of anti-Muslim rhetoric in the country. Rev. Dominic Monti, OFM and Rev. John O'Conner, OFM have encouraged Catholics to think and pray about their relationships with Muslims. In an article published on St. Bonaventure University website on September 8, 2010 titled: "September 11th anniversary prompts Franciscans to encourage respect," the Franciscan friars have stated that in the 19th century, there was a similar outcry against Roman Catholics.

They were considered a foreign inassimilable mass within the nation, and their religious practices and values were considered contrary to American way of life. Those were later proven wrong. The priests urged that Muslims Americans must be given the same opportunity as anybody else, and that they be accepted as fellow-worshipers of our common God.

The writers also stated that The Second Vatican Council's dogmatic constitution on Church, Lumen Gentium, after mentioning Christians and Jews, goes on to state "God's plan of salvation also includes those who acknowledge the Creator, first among whom are the Muslims: they profess to hold the faith of Abraham, and together with us they adore the one merciful God, who will judge all human beings on the last day." Rev. Monti and Rev. O'Conner explained that the Church teaches that Muslims are not "pagans" or "idolaters" but children of the same loving God as Christians and Jews.

They demanded that religious groups must be allowed to

honor the Supreme God in public worship, and they must be allowed to promote institutions in which their communities may organize their own lives. They declared that the religious communities' right to purchase land and build their houses of worship must not be hindered by legislations and administrative authorities. They added that this could have implications for how Catholic Americans should accept Muslims in the society. They also added that a fanatical minority must not be allowed to define an entire religion.

The Franciscan priests recounted the story of Saint Francis visiting the Sultan of Egypt to deliver a message of peace at a time when crusaders were attacking Muslim lands. At the time, some preachers were urging Christians "to kill a Muslim for Christ." They state that St. Francis boldly defied the prejudices of his era to demonstrate to the Sultan of Egypt that Christianity had another face than that of the Crusaders who faced him in battle, and although he was not able to convert the Sultan to Christianity, he returned to Europe impressed by the strong faith of the Muslims he met. It convinced him that he had met other worshipers of God like himself.

As the Muslim community is singled out for particular scrutiny, it is receiving support from American Catholics. Most Rev. Wilton D. Gregory, Archbishop of Atlanta, and Chairman, Committee for Ecumenical and Interreligious Affairs of the United States Council of Bishops wrote a letter of support on March 9, 2011 to Dr. Zahid Bukhari, President, Islamic Circle of North America (ICNA) in which he expressed his support to Members of ICNA.

He pointed out that American Catholics were subjected to similar prejudice in this country when Catholics began to arrive in large numbers in the late 19th and early 20th centuries. On behalf of American Catholics, he expressed solidarity with American Muslims.

In an article written in the March 8, 2011 issue of National

Catholic Reporter, and titled: *"Why Catholics must speak out against Islamophobia,"* Jeanne Clark[100] wrote:

"My Congressman, Rep. Peter King (R-NY), continues his shameful tradition by sponsoring hearings on Capital Hill this week that will demonize Muslim Americans, undermine interfaith dialogue and distract us from practical efforts to confront violent extremism. As a Catholic sister from Long Island, I stand with a broad spectrum of faith leaders who believe that fighting terrorism must never mean compromising our nation's core values and highest ideals.

Catholics, whose ancestors here battled vile stereotypes and even charges of disloyalty, should especially denounce King's sweeping investigation of "radicalization" in the American Muslim community.

Today, a toxic climate of Islamophobia stigmatizes Muslims. Many women of Long Island who wear hijab (head covering) are afraid to go to the grocery store alone. Muslim children in a local school are shunned by students. Across the country, hate crimes against Muslims are on the rise and many communities have opposed mosques.

This prejudice diminishes us all and undermines our nation's commitment to equality and religious pluralism. In my experience relating to and working with Muslims on Long Island, I'm inspired by my neighbors' commitment to worship in peace and teach their children to love America. I have seen their dedication to serve others, especially those with few resources, and a desire to work in solidarity with Christians and Jews for nonviolent solutions to conflicts.

Muslims are doctors and teachers, police officers and business owners. They are a part of American family and should be treated with dignity.

As King convenes his misguided hearings this week, Pax Christi Long Island is preparing to present out 2011 Pax Christi Award to Habeeb U. Ahmed—the board chairman of the Islamic Center of Long Island and a member of the Nassau County Human Rights Commission—and his wife Seemi Ahmad, the New York State co-chair of the Muslim Peace Coalition.

These inspiring leaders give back to their community and serve the common good. At this time of division and fear, we hope this honor will serve as a reminder that our nation is stronger when we unite behind shared values in a spirit of respect and cooperation.

Despite false perceptions shaped by stereotypes, Muslim American leaders have consistently denounced terrorism and worked with law enforcement groups to prevent violence. In recent months, Muslims foiled attempted bombings in Times Square and a Portland, OR Building. Maintaining trust with the Muslim community is crucial to furthering this cooperation.

King should choose a more constructive approach to strengthening the bonds of trust that bolster our security and protect our values by convening a dialogue between faith leaders, law enforcement, and elected officials.

Over 80 religious leaders, social justice advocates and people of faith on Long Island sent the congressman a letter urging him to cancel these misguided hearings. Many of us recently gathered in prayerful protest in front of his office.

Although Congressman King has insisted that his hearings will focus on Islamic extremism, his own rhetoric suggests that he will cast a cloud of suspicion over the entire Muslim community. He told a radio host that radicals lead 80 percent of mosques and once described Muslims as "an enemy living amongst us."

Leaders across the political spectrum agree that we must work together to prevent terrorist attacks. My opposition to King's hearing isn't motivated by "political correctness" or a naïve belief that evil does not exist in the world. Rather, we need a different approach because I fear these hearings will undermine practical approaches to confronting violent extremism in all its forms and threaten our most inspiring ideals as a nation."

On March 29, 2011 Senate Majority Whip, Senator Dick Durbin (D-Ill), Chairman, Senate Judiciary Committee of the United States Senate, Sub-Committee on Constitution, Civil Rights and Human Rights, held a hearing on "Protecting the Civil Rights of American Muslims." One of the witnesses at this hearing was Cardinal Theodore McCarrick, Archbishop Emeritus of Washington. His testimony was termed as a landmark rebuke of bigotry in American politics from the highest levels of the Catholic Church.

Cardinal McCarrick stated that as a community that has been the target of religious discrimination, Catholics understand the need to bring attention to protecting the civil rights of American Muslims. He said a justified concern for security and appropriate pursuit of those who pervert religion to attack others cannot be allowed to turn into a new form of religious discrimination and intolerance.

For this reason, Cardinal McCarrick said, Catholics stand with "their Muslim brothers and sisters" in defense of their dignity and rights. Religious freedom is destroyed by attacks on people, and it is a terrible misuse of religion to incite hatred and justify violence. Attacking people of differing religious beliefs can sometimes be used to promote fear and suspicion of all people associated with that particular faith.

Cardinal McCarrick urged that in an atmosphere in which other countries wrestle with how to treat religious minorities, we should let them look to America, where we strive to ensure that our religious minorities are treated with dignity and their religious identity and beliefs are treated with respect. Let them see a people blessed with hard won religious freedom living out our commitment to the rights of all by demonstrating full respect for the identity, integrity and freedom of all religions.

Another group who has raised their voices in support of American Muslims are the Religious Society of Friends (Quakers). In a letter to editor of OakLeaves (Member of Sun-Times Media) on March 3, 2011, Wil Rutt[101] stated that as fears about Islam grow in the United States, Religious Society of Friends (Quakers) welcome Muslims and voice their support for them within their community and nation.

He called for people to work together to stem the tide of fear and the threat of persecution and violence. The Quakers also called for an end to political posturing and misstatements that poison dialogue, create divisions in the society, and promote an anti-Islam image of America.

He added that in the 1600s, Quakers were also feared, and the practice of their faith was unlawful. Their religious freedom was also threatened and they had to struggle for acceptance. He stated that freedom of religious is a cornerstone of American democracy, and we all have an opportunity to make this ideal a reality in our communities.

In a statement issued on August 16, 2010, LA Jews for Peace organization has supported the Cordoba Initiative, i.e., building of the community center at Park 51. The statement said "this initiative is dedicated to bridging gaps between Muslims and the West. It referred to President Obama's statement in which he said that as a citizen and a President he believed that Muslims have the same right to practice their religion as the other Americans, and it includes the right to build a place of worship and a community center on private property in Lower Manhattan, in accordance with local laws and ordinances. He said this is America, and our commitment to religious freedom must be unshakeable."

Rabbi Bruce Warshal[102] wrote an article titled "*Shame on*

America, Jews and the ADL" published in the September 1, 2010 issue of Florida Jewish Journal. In the article, he said that the community center planned for building at Park 51 site is not designed to be a mosque, but a 13-story community center with a swimming pool, 500-seat performing arts center, a gymnasium, a restaurant, and a prayer room for Muslims, which already exists in the current building.

He said that originally the proposed building was to be named Cordoba House, to send out a message that Islam was a religion of peace and tolerance. It is more tolerant of Jews, Christians and other people than any other faith. It took this name from the city of Cordoba in medieval Spain under Muslim rule, where people of all religions lived together and respected one another. The Muslim ruler, Caliph Abd al-Rahman III, had a Jew as his foreign minister and a Greek bishop in his diplomatic corps. However, the opponents of the project started criticizing, and the name was changed to the address of the building Park 51.

Rabbi Warshal calls the present state of Islamophobia a perfect storm of hate against Islam, with right-wing Christians and right-wing Jews demonizing Muslims, and political leaders trying to take advantage of the situation. He said the outpouring of hate against Muslims is based on the concept of collective guilt, which means if one individual commits a crime, the blame goes to the entire community he belongs to. He cautioned Jews against falling victim to the concept of collective guilt and against demonizing entire communities for the sins of a few.

The LA Jews for Peace statement also pointed out that the fact that the Park 51 site is located two blocks from the World Trade Center is of lesser importance than maintaining the guarantee of the U.S. Constitution, specifically the First Amendment to "the free exercise" of religion.

In another statement issued on September 20, 2010, LA Jews for Peace condemned the smear campaign and hateful and divisive statements by the right wing bigots against Muslims and the Council on American Islamic Relations (CAIR). It said this ongoing national campaign is manifested in attacks on the rights of Muslims to build mosques, attempts to burn copies of the Qur'an, and the hate mongering in the media and by many politicians.

It said the activities of the Republican Jewish Committee (RJC), and other right-wing, pro-Israel groups, defame the peaceful, moderate Muslim-American community, and undermine its political activities. If these activities are allowed to continue, they will marginalize Muslim-Americans by discouraging and intimidating politicians from working with that American community.

In an article titled: "*Nascent effort to combat anti-Islam sentiment running into strong headwind*," published in The Jewish Week on September 16, 2010, James Besser[103] has stated that many major Jewish groups have supported the right of Imam Feisal Abdul Rauf to build the cultural center two blocks from the WTC site. Groups such as the Reform movement, the National Council of Jewish Women, and the Jewish Council for Public Affairs (JCPA) have been at the forefront of the nascent effort to combat the anti-Islam eruption. The reaction in Jewish communal circles against the proposed threat to burn the Qur'an by an obscure Florida pastor ranged from the negative to the appalled.

Besser quoted Rabbi Steve Gutow, president of the JCPA, who said: "Suggestions that Islam is somehow outside America's traditional protection of religious freedom represents a big shift, and it may ultimately endanger Jews and other religious minorities. We should be outraged by what is happening in America because some of our most fundamental tenets are being challenged."

Another Jewish leader, Rabbi Haim Dov Beliak, founder and director of JewsOnFirst.Com, a web-based First Amendment group, has commented: "Jews were accused of killing Christ for 2000 years; now some of us are supporting those who say all Muslims are responsible for September 11."

Rabbi David Saperstein has also spoken out against anti-Muslim discrimination. Similarly, Nathan Diament, Washington director for Orthodox Union, has expressed outrage at the notion of burning Qur'an. He said the notion of burning holy text (Qur'an) should not only offend, but send chills down the spine of anybody, especially the Jewish community, which has seen its own holy texts burned over the centuries. He said there is no place for such a thing in the United States.

On September 15, 2010, Rabbi Arthur Waskow of the Shalom Center posted his comments on James Besser's article. He said the Shalom Center held the first public support vigil for and at Park 51. They also initiated a strong Jewish statement, signed by hundreds of rabbis and other Jews, in which they supported the creation of a Muslim-based cultural center, and rebuked the anti-Defamation League for its opposition to the center.

Rabbi Waskow said his own feelings on this issue went back deep into his childhood, when he was seven years old. His grandmother interrupted other Jewish women who were talking contemptuously about the African Americans. She reminded them: "That's the way they talked about us in Europe. This is America, and we must not talk like that."

On September 7, 2010 an interfaith summit was organized by the Islamic Society of North America (ISNA) in Washington, D.C. Members in attendance held a press conference, issuing a joint statement to the public regarding unified action for faith communities to promote tolerance and combat anti-Muslim rhetoric, hate crimes, and Islamophobia.

The press conference included statements from Jewish, Christian, and Muslim members to discuss the critical need for members of all faiths to protect the safety and civil rights of Muslims.

A member of the interfaith summit stated: "Hate is neither a religion nor a democratic value."

The statement said that the religious leaders had come together to denounce categorically the derision, misinformation and outright bigotry directed against America's Muslims community. The religious leaders have a sacred responsibility to honor America's faith traditions and to promote mutual respect and assurance of religious freedom for all. They announced a new era of interfaith cooperation.

The statement said Jews, Christians, and Muslims are grateful to be living in this democracy whose constitution guarantees religious freedom for all. These freedoms include freedom to worship in congregations of our own choosing and to maintain institutions that carry out our respective missions. These are the freedoms that must be guarded and defended, otherwise they face peril.

The United States of America has been a world leader in defending the rights of religious minorities, yet at times in its history, particular groups have been singled out for unjust discrimination by those who have either misconstrued or intentionally distorted the vision of our founders.

The statement said that it is alarming to see an anti-Muslim frenzy in recent weeks that has been generated over the plans to build an Islamic community center and mosque at the Park 51 site. The religious leaders attending the summit recognized that the grounds around the former World Trade Center, where 2,606 innocent people were killed on 9/11, remains an open wound in our country. However, their concern was to respond to the atmosphere of fear and contempt for fellow Americans of the Muslim faith that the controversy has generated.

The leaders attending the summit also expressed their profound distress and deep sadness at the incidents of violence committed against Muslims, and at the desecration of Islamic houses of worship. They pledged to stand by the principle that to attack any religion in the United States is to do violence to the religious freedom of all Americans.

The burning of the Holy Qur'an was an offense that demanded condemnation in the strongest possible terms by all who value civility. Religious leaders said they were appalled by such disrespect for a sacred text that for centuries has shaped many of the great cultures of the world, and that continues to guide the lives of more than a billion Muslims today.

The religious leadership emphasized the need to build a future in which religious differences would no longer lead to hostility or division between communities. Rather, such diversity could serve to enrich public discourse about the great moral challenges that America faced. The leaders demanded that no religion should be judged on the words or actions of those who seek to pervert it through acts of violence, and that politicians and members of the media must not exploit religious differences as a wedge to advance political agendas or ideologies.

They also stated that bearing false witness against the neighbor—something condemned by all three of our religious traditions—is inflicting particular harm on the followers of Islam, a world religion that has lately been mischaracterized by some as a "cult."

The Jewish, Christian and Muslim religious leaders called for renewed commitment to mutual learning among religions. They emphasized that leaders of local congregations have a responsibility to teach with accuracy, fairness and respect about other faith traditions.

They appreciated that the partnerships that had developed in recent years between synagogues and churches, mosques and synagogues, and churches and mosques should provide a foundation for new forms of collaboration in interfaith education, inter-congregational visitations, and service programs that redress social ills like homelessness and drug abuse.

The leaders stated that what can be accomplished together is far more than what can be achieved working in isolation from one another. The achievements from collaboration between religious congregations and national agencies will help to heal our culture, which continues to suffer from the open wound of 9/11.

They emphasized that Jews, Christians and Muslims should work together based on deeply held and widely shared values, each supported by the sacred texts of their respective traditions. They acknowledge with gratitude the dialogues between their scholars and religious authorities that have helped them to identify a common understanding of the divine command to love one's neighbor. Judaism, Christianity, and Islam all see an intimate link between faithfulness to God and love of neighbor; a neighbor who in many instances, is the stranger in our midst.

The statement released to the press by leaders of the three Abrahamic faiths said that the spiritual leaders representing the various faiths in the United States have a moral responsibility to stand together and to denounce categorically derision, misinformation, or outright bigotry directed against any religious group in this country. Silence is not an option. Only by taking this stand, can spiritual leaders fulfill the highest calling of their respective faiths, and thereby help to create a safer and stronger America for all of the people.

This summit was attended by leaders of the Greek Orthodox Archdiocese of America, the Armenian Church in America, Progressive National Baptist Convention, National Association of Evangelicals, New Evangelical Partnership for the Common Good, Providence Missionary Baptist Church, Islamic Society of North America, Anti- Defamation League, Reconstructionist Rabbinical College, Interfaith Alliance, Jewish Council for Public Affairs, Religions for Peace, Council of Bishops of the United Methodist Church, National Religious Campaign Against Torture, National Council of Churches (NCC), Orthodox Church in

America, The Interfaith Conference of the Metropolitan Washington, United States Conference of Catholic Bishops (USCCB), Archdiocese of Washington, Evangelical Lutheran Church in America (ELCA), American Baptist Churches, Rabbinical Assembly, Episcopal Diocese of New York, Muslim-Jewish Relations Program Office of Foundation of Ethnic Understanding, The Union for Reform Judaism (URJ), Center for American Progress, Religions for Peace, United Methodist Church, and Arab American Institute.

Japanese Americans have also voiced their support for American Muslims. In an article published in the March 8, 2011 issue of Washington Post under the title: "Japanese Americans: House hearing on radical Islam sinister." David Nakamura[104] stated that as House Homeland Security Committee Chairman Peter King (R-NY) prepared to launch a series of controversial hearings on Radical Islam in the United States, the bonds between Muslim Americans and Japanese Americans became stronger.

This is spurred by memories of the internment of 110,000 Japanese Americans during World War II. For this reason, they have been the most vocal supporters of Muslim Americans. Japanese Americans have shown their support by rallying against hate crimes at mosques, opposing the government's indefinite detention of Muslims, organizing cross-cultural trips to the Manzanar internment camp memorial, holding seminars on race, religion and ethnicity, and by holding "Bridging Communities" workshops at Islamic schools and colleges.

Japanese American Congressman Rep Michael Honda (D-Calif) has also denounced King's hearing as "something similarly sinister," comparing it to wartime roundup of the Japanese, and anti-Communist hearings staged by Sen. Joseph McCarthy. In 1988, Congress apologized to the Japanese Americans and blamed the roundup on race prejudice, war hysteria, and a failure of political leadership.

In an article titled *"On the 10th Anniversary of Sept. JA, Muslim American Friendship Grows*, published in the September 2, 2011 issue of Pacific Citizen—News and Information for the Asian American Community, Christine McFadden wrote that JACL (Japanese American Citizens League) was the first national organization in the country to come to publicly offer support to the Muslim and Arab Americans in the midst of the emotions of the 9/11 terrorist attacks.

Their representative issued a press release to every major news outlet in the country urging the nation not to scapegoat Arab and Muslim communities, and contacted government authorities to remind them of the victimization of Japanese Americans after Pearl Harbor. From that initial support began a relationship between the two communities that has been growing ever since.

Several joint programs have been initiated to foster close relationship between the two communities. For example, one of the programs is named 'Bridging Communities." It brings together high school students from Japanese American and Muslim American communities to further expand their relationship.

Their bond has brought with it positive results in protecting civil rights and educating the public to ensure that Arab and Muslim Americans do not suffer the same mass incarceration that Japanese Americans endured during World War II.

Writing in the Op-Ed section of August 21, 2010 issue of the New York Times, Nicholas Kristof[105] wrote an article under the title of "Taking Bin Laden's Side." In it, he said that opposition to the building of Park 51 community center and mosque would play right into the hands of (the followers of) Osama Bin Laden, Anwar al-Awlaki and other extremists who share with many American Republicans the view that the West and the Islamic world are caught in a "clash of the civilizations." They could use this opposition to the community center as a slogan and try to recruit more terrorists.

Another Christian leader who came to defend the Muslims against Islamophobia is Reverend Deborah C. Lindsay. In her Sunday August 29, 2010 sermon, which was also broadcasted on www.youtube.com/user/dekhosuno, she talked about the wave of Islamophobia in United States, and recommended to her audience to remember the following things:

1. All scriptures have some stories which may appear to teach violence, so one should not just single out one scripture or the other. The predominant message of the Qur'an and the Bible is about peace, justice, love of God, and love of the fellow human being. There are similarities in the messages of the scriptures: The Bible teaches "Thou shalt not kill;" the Qur'an teaches: "Whoever kills another without a justifiable cause, surely he kills the entire mankind, and whoever saves another one, surely he saves the entire mankind." These are words of peace and faith that could save the world.

2. If someone sends you an email demonizing Muslims or followers of any other faith, don't forward it to anyone else, delete it. Don't give in to your fears.

3. Don't focus on a tiny minority of extremists who commit acts of violence, focus on overwhelming majority of peace-loving Muslims who are working hard for their families, like you are.

4. When you think of a Muslim, think of a doctor who may treat you when you go to a hospital emergency room, an engineer who works in Honda Company, or a Muslim professor at your local university who teaches your child. When you think of those who died on 9/11, don't forget

to think about the Muslims who also died in that tragedy, not the hijackers but the people and families for whom the attacks were a personal tragedy.

5. Try to remember Mohammed Salman Hamdani, a Pakistani American, who played high school football, attended college, and drove an ambulance. He was 23 years old when he died at Ground Zero. At a House Homeland Security Committee hearing on 'radicalization of Islam in America,' Congressman Ellison, who spoke as a witness, tearfully described the sacrifice of Mohammed Salman Hamdani, a volunteer medical technician who died trying to help rescue victims in the World Trade Center on Sept. 11, 2001 — pointing out that Mr. Hamdani was wrongly suspected of being part of the plot until his remains were discovered.

6. Remember Mohammad Salahuddin Qadri, a waiter in a restaurant in the World Trade center. He died in that tragedy and two days later his wife gave birth to their first child. Also, remember Tariq Amanullah, who was an active member of the Islamic Circle of North America (ICNA) and worked in the World Trade Center on September 11. And also remember Rahma Salie, a 28 year old young Muslim woman who died as a passenger on American Airlines Flight 11. She was 7 month pregnant.

Reverend Deborah Lindsay has also suggested that people of all faith traditions should commit to talk to each other instead of talking about each other. A survey of public opinion conducted by Genesis Research and commissioned by CAIR in August 2004 indicated that personal relationships between Muslims and non-Muslims is a major factor in shaping positive public attitudes about Islam. Those non-Muslim Americans who knew or had a relationship with any Muslims, had more favorable opinion when asked if Muslims were friendly and hospitable, had family oriented values, taught and practiced compassion, and cooperated in war on terror.

The non-Muslim reader is advised to know that Islam is a major religion, with the second largest number of followers (about 1.5 billion) in almost all parts of the world. It is one of the three monotheistic Abrahamic faith traditions, and its followers, Muslims, worship One and the Only True God, called Allah in Arabic language. Muslims do not hate non-Muslims of any faith or no faith at all. They believe in love of God and love of the neighbor, and the neighbor includes all humanity.

Islam teaches interfaith harmony, and Muslim history shows that they have reached out to non-Muslims in peace and friendship throughout their history. American Muslims are as patriotic as any other Americans are, and many serve in the United States armed forces. All American Muslims love their country and are actively participating in the American experience. It is important that those who wish to learn more about Islam and the Muslims choose their source of information carefully.

29

WHAT ATTRACTS PEOPLE TO
ISLAM?

IN THE UNITED States, there are an estimated 7 to 8 million Muslims. Islam is commonly known to be the fastest growing religion in America and the world.[3, 106-109] In this chapter we will explore the phenomenon of conversion to Islam, and find out why people are converting to Islam despite Islamophobia and a relentless campaign in the West to discredit Islam.

The Council on American-Islamic Relations estimates that some 20,000 Americans convert to Islam each year, with women outnumbering men approximately four to one. According to Georgetown University professor Yvonne Haddad, coauthor of *Muslim Women in America*, some are inspired by the rules of the Qur'an, which they find empowering. Some are seeking a community that endorses a woman's more traditional role as homemaker. Others are purely on a spiritual quest. "I think Americans should see them as women who have found themselves," says Haddad.[110]

Why are so many people choosing to convert to a religion increasingly associated with terrorism, videotaped beheadings, oppression of women, and dictatorial governments?

The converts give a variety of reasons for embracing Islam. The foremost reason is simplicity of the creed of Islam: "There is no one worthy of worship except God, and Muhammad is His servant and (last) messenger." There are no mysteries and unexplainable dogmas in it. Other reasons include disillusionment of the converts with their previous religions; and reaction to moral degradation of the West and its culture of excessive materialism and consumerism, shameless indulgence and greed, sexual perversion, and addiction to alcohol and drugs. One convert stated that American political leadership was preaching about freedom and democracy, and it was not truthful. He said he was looking for something that is real truth and he found that truth in Islam.

Some converts were attracted to strong family structure and system of social justice in Islam; others were fascinated with Arabic language, words, and recitation of the Qur'an, and the Islamic world. Some converts converted because they underwent unexplainable spiritual experiences.

Britain's former Prime Minister Tony Blair's sister-in-law Lauren Booth converted to Islam because she had an intense feeling during a visit to a mosque in Qom, Iran. The feeling stayed with her even after she had left the mosque. That special (spiritual) feeling was her reason to accept Islam.

One example of a white American male converting to Islam is that of Dr. Lawrence Brown, whose story on conversion to Islam was published in the November/December 2010 (volume 1) Issue 2 of American Muslim Magazine.[111] Dr. Laurence Brown graduated from Cornell University, Brown Medial School, with specialization in ophthalmology. He has served in the United States Air Force for 16 years, with 8 years as a reserve and another 8 years on active duty. Currently, he is the medical director of a major eye center, and specializes in cataract surgery. In addition, he is a writer and has authored several books.

Dr. Brown is the son of Quaker parents, but grew up as an

Atheist. He tried to become Christian but in each sect he found some objections the clergy could not satisfactorily answer. As soon as he learned about Islam, things fell into place and made sense for him. There was one incident in his life that became the reason for him to accept Islam, which is described on his website: www.LevelTruth.com.

His daughter was born with a lethal heart defect, making him realize that he did not have control of his life. He was desperate, but still an Atheist. He prayed the prayer of a skeptic: "Oh, God! If there is a God, save my soul, if I have a soul." He told God that he did not know if He was there or not, but if He was, then he needed help. He asked God to save his daughter, and he promised that if his daughter was saved, he would follow the religion that was most pleasing to God, and to which God led him. A short time thereafter, his daughter's condition miraculously reversed. The doctors tried to explain, but Lawrence Brown knew the real reason. Fulfilling his promise to God, he accepted Islam.

Another convert to Islam, Kevin James is a Supervising Fire Marshal in the Fire Department of New York (FDNY). He converted to Islam because he felt personal kinship with Prophet Muhammad. He was impressed with the universality of Islam and the Qur'an's teaching about obedience to One God. The Qur'an's teaching where it says that 'if you save one life, it is as if you have saved the entire mankind' also impressed him. This particular teaching of the Qur'an was one of his reasons to become a fire fighter with FDNY. It made him think, "what could be more important than saving a life?"

The fast growth of Islam in the West indicates that Islam is truly a religion from God. It is unreasonable to think that so many Americans, Europeans, and people from other countries have converted to Islam without careful consideration and deep contemplation before concluding that Islam is true. The converts have come from different countries, races, and lifestyles. They include scientists, journalists, professors, philosophers, politicians, diplomats, athletes, and religious scholars.

One has to be searching for the 'Truth' to be inclined towards Islam. There has to be an incentive, not for economic or material gain but to know the 'Truth'. The example of Islam is like that of a complete and perfect geometrical pattern, whose every part completes and complements other parts.

Its real beauty lies in the harmony and cohesion of these parts. It is an incomparable guide for everyday life, based on true ethical and moral values and on the principles of justice and real equality. It is not a blind faith. The Qur'an repeatedly implores man to think and reflect. The faith of Islam is based on reason and logic.

Margot Patterson[112] quoted Kevin Jaques, an assistant professor of religious studies at the University of Indiana, who noted that more Latinos and Native Americans are now embracing Islam. What is leading Americans to Islam, according to Professor Jaques, is that as the United States is changing, and churches are failing in their traditional role.

Converts are looking for something that the church isn't giving them, especially for second- and third-generation Latinos, who are looking for a religious tradition that gives them a bigger sense of community. Summing up the reasons for conversion to Islam, Professor Jaques said: "one of the things you hear most in mosques is community, community, community—which is a major attraction for a lot of people."

REFERENCES

1. Huston Smith, Islam: A Concise Introduction, Harper Collins Publishers, Inc., N.Y., 2001.
2. John Kaltner, Islam—What Non-Muslims Should Know, Augsburg Fortress, Box 1209, Minneapolis, MN 5540, 2003.
3. John Esposito, What Everyone Needs to Know About Islam; Oxford University Press. 2002.
4. Council of American Islamic Relations, CAIR calls on mainstream leaders to repudiate evangelist's remarks. CAIR, Washington, D.C. May 2, 2005.
5. Ahmed Shihab-Eldin, Arabs in America: Misrepresented and Misunderstood, Daily Free Press, Boston University, April 26, 2005.
6. Tim Aylsworth, Americans don't understand Islam, The Battalion, Texas A&M, Texas, April 26, 2005.
7. The Council on American-Muslim Relations (CAIR), Report: Anti-Muslim Hate Crimes Jump 52 percent—Total number of Muslim civil rights cases tops 1,500 in 2004, CAIR, Washington, D.C. May 11, 2005.(http://www.cair-net.org/asp/2005CivilRightsReport.pdf)
8. Karen Armstrong, Islam- A Short History. Weidenfeld and Nicolson, U.K., 2000.
9. Douglas, NIV Compact Dictionary of the Bible, p. 42; quoted in www.islam-guide.com/ch3-2.htm
10. Karen Armstrong, A Histroy of God, Ballantine Books, The Random House Publishing Group, Inc., New York, 1993.

11. Susan Olp, Scholar links Islam with healing, Billings Gazette; Billings, Wyoming, May 11, 2005.

12. Ken Camp, Professor's comments on Islam spark controversy in Texas, Associated Baptist Press, May 08, 2007, www.abpnews.com/content/view/2247/120/.

13. Anonymous, Some Evidence for the Truth of Islam, Chapter 1: The Scientific Miracles in the Holy Qur'an, on website http://www.islam-guide.com.

14. Jerry Markon, Burned Korans Found at Va. Islamic Center, Washington Post, Friday, June 17, 2005.

15. Anonymous, Feces-covered Qur'an left at Tennessee housing complex, News release by Council on American-Islamic Relations (CAIR), Washington, D.C. (http//www.cair-net. org), June 23, 2005

16. Reuters, Jailers splashed Koran with urine—Pentagon, Reuters News Service, ABC News Internet Ventures, June 3, 2005.

17. Abdul Hamid Siddiqui, Selection From Hadith, Islamic Book Publishers, P.O.Box 20210, Safat, Kuwait, 1983.

18. Thomas Carlyle, "On Heroes and Hero-Worship, and the Heroic in History"; Lecture II. The Hero as Prophet. Mahomet: Islam. London; 1840. www.gutenberg.org/files/1091/1091.txt

19. Professor K. S. Ramakrishna Rao, Muhammad–The Prophet of Islam, New Crescent Publishing Co., Delhi, India, 17th ed. 1997.

20. Martin Lings, "Muhammad - His Life Based on the Earliest Sources", Islamic Texts Society, London, UK, 1994.

21. Mahatma Gandhi, quoted by K. S. Ramakrishna Rao in Muhammad—The Prophet of Islam, New Crescent Publications Co. Delhi, India, 17th ed. 1997.

22. Huston Smith, The World's Religions, HarperCollins Publishers, New York, NY 1991.

23. Stanley Lane-Poole, "The Speeches and Table Talk of the Prophet Mohammad", quoted in "Islam and Christianity" by U. A. Samad, Begum Aisha Bawany Wakf Publications, Karachi, Pakistan, 1970.

24. Alfonso De LaMartaine, Histoire de la Turquie, Paris, 1854, Vol. II, pp. 276-277.

25. Hurgronje, C. Snouck, quoted by R. K. Ramakrishna Rao, in Muhammad, The Prophet of Islam, New Crescent Publishing Co. New Delhi, 17th ed. 1997.

26. John William Draper, "A History of the Intellectual Development of Europe", London, 1875, Vol 1, pp 329-330.

27. Sir George Bernard Shaw, "The Genuine Islam" Singapore, Vol. 1, No. 8, 1936.

28. Montgomery Watt, Muhammad at Mecca, Clarendon Press, Oxford, 1960.

29. Edward Gibbon and Simon Ockley, History of the Saracen Empires, London, 1870, p. 54.

30. James Michener, Islam: The Misunderstood Religion, Reader's Digest, May 1955.

31. Washington Irving, Mahomet and His Successors. Belford Clarke Publisher, Chicago, 1849.

32. Rev. Bosworth Smith, quoted by Rama Krishna Rao in Muhammad—The Prophet of Islam, New Cresent Publishing Co. Delhi, India. 17th Ed. 1997.

33. Michael Hart, The 100, A Ranking of the Most Influential Persons in the History", Hart Publishing Company, Inc., New York, 1978, p.33.

34. The Holy Bible, Revised Standard Version, Preface, p iv and vii.

35. Bart D. Ehrman, Misquoting Jesus—The Story Behind Who Changed the Bible and Why. Harper Collins Publishers, New York, NY, 2005.

36. Bertrand Russel, History of Western Philosophy, London, 1948, p. 419.

37. A. M. Stoddard, Quoted in Islam, The Religion of all Prophets by U. A. Samad, Begum Bhawani Waqf, Karachi, Pakistan, p. 56

38. Arnold J. Toynbee, Civilization on Trial, New York, 1948, p. 205.

39. H. A. R. Gibb, Whither Islam, London, 1932, p 379.

40. Sarojini Naidu, Ideals of Islam, in Speeches and Writings of Sarojini Naidu, Third ed., G. A. Natsan & Co., Madras (India), 1918, p. 105.

41. Montgomery Watt, Islam and Christianity Today, Londin, 1983, p ix.

42. Edward Montet, La Propagande Chretienne et ses Adversaries Musulmans, Paris, 1890, quoted by T. W. Arnold in The Preaching of Islam, London, 1913, p 413-414.

43. Phillip K. Hitti, 'History of the Arabs, Palgrave Macmillan Publishers, 2002, quoted by A. Zahoor on website http://www.cyberistan.org/Muslim History, 1997.

44. Hugh Salzberg, From Caveman to Chemist—Circumstances and Achievements, American Chemical Society, Washington, D.C. 1991.

45. De Lacy O'Leary, Islam at the Crossroads, London, 1923, p.8.

46. Lawrence E. Browne, The Prospects of Islam, London, 1944

47. Jerald F. Dirks, Muslims in American History: A Forgotten Legacy, Amana Publications, Beltsville, MD 20705, First Ed. 2006.

48. Mark Graham, How Islam Created the Modern World, Amana Publications, Beltsville, MD 20705, 2006.

49. Jonathan Lyons, The House of Wisdom –How the Arabs Transformed Western Civilization, Bloombury Press, New York, 2009.

50. Dunlop, D. M., Arabic Science in the West, Pakistan Historical Society Publication No. 35, Azeemi Printers, Karachi, Pakistan, 1988.

51. Duncan Townson, Muslim Spain, Lerner Publications Company, Minneapolis, 1973.

52. Thomas Abercrombie, When the Moors Ruled Spain, National Geographic, Vol. 174, No. 1, July 1988, p. 93.

53. James S. Aber, History of Geology Syllabus, Emporia State University, http://academic.emporia.edu/aberjame/histgeol/syllabus.htm

54. Salim T. S. Al-Hassani, 1001 Inventions—Muslim Heritage in Our World, 2nd ed., Foundation for Science, Technology and Civilization, Manchester, UK. 2006.

55. Khurshid Ahmad, Family Life in Islam, The Islamic Foundation, Leicestershire, U.K., p 16.

56. Clifford Longley, Islam Strengthens Family Life. The Times of London, December 23, 1974.

57. Rafiq Zakaria, The Trial of Benazir—an insight into the status of woman in Islam, Popular Prakashan Private Ltd., Bombay, India, Second Ed. 1990.

58. The Sunday Star-Ledger, Newark, New Jersey, May 16, 2004, Section One, p.14.

59. Donald Neff, The Washington Reporter on Middle east Affairs, May/June Issue.

60. Bruce Hoffman, A. B., "Terrorism," Microsoft® Encarta® Online Encyclopedia 2005, http://encarta.msn.com © 1997-2005.

61. Robert Pape and James Feldman, Cutting the Fuse: The Explosion of Global Suicide Terrorism and How to Stop it; University of Chicago Press, 2010.

62. BBC World News. Ten Pakistani army personnel including a Major killed in operation against Al-Qaida and Taliban in Southern Waziristan (Pakistan) along Pakistan-Afghanistan border. June 26, 2002.

63. Hafiz Wazir, Reuters News Agency "Pakistan Army pounds surrounded militants." Sixteen (Pakistani) soldiers and 24

militants, including some foreigners, were killed on Tuesday (March 16, 2004), first day of fighting. Fifteen more soldiers have been killed since Thursday, March 19, 2004.

64. Anonymous, Fiqh Council of North America's Fatwa against Terrorism, The Message International, January—February, 2010 issue, ICNA, 166-26 89th Avenue, Jamaica, N.Y. 11432-4254.

65. Chrley Reese, in Orlando Sentinel, August 24, 1998 Issue.

66. Enver Masud, The War on Islam, Published by The Wisdom Fund, Washington, D.C. April 17, 2010

67. Shaykh Muhammad Hisham Kabbani, Illuminations—Compiled Lectures on Shariah & Tasawwuf, Islamic supreme Council of America (ISCA). Fenton, Mi, USA, 2007.

68. Abul A'la Mawdudi, Towards Understanding Islam, Printed by Islamic Circle of North America (ICNA), 10th ed., 2001. ISBN 1-883591-01-05.

69. Shaykh Hakim Moinuddin Chishti. The Book of Sufi Healing, Inner Traditions International, Ltd. New York, N.Y. 10016, 1985. (reprinted poem of Hazrat Khwaja Moinuddin Chishti by permission from Inner Traditions• Bear & Company, One Park Street, Rochester, VT 05767 www.InnerTraditions.com

70. Ahmad Zarruq, Zaineb Istrabadi, Hamza Yusuf Hanson, "The Principals of Sufism." Amal Press, 2008

71. Sirdar Ikbal Ali Shah. Islamic Sufism, Samuel Weiser, Inc. New York, NY, 1971.

72. R. J. McCarthy, English translation of Al-Ghazali's Path to Sufism—His Deliverance from Error- al-Munqidh min al-Dalal, Fons Vitae, Louisville, KY., 2006

73. Shaykh Muhammad Hisham Kabbani, Classical Islam and the Naqshbandi Sufi Tradition, Islamic Supreme Council of America (ISCA), Fenton, Mi, USA, 2004.

74. Shaykh Nazim Adil Al-Haqqani, Liberating the Soul- A Guide for Spiritual Growth, Volume 1, Published by Islamic Supreme Council of America (ISCA), Washington, D.C. 20036, 2002

75. Imam Feisal Abdul Rauf. What's Right with Islam—a New Vision for Muslims and the West, Harper Collins Publishers, Inc. New York, N.Y., 2004.

76. W. Montgomery Watt, The Faith and Practice of al-Ghazali, London, UK, 1970.

77. Nuh Ha Mim Keller, Reliance of the Traveller, Amana Publications, Beltsville, Maryland, USA, 1994.

78. William Wan, After the Fort Hood Shootings, a Muslim American Soldier Battles on Friendly Ground, The Washington Post, March 24, 2010.

79. Anonymous, American-Israeli Relations—Where did all the love go, The Economist March 20th – 26th 2010, p 45.

80. Qazi Hussain Ahmad, Address to the opening session of USA-Islamic World Forum, Doha, Qatar, January 11, 2004.

81. Dr. Muzammil H. Siddiqi, Quran and Violence, The Muslim Observer Volume III Issue 41, October 19-25, 2000, p 24.

82. Phil Lawler. The Forum: The Pope's Challenge to Islam and the West (analysis). CWNews.com September 27, 2006.

83. Robert Pigott. Emerging voice of mainstream Islam. BBC NEWS, October 12, 2007. http://news.bbc.co.uk/go/pr/fr/-/2/hi/europe/7038992.stm

84. Michelle Boorstein. Muslims Call for Interfaith Peace. Washingtonpost.com October 12, 2007

85. Emily Flynn Vencat. A Muslim Letter to Christians—In an unprecedented letter, Muslim leaders across the globe invite the world's Christians to the table. Newsweek, October 11, 2007.

86. Louis Werner, Prince of Brotherhood, Saudi Aramco World magazine, July/August 2010 issue, Saudi Aramco World, Houston, Texas 77252-2106.

87. Iftikhar U. Hyder. Spiteful stereotyping of religious Mus-
     lims, Dawn- the Internet Edition, March 4, 2006, Karachi,
     Pakistan, http://DAWN.com

88. Sarah Joseph, The Guardian, London, U.K. February 3, 2006.

89. Martin Jacques, The Guardian, London, U.K. February 17,
     2006

90. Aysha Akram, The Chronicles, San Francisco, USA Feb., 12,
     2006.

91. Susilo Bambang Yudhoyono, President of Indonesia, in
     www.theage.com Feb. 12, 2006

92. Agence France-Presse, 9/9/06, http://news.yahoo.com/s/afp/
     20060909/ts_afp

93. Anonymous, Discover Islam Poster; Discover Islam;
     Orlando, Fl.

94. Ted Widmer, People of the Book—The true history of the
     Koran in America, The Boston Globe , September 12, 2010
     Issue.

95. Jonathan Curiel, The Life of Omar ibn Said, Saudi Aramco
     World magazine March/April, 2010 Issue, Aramco Services
     Company, Houston, Texas 77096.

96. Alex Haley and Malcolm X. The Autobiography of Malcolm
     X, Ballantine Books, New York, 1965, pp 391.

97. Bobby Ghosh, Time Magazine, August 30, 2010 Issue.

98. Dick Cavett, Opinionator, New York Times, August 20, 2010.

99. Christian Salazar, Associated Press, Yahoo News, August
     25, 2010.

100. Jeanne Clark, Why Catholics must speak out against Islamo-
     phobia, National Catholic Reporter, March 8, 2011(Reprinted
     by permission of National Catholic Reporter, 115 E Armour
     Blvd, Kansas City, MO 64111 www.ncronline.org.)

101. Wil Rutt, OakLeaves (Member of Sun-Times Media), March
     3, 2011

102. Rabbi Bruce Warshal, Shame on America, Jews, and the ADL, Florida Jewish Journal, September 1, 2010.

103. James Besser, Nascent effort to combat anti-Islam sentiment running into strong headwind, The Jewish Week, September 16, 2010.

104. David Nakamura, Japanese Americans: House hearing on radical Islam 'sinister.' Washington Post, March 8, 2011.

105. Nicholas Kristof, Taking Bin Laden's Side,New York Times, August 21, 2010.

106. Larry B. Stammer, Times Religion Writer, "First Lady (Hillary Rodham Clinton) Breaks Ground With Muslims," Los Angeles Times, Home Edition, Metro Section, Part B, May 31, 1996, p. 3.

107. Timothy Kenny. Elsewhere in the World, USA Today, Final Edition, News Section, February 17, 1989, p. 4A.

108. Geraldine Baum. For Love of Allah, Newsday, Nassau and Suffolk Edition, Part II, March 7, 1989, p. 4.

109. Ari L. Goldman. "Mainstream Islam Rapidly Embraced By Black Americans," New York Times, Late City Final Edition, February 21, 1989, p. 1.

110. Sandra Marquez. People, 9/4/06 http://people.aol.com/people/article/0,26334,1328839,00.html

111. Dr. Lawrence Brown, Why I became a Muslim, American Muslim Magazine, November-December 2010 (volume 1) Issue 2, Islamic American Universal, Southfield, Michigan 48075.

112. Margott Patterson, 6/30/06   http://ncronline.org/NCR_Online/archives2/2006b/063006/063006a.php

GLOSSARY

Akhirah	Life in the hereafter
Al-Ameen	Title of Prophet Muhammad, meaning 'the trustworthy'
Allah	Arabic word for God Almighty
Al-Sadiq	Title of Prophet Muhammad, meaning 'the truthful'
Barzakh	A state between the time of death and the Day of Resurrection
Bedouins	Nomad Arab inhabitants of the desert
Burqa	A head-to-toe overall covering used by some women
Da'wa	Work for the propagation of Islam
Deen	Arabic word for religion or 'way of life'.
Dopatta	A scarf worn by women in India and Pakistan
Eid-ul-Adha	An Islamic holiday commemorating willingness of Abraham to sacrifice his son at the Command of God
Eid-ul-Fitr	An Islamic holiday marking the end of fasting during the month of Ramadan
Falah	Well being
Fatwa	Islamic religious edict issued by an Islamic religious authority
Hadeeth	Historical recording of the traditions of Prophet Muhammad

Hafiz   A person who has memorized the entire Qur'an by heart

Hijab   A covering used by women to cover their head

Iftar   A meal for breaking fast of the month of Ramadan

Ijma   Consensus—solution to problems faced by Muslims based on the largest number of opinions (or votes).

Ijtihad   Independent thinking as an aid to finding solutions for the problems faced by Muslims.

Imam   An individual who leads Muslim prayer (in a mosque). In Shiite Islam, it is a title for a religious leader.

Jihad   Struggle by Muslims to put God's Will into practice in daily life, including (but not limited to) military action.

Ka'ba   A cubicle structure built by Abraham as the house for the worship of One God, and located in the grand mosque in the city of Mecca.

Khutbah   Sermon given by an Imam as a part of the Muslim prayer

Madrassa   Arabic equivalent of the English word school. Curriculum may include exclusively religious education or religious as well as secular education.

Mahomet   Name used by Orientalists for Prophet Muhammad

Makkah   Arabic word for Mecca

Marwa   One of the hills near Ka'bah in Mecca

Mosque   A Muslim house of worship

Muazzen   An individual who chants out the Muslim call for prayer

Qur'an   Holy book of Islam, compilation of words and verses directly revealed by God to Prophet Muhammad

Raka	A cycle of ritualistic movements (standing, kneeling, bowing, and sitting) during the mandatory Muslim prayer or salat.
Salat	Mandatory Muslim ritualistic prayer—performed 5 times each day
Safa	One of the hills near Ka'ba in Mecca
Sawm	The Muslim fast—requires abstinence from food, drinking and sex from dusk to dawn .
Shahadah	Declaration that there is no one worthy of worship except God and Muhammad is His Messenger.
Sharia	Islamic law based on the teachings of the Qur'an and sayings of Prophet Muhammad.
Suhur	A meal taken before dawn before starting the fast of Ramadan
Sufi	A Muslim who seeks most direct way to God through spiritual purification.
Taliban	Plural for Arabic word Talib meaning 'student.' A political movement in Afghanistan and Pakistan of fundamentalist Muslims who want to govern according to strict and fundamental teachings of Islamic law or Sharia.
Ummah	Arabic word for an undivided nation/community (of Muslims)
Veil	A facial covering used by some Muslim women.
Wu'du	Ritualistic cleaning/washing in preparation for Muslim prayer
Zakah	One of the five forms of worship in Islam—involves payment of a fixed amount of money to the deserving persons.

INDEX

ABOUT THE AUTHOR

MANZOOR HUSSAIN RECEIVED his PhD from the University of California, Riverside and worked, first as a Senior Research Scientist in American chemical industry in New Jersey, and later for 12 years at the International Atomic Energy Agency (IAEA) of the United Nations in Vienna, Austria. At the IAEA, he was Head of a Unit of the Agency's Laboratories. His contribution to the work of the IAEA was recognized on the occasion of the award of the 2005 Nobel Peace Prize to IAEA. For the last 11 years he has been teaching chemistry at a university and Islamic Studies at an Islamic High School in New Jersey. He has been active as a volunteer in several social service activities, and is currently involved in interfaith dialogue programs. He is married to Jana Catherine Hussain, who comes from a Christian family from California, and they live in New Jersey.

Made in the USA
Middletown, DE
01 April 2023

28063501R00203